Chris and Emily's story will inspire you and infuse your life with the courage to face the challenges of life.

DR. THOMAS MULLINS, FOUNDING PASTOR
OF CHRIST FELLOWSHIP CHURCH

In life, everything happens for a reason, and meeting Chris reassured me of that. His positive attitude and desire to make a difference in other people's lives are infectious. This book will not only inspire you but will make you take action to bring positivity into this world.

ERIC LEGRAND, FORMER RUTGERS FOOTBALL
PLAYER, MOTIVATIONAL SPEAKER

The Seven Longest Yards will have you laughing, crying, and feeling challenged to keep moving forward in life. You'll be ready to take on those things you thought you could never accomplish. Chris and Emily have given us a gift of encouragement and practical inspiration in the pages of this book. This is a must-read.

TODD AND JULIE MULLINS, SENIOR PASTORS
OF CHRIST FELLOWSHIP CHURCH

When I meet someone who can take steps after a serious fracture to their neck, I always say, "You're a walking miracle!" That describes Chris Norton. This man refused to accept his doctor's prognosis and found the will to move forward despite adversity. If you like stories that inspire you to fight against the odds, *The Seven Longest Yards* should be your next read!

JONI EARECKSON TADA, JONI AND FRIENDS
INTERNATIONAL DISABILITY CENTER

Our brains need stories of overcoming so we might know our own stories can be ones of overcoming too. Chris and Emily's book and hard-won lessons learned remind us that our most difficult challenges can also be our most powerful assignments in life.

KATHERINE AND JAY WOLF, COFOUNDERS
AND COAUTHORS OF *HOPE HEALS*

This book takes you on a powerful, emotional journey. I simply love Chris and Emily and the way God is using their lives in incredible ways. This book will make your heart soar, your spirit rise, and your problems seem, well, momentary. Which is exactly what they are. Let Chris and Emily show you how God works hope into even the most trying of circumstances.

CAREY NIEUWHOF, FOUNDING PASTOR OF CONNEXUS
CHURCH, AUTHOR OF *DIDN'T SEE IT COMING*

The old adage that life is 10 percent what happens to us and 90 percent how we react to it has more validity than most perceive. Chris and Emily have faced some of life's most jagged twists head-on and sculpted them into opportunities. Paralysis envelops a life and those around it with pain and suffering. The ability to recultivate that life and find a positive journey is something we all can learn from.

MIKE BARWIS, MS, CSCS, RSCC*E, NASE, BMI,
CEO OF BARWISMETHODS CORPORATIONS

Without question, *The Seven Longest Yards* is one of the best books I've ever read on overcoming hardship and the unexpected in life. Seriously. I laughed. I cried. I fist-pumped a lot while reading this incredible and very encouraging book by Chris and Emily Norton.

KURT W. BUBNA, PASTOR AND AUTHOR

If you are struggling in some way right now, do your best to keep in mind that although it might not seem so, better days are coming. No one knows this better than Chris and Emily Norton. Their story, told though *The Seven Longest Yards*, will remind you that the test always comes before the merit. The struggle always precedes the strength. You have to endure breakdowns to break through them. Take it one day at a time, and trust the journey. Just as Chris and Emily did.

MARC AND ANGEL CHERNOFF, *NEW YORK TIMES*
BESTSELLING AUTHORS OF *GETTING BACK TO HAPPY*

Chris and Emily Norton embody the spirit of overcoming. They are living proof that we can become better as a consequence of whatever it is that we face!

KYLE MAYNARD, BESTSELLING AUTHOR OF *NO
EXCUSES*, TWO-TIME ESPY AWARD WINNER

Chris's determination is a true testament to the warrior mentality he portrays. He is a beacon of hope. His fight and will to never give up inspire so many.

ANTHONY PURCELL, EXECUTIVE DIRECTOR OF
THE WALKING WITH ANTHONY FOUNDATION

Your greatest struggles can become your greatest strengths. This book will show you this truth and inspire you to live your best life.

JOHN O'LEARY, BESTSELLING AUTHOR AND SPEAKER

Sometimes life will give you challenges you can't get away from. This book will encourage you to face any and all obstacles in your path by using the inner strength you possess. Chris exemplifies how you can overcome all life's adversities. Chris is an outstanding husband, father, and friend who truly inspires everyone he crosses paths with.

TRAVIS MILLS, RETIRED UNITED STATES ARMY STAFF
SERGEANT, NEW YORK TIMES BESTSELLING AUTHOR

Unashamedly honest, confident, and humble, Chris and Emily show us how to find lasting hope amid unending challenges. Their story confirms that internal fortitude is developed through dedication and determination. Their tenacity is contagious. This is a must-read for anyone seeking to live a rewarding life that leaves a legacy for others to follow.

COLLEEN SWINDOLL-THOMPSON, FOUNDER AND
DIRECTOR OF REFRAMING MINISTRIES

The
SEVEN
LONGEST
YARDS

*Our Love Story of Pushing the Limits
while Leaning on Each Other*

CHRIS & EMILY NORTON

WITH MARK TABB

ZONDERVAN®

ZONDERVAN

The Seven Longest Yards
Copyright © 2019 by Chris and Emily Norton

Requests for information should be addressed to:
Zondervan, *3900 Sparks Dr. SE, Grand Rapids, Michigan 49546*

ISBN 978-0-310-35692-9 (hardcover)

ISBN 978-0-310-35694-3 (audio)

ISBN 978-0-310-35693-6 (ebook)

The authors are represented by Rick Richter, Aevitas Creative Management.

Art direction: Curt Diepenhorst
Cover photo: Sarah Kate
Interior design: Denise Froehlich

Printed in the United States of America

19 20 21 22 23 /LSC/ 10 9 8 7 6 5 4 3 2 1

*To all the people who have loved us and
helped us throughout our journey*

---

*To our five beautiful daughters, Whittley,
Ava, Liliana, Isabella, and Ariana, who
inspire us and make us so proud*

Contents

Foreword

Years ago, after football practice with the Denver Broncos, I got a call from my former college coach, Urban Meyer. He told me about a college football player who had been dramatically injured on the field, who was given a slim 3 percent chance of ever regaining movement below his neck. But Coach Meyer also told me this guy wasn't going to let this prognosis stop him. And that's how I met one of the most inspiring guys I know—Chris Norton.

As I learned later, Chris was spending part of his hospital stay with the TV on, watching my training as I prepared for the NFL draft. He said it was my hard work and dedication that inspired him to hold on to hope when he needed it most. But I'll tell you what, when I got on the phone with him, it was *he* who inspired *me*.

Here was this eighteen-year-old college football star who was being told he would never walk again. Yet Chris didn't let this steal his hope. What's more, he matched this relentless hope with action, pushing himself hard every single day to meet his goals.

That day after football practice, I only talked with Chris for fifteen minutes. In my very first yet short impression of Chris, I was blown away by his determination to stay positive, to do the work, and to trust that God had a bigger story in mind.

We kept in touch during Chris's recovery, and sure enough, his story continued to unfold in incredible ways. When he met his wife, Emily, when they walked across that graduation stage together, when their video went viral, I was so happy for them. When Chris launched his charity foundation, I sent them an auction item to help out. Years later I got to meet their amazing family in person—Chris, Emily, and their five beautiful girls, who could not have better examples of parents who live out faith and determination every day.

I'm excited for you to be holding this book in your hands because you are about to begin a master class in the power of perseverance. Chris and Emily have fought so many battles together, and through it all, they've demonstrated an incredible reserve of resolve. They know that viral videos and highlight reel moments never show the half of it. The real story is built in the behind-the-scenes work of stretching yourself, doing the next right thing, refusing to give up, and trusting God. They know the power of putting one foot in front of the other, both literally and figuratively. And this book is meant to inspire you to do the same.

TIM TEBOW

Acknowledgments

Thanks to the many people who have helped us through the book writing and publishing process. To name a few: Rick Richter, Mark Tabb, Lauren Koeller, Katie and Reece Norris, Michael Port, Carey Nieuwhof, John O'Leary, Joey Coleman, and the Walking With Anthony Foundation.

First Steps into Forever

· CHRIS ·

My heart beat in my ears as I nervously adjusted my tie and waited. One bridesmaid after another slowly made their way down the aisle one step at a time, escorted by my groomsmen. I smiled at each, but I wished they'd all move a little faster. I'd waited for this day my entire life, and there was only one person I wanted to see. Finally, the last bridesmaid took her place. The string quartet's music swelled, which sent a buzz through the crowd that had gathered to share this day with Emily and me. I glanced up at the overcast sky, thankful for the clouds that kept the Florida heat from becoming overwhelming. We couldn't have asked for a more perfect day for our wedding.

The music built. Little girls swiveled in their seats, craning their necks for a first glimpse of the much-anticipated white dress. In a few minutes, Emily and I would become husband and wife. We'd say our vows and then walk together down that aisle. It was only seven yards, but that distance represented something special to us: the first steps in our journey together.

Sitting in my wheelchair, I didn't take those seven yards for granted. Just seven and a half years ago, lying in a hospital bed, I doubted I would ever take another step. My dreams crumbled as my life as I knew it was over. More than once I cried out to God, *Why is this happening to me? This has to be a mistake.* I looked ahead and could not see a future I wanted to live. Every goal I had ever set for myself—every dream, every plan—ended in a split second. Even worse, I feared I'd have to spend that empty future alone.

But God knew better.

I could not have imagined the life he had in store for me. I never expected to be given a public platform—not to shine a spotlight on myself, but to point people toward God and to give them inspiration and hope. And I hadn't allowed myself even to hope that a woman like Emily could look at me with pure love and devotion in her eyes—that she could see me, and not my wheelchair. Emily not only encouraged me to keep training and keep working when I felt like giving up but also opened my eyes to the needs of others and showed me how fulfilling it could be to sacrifice my comfort to help them.

It had been seven years, and they all led up to the seven-yard aisle at our wedding.

Our flower girls came walking up the aisle now, scattering petals from their baskets as the ring bearers walked solemnly beside them. Emily was next. A lump formed in my throat as I strained my eyes, looking for the first sign of her.

Emily and I hadn't just overcome my physical condition together. Just one year ago, I wasn't sure if there would ever be a wedding. A deep depression had wrapped Emily in its clutches, choking the light and passion that defined her and sparking constant fighting between us. More than once Emily had told me that we were through, but she could never give up on me, and I could never give up on her.

Thankfully, God never gave up on either of us. Our wedding today was proof that he could overcome any obstacle we faced and lead us into a life that exceeded anything we had ever imagined—not only for us but also for the fifteen foster children he has brought in and out of our home. Our wedding walk was our way of telling the world that with God, all things truly are possible. We should know. We've lived it.

1

In an Instant

· CHRIS ·

"Get up, Norty. Come on, man. Let's go," my teammate Josh Patterson said to me.

But I couldn't get up. I told my arms to push up off the ground. Instead, I lay there facedown. Then it hit me: I couldn't feel my arms. Or my legs. Or the ground underneath my body. I couldn't feel anything below my neck. *Okay, here we go again. It's just a stinger,*[1] *like the one I got in a game in high school when my right side went numb. I've just got to give it some time and I'll be fine.* I was embarrassed to be lying on the field for so long after the whistle had blown the play dead.

"Get back! Don't touch him!" Chris Kamm, our head athletic trainer, shouted.

Great. The athletic trainer's coming out. Get up before you embarrass

---

1 "Burners and stingers are injuries that occur when nerves in the neck and shoulder are stretched or compressed after an impact. These injuries are common in contact or collision sports, and are named for the stinging or burning pain that spreads from the shoulder to the hand. A burner or stinger can feel like an electric shock or lightning bolt down the arm. In most cases, burners and stingers are temporary and symptoms quickly go away." https://orthoinfo.aaos.org/en/diseases--conditions/burners-and-stingers/

yourself any more than you already have. I tried again to move my arms, but nothing happened.

Kamm crouched down with his head nearly touching the field to get low enough to look me in the eyes. "What are you feeling, Chris?" he said.

"Nothing."

"Are your ears ringing?"

"No."

"Can you see me?" Kamm asked.

"Yeah. My vision is clear. I think I'm okay. I just can't move anything right now. Probably just a stinger. Give me a second," I said.

Out of the corner of my eye, I saw our defense huddled up on the sideline with the head coach. We'd just scored a touchdown that got us back in the game about midway through the third quarter. Our hometown crowd was still buzzing. We had to make a defensive stop and get the ball back. The best way to do that was to pin Central College deep in their own territory by making a big stop on the kickoff. That's what had left me lying on the field.

Officially I played free safety, which is a defensive back. But as a freshman, most of my playing time came on special teams, especially kickoffs. On kickoffs I lined up on the far right side of the field. After our kicker kicked the ball, my job was to make sure the guy who caught it did not get "outside," with a clear running lane down the sideline. I was supposed to turn him toward the middle of the field to the rest of our coverage team.

On this play the kick was short but to my side of the field. At only five feet eleven, 185 pounds, I was undersized for a free safety, but I knew how to tackle. I sprinted down the field as fast as I could and went straight toward the ball carrier. At six feet two, 230 pounds, he had the size advantage, but I knew that didn't matter. I couldn't tackle him straight up, so I planned on turning my body into a 185-pound missile aimed straight at his knees. Unfortunately, I mistimed the dive. I still got the tackle, but instead of hitting his knees with my shoulder, my head collided with his thigh, and his knee hit me directly in the neck. I didn't hear anything snap. I didn't feel any sharp jab of pain. The play was just like any other play. After I made contact with the ball carrier, I slammed face-first into the turf. The ball carrier flipped over me, and I heard the *pop* of other collisions as more guys made contact. The referee blew his whistle, and everyone got up. Everyone but me.

"All right, Chris. Listen. I want you to stay as still as you can. Don't move your head," Kamm said. "Is your breathing okay?

"Yeah," I said, puzzled as to why he'd ask me that.

"Can you wiggle your fingers for me?"

I tried. "Not yet," I said.

"I'm going to grab your hand. Let me know if you can feel it." Kamm said.

"I don't feel anything."

"Okay. Can you move either of your feet?"

"No. I'm sorry." I said. I was so embarrassed. *Okay, joke's over,* I thought. *It's time for everything to start working now.* The buzz of the stadium had died down. Five thousand people were suddenly eerily quiet.

Our Luther College team doctor joined Kamm next to me. She asked me more questions: "Can you move the fingers on your right hand? How about your left? Can you make a fist?" The fact that she asked me basically the same questions that Kamm had just asked made fear rise up inside me. I pushed it back as best I could, telling myself again that this was just a stinger. In a minute or two, the feeling would return, and I'd be up and off the field. Still, I had to answer the team doctor's questions, so I told her the same thing I told Kamm, "No, I can't feel or move anything."

"Let's get him rolled over," Kamm said. "I've got his head. You two, take his legs. You, on his side." I knew from Kamm's instructions that the rest of the student athletic training staff was all around me. I also knew they must have grabbed hold of my arms, legs, and body, but I couldn't feel it.

"On my count," Kamm continued, "Careful. One. Two. Three. Roll."

I found myself staring straight up at a bright, blue October sky. The student trainers crowded around me, fear on their faces. Kamm crouched down over me with his knees on either side of my helmet to keep me from moving my head. Even so, I could see a few of my teammates not far away. They were all down on one knee. That's a bad sign. Anytime an injured player stays down on the field too long, the rest of the players go down on one knee. But not just out of respect; a lot of them start praying.

"Chris," the team doctor said, "can you feel me touching your legs?"

I wanted to scream out, Stop asking me that! I am naturally an optimistic person. To me, the glass is always half full. That optimism was slowly being swallowed by panic. "No," I said.

"How about now?"

"No."

"What about now? Can you feel me touching your shoulder?"

"No. Not yet," I said, fighting to hold myself together. I'd reached my breaking point. No matter how hard I tried to think positively, I knew I was in trouble. My mind scrambled to find some best-case scenario, but the longer I lay there with doctors and trainers reminding me that I couldn't feel anything below my neck, the harder it was to find anything good to focus on. I did the only thing I could. Since pretty much the only things on my body that worked were my mouth and my eyes, I shut my eyes tight, and I tried to check myself out of the situation completely. I also prayed. "God, just let me walk off. This is starting to scare me. The joke's over. I've had enough. Let's move on. Please let me get up, and let's just have this whole thing be over." At that moment I did not want to think I'd suffered any kind of major injury. I could not let my mind go there.

"You still with us, Chris?" Kamm asked. Since my eyes were closed, I'm sure he thought I was slipping in and out of consciousness from a concussion. I didn't think I had a concussion because my head was clear.

"Yeah," I said without opening my eyes. I still refused to believe this was happening. In my eighteen years of life, everything had always worked out for me. I'd lived my life without any major hiccups. On top of that, I'm from a small town in Iowa. Bad things like this don't happen to guys from small towns in Iowa or on the football field of a small college like Luther. No, these are the things you see on television to people far away. "I'm still here," I said.

"Okay, good," Kamm said. "We're going to cut your face mask off so we can get your helmet off," he added.

"Okay," I said without opening my eyes. I didn't see it at the time, but later I learned that the team doctor originally was going to be the one to cut off my face mask, but her hands shook so much that she couldn't do it. Instead, she switched places with Kamm, who did the job himself. It took forever. After they cut off my face mask, they removed my helmet. They basically had to break it into pieces to get it off my head without moving my neck. Once my helmet was off, they slipped on a neck brace to stabilize my head and neck.

A new voice chimed in. "How are you feeling, Chris?" The paramedics had arrived.

"I'm good," I said without opening my eyes.

"Good, Chris. That's real good. Now I need you to try to do something for me," one of the EMTs said.

"Okay," I said.

"I want you to try making a fist."

I knew my hand wouldn't work, but I tried anyway. No luck.

"Okay. Can you feel me touching your leg?"

Not again, I thought. "I still can't feel anything," I said, annoyed, but it was hard to get the words out before I ran out of air. *That's weird*, I thought to myself. I tried to take a deep breath, but I couldn't.

"Are you breathing okay?" Kamm asked.

I took another breath that wasn't nearly as deep as I wanted it to be. "Yeah," I said, trying to convince myself. "I think so."

"Hang in there, Norty," a voice said. I opened my eyes to see our head coach, Mike Durnin, leaning into the huddle of people working on me.

"Thanks, coach," I said.

Jeff McMartin, the head coach of Central College's team then added, "You'll be all right. You're in good hands."

I squeezed my eyes shut again and tried to believe them.

At least fifteen minutes had passed since the whistle blew, but to me every minute felt like an hour. If I didn't know better, I'd have thought the stadium had emptied out and everyone had gone home. The only sounds were the voices of the EMTs asking me more questions and the squawk of their radios. Then I heard a welcome voice.

"Chris."

"Dad?" I wished my parents hadn't been here to see this. I didn't want them to get all worried for no reason.

"You're doing good, son. Your mom and I are right here."

"Thanks, Dad." His voice sounded strong, but his eyes told me he was scared for me.

My father knelt down close to me and said, "You're going to be okay. You're going to be all right."

I wanted to say I believed him, but I didn't say anything. "Listen, we're going to get you on a backboard and load you into an ambulance to get you some help. Okay?" one of the EMTs said.

"Okay," I said.

The EMTs around me worked fast. They lifted my body slightly on one side, then back on the other, to slide the backboard under me. But I had no idea they had done it. My only sensation came when they put blocks on either side of my face and strapped my head to the board. Claustrophobia came over me, like I was trapped in a very small place. And I was. I felt as if I were trapped inside someone else's body. I saw the EMTs moving my arms and legs, but I had no sensation that these were my arms and legs. It was as if my head had been completely severed from my body.

"On my signal," one of the EMTs said. They then lifted me up and placed me on the stretcher. I heard Velcro ripping as they strapped me to the stretcher.

"Where are my legs?" I asked.

"They're right here, Chris," one of the EMTs said.

"Are they pointed up? I feel like they're in the air," I said.

"No, they're down," I was told.

"Are you sure?" I asked.

"Yeah," one said.

"Chris," my dad said.

"Dad."

"They're going to load you into the ambulance and take you to the hospital. Your mom and I will meet you there."

"Okay," I said.

"I love you, son," my dad said.

"I love you too."

The EMTs rolled me off the field toward the waiting ambulance. The crowd clapped like they do every time an injured player is helped off the field. Typically, in these situations, the athlete gives the crowd a thumbs-up to let them know he's going to be okay. I tried to force my thumb to rise, but it didn't respond. I tried again and again and again.

At that moment I wanted to give the crowd a thumbs-up more than any-thing in the world. I wanted to tell them, and myself, that I was going to be okay. But I couldn't. I had been to a lot of sporting events in my life in which players went down with an injury and had to be helped off the field. I had never seen one, not a single one, fail to give a wave or a thumbs-up or some little sign to the crowd that he was going to be okay. If I knew then what I know now, I'd have given the crowd a thumbs-down. Of course, I couldn't do that either. *Oh no! Why is this happening? When will this stop?*

Twenty or twenty-five minutes had gone by since I hit the ground. My "stinger" had not gone away. I had no more feeling in any part of my body below my neck than I did the moment I hit the ground. Even worse, I couldn't get enough air. I felt as though I was breathing through a straw. Fear rose up inside me. *Please, God, make this go away. Let me get up off this thing. I don't care if I ever play football again. Just let me get up off this and walk.*

The EMTs lifted me into the ambulance. As soon as they had me loaded inside, one of them said into his radio, "We need to get a chopper started." Then turning to me, he asked, "Mayo or La Crosse?"

"What?" I asked. "Do you want to go to the Mayo Clinic in Rochester or Gundersen in La Crosse, Wisconsin?" The two were about the same distance away.

"Mayo, I guess," I said. I didn't know which to choose, so I went with the name I recognized.

"Okay," the EMT said. Then into his radio, he said, "We need the chopper to transport to Mayo."

Holy crap, this is real, I thought. I tried closing my eyes again to shut everything out, but it was too late. Panic set in. My head felt like it might explode as the ambulance sped through the streets of Decorah, siren blaring, on our way to Winneshiek Hospital. My natural optimism gave way to full-blown fear. *What's going to happen to me?* I wondered. I didn't know if I really wanted to find out.

2

A Passion to Make a Difference

· EMILY ·

Growing up in Muscatine, Iowa, I wouldn't say my life was perfect, but it was about as close as you can get. My two brothers, my sister, and I grew up in a middle-class neighborhood, went to church every Sunday, and had a mom and dad who showed us that living out your faith means more than just being a good person and doing the right thing. Real faith acts. I took them seriously from an early age, beginning one night when I saw a television show about international adoption that changed my life.

A lot of the details are fuzzy, but I vividly remember seeing baby after baby lined up in small cribs stacked on racks, like some sort of human warehouse. A single light bulb hung over the bare room with a dirt floor. The sight of suffering children devastated me. "Mom and Dad, we have to do something!" I cried. "We have to adopt them!"

My parents empathized with the situation of these children, but they didn't phone an agency and try to adopt them. At the time I was far too young to understand the challenges of international adoption, but that didn't make me stop asking my mom and dad to do something. It wasn't only the children on television that broke my heart. I constantly watched for kids who needed to be adopted. My mom and dad patiently listened as I told them about the latest desperate child I thought we could rescue. My parents may not have adopted any of the children I told them about, but they taught me by example that following Jesus means helping others.

When I was young, I thought about kids from other countries who needed help. I didn't realize that kids in my own country might also be living in terrible situations without families who love them—much less kids at my own school.

My sheltered worldview was blown out of the water when I signed up for a student-to-student mentoring program. Our local police department worked with the high school to match up students with elementary kids. It seemed like a natural fit for me, so I signed up during my freshman year to meet with kids at Franklin Elementary School.

One day I was on my way into the cafeteria for mentoring when a teacher stopped me. "If you don't mind, I'd really like you to talk to that girl over there. Her name is Whittley." I glanced over and saw a fourth-grade girl whose eyes were caked in white and blue eyeshadow. Her chin line had that distinct look of a too-dark foundation that hadn't been blended from her face to her neck. No one told me anything about Whittley's home environment or what could possibly make an eight-year-old think she needed to wear that much makeup. I also had no idea that two weeks earlier Whittley had tried to kill herself. I really didn't know anything about her when I sat down in front of her and smiled. "Hi, I'm Emily! Is it okay if I sit with you?"

Whittley shrugged and looked down at the cafeteria table. "Sure, I guess."

I wasn't sure what I should say. Most kids her age were thrilled to hang out with high schoolers, but Whittley kept staring at the table and didn't say a word. Normally, I might have felt uncomfortable with someone who clearly didn't want to talk to me. Today was different. Something drew me to Whittley. Finally, I broke the silence. "Hey, do you like makeup?"

She looked up at me suspiciously. "Yeah, it's alright."

I dug into my backpack and pulled out a compact. "I just got some new eye shadow that's really pretty. You want to see how I put it on?" Whittley didn't move, so I opened the compact and took out the applicator. Then I paused. "You know, this color might look better on you. I have some makeup wipes with me. Want to take off your eyeshadow so you can try it on?" Now I had her attention. She nodded slowly, a smile starting to form.

I handed her a wipe and helped her scrub off the eye shadow and foundation. When her face was clean, I did an exaggerated double take. "Oh my gosh! Look at you! You are gorgeous! Why would you ever want to cover that up?" Whittley smiled.

"My mom always told me the trick to wearing makeup is to look like you're not actually wearing makeup," I said. "You just want to highlight your natural beauty. *Clearly* that's not going to be a problem for you!" Whittley beamed.

We finished our makeup lesson, the program ended for the day, and I went home feeling so much joy knowing that even if I only made a small impact on Whittley that day, that one small act of kindness was worth it. Whittley and I continued meeting through the after-school mentoring program for the rest of the year. School ended, and I didn't see Whittley through the summer. The next fall I continued with the mentoring program, but the leaders put me in a classroom with a few other kids who needed extra help. Whittley also continued in the program, but I only saw her a few times that year. From time to time, we ran into one another either in the hallway or library. After that year we lost contact with one another.

At the beginning of my junior year, I wanted to do something for middle school girls. I heard about a national program called Girl Talk, in which high schoolers serve as role models for middle schoolers and meet with them once a week after school to talk about everything from bullying and difficult home situations to boy problems and working hard at school. The principals and counselors at both the middle and high school gave me the green light, so I went to work setting everything up. The day before the program's launch, I met with the middle school counselor to iron out the final details when she said, "There's this girl, Whittley, who would do really well in this program. She needs it."

"Oh my gosh," I said. "I know Whittley."

The little girl I remembered was now a sixth-grader. When she walked into the program, I gasped. Her head hung down, but I could see that it was shaved completely bald. The look on her face told me she didn't choose this style. Later I learned that Whittley had a friend try to cut her hair. The friend messed up Whittley's hair so badly that her stepdad ended up shaving it off.

Us reconnecting is not a coincidence, I thought. *This is a divine appointment. Do not lose contact with her again!* Our initial conversation that afternoon was a little awkward, but I made sure I got her phone number. Then I started giving her rides home after Girl Talk. Eventually we hung out together, sometimes at my house and other times at the trailer park where she lived.

Since I was the Girl Talk leader, I tried to get involved with other girls in the program as well. I'd strike up conversations and let Whittley talk to other high school students. Every once in a while, though, I'd look up and see Whittley glaring at me. Once, when we hadn't talked much during a session, she climbed in my car for her ride home and let out a huge sigh. She wouldn't even talk to me until I finally asked, "Is something bothering you?"

She whipped her head around and scowled. "I thought you were supposed to be my friend."

"Of course I'm your friend," I said. "Why would you say that?"

"Then why are you talking to all those other girls? Don't you want to talk to me?" Her voice was angry, and I could tell she genuinely didn't know the answer.

"Oh, Whittley, talking to other girls doesn't mean I care less about you. I care more about you than you will ever know." I patted her shoulder reassuringly. "I have to make sure other girls feel included because that's part of Girl Talk, but that will never take away from our friendship." In that moment I felt a love for her that I had never felt for anyone. Even so, no matter how much I reassured her, she refused to believe me. Over the next few weeks, she continued to try to push me away.

I didn't understand why she was so jealous until one evening I knocked on her trailer door to pick her up to come to my house. I waited and waited, but no one came. I was about to head back to my car when the door creaked open. "Yeah?" a woman said, a cigarette in her hand. I assumed correctly that this was Whittley's mom.

I tried not to breathe in the smoke as I said, "Hey, is Whittley here?"

"I don't know where she is," she said in a flat voice, as if she couldn't be bothered with something so trivial as keeping up with her eleven-year-old daughter.

I stared at her. "You don't know where she is?"

She shrugged like it wasn't worth the effort to keep talking. "She's at a friend's house somewhere. But I don't know where she is."

I couldn't even speak I was so angry. Whittley had told me enough about her home life for me to know that things were bad. But young and naive me thought she must have been exaggerating. Meeting her mom for the first time and finding her so emotionally detached from her daughter told me that Whittley was telling the truth. I wanted to yell, Hey, it's a little weird that you don't know where your daughter is, and you're supposed to be *her mother*! But I kept my mouth shut. I knew if I made Whittley's mom mad, she might not let me see Whittley anymore. Instead, I forced a smile. "Okay, well tell her Emily stopped by."

Later I learned that Whittley had opened up to a friend about the physical and sexual abuse she was suffering. The friend's mom had called the Department of Human Services, who had removed Whittley from her mom's house and placed her in a group home thirty minutes away. I tried to go see her, but because I wasn't family, I was not allowed. However, I heard that her mother needed a ride to visit the group home, so I volunteered.

The drive over was miserable. Through the entire drive, Whittley's mom complained about her life and how Whittley was to blame. I tried to tune her out by thinking of song lyrics, homework, and anything else to drown out the negative stream of words spoken against my dear friend, but nothing worked. The more Whittley's mom complained about her daughter, the angrier I became. I'd never hated anyone in my life, but I was starting to during that car ride.

The visit with Whittley did not improve my view of her mom. During the visit I had a nice talk with Whittley. In a common area where visitors could hang out with the girls, the two of us played a board game and discussed how she was doing. Her mom didn't join in the game, nor did she say much of anything the entire time we were there. When we stood up to leave, Whittley sobbed. "Please don't leave," she begged her mom. "I love you. I love you so much. Please take me home with you."

I started crying too, but then I realized that Whittley's mom seemed unmoved. Her child was standing right in front of her, crying that she loved her, and she couldn't bring herself to say it back.

I couldn't take it anymore. After Whittley was taken back to the group home, I turned and looked her mom right in the eye. "Doesn't it make you sad that you're leaving your daughter here?"

She stared at me, completely emotionless. "I've dealt with this with my other daughter. I'm used to it."

By the time we got home from the visit, I was so emotionally exhausted that I had to take a nap. I didn't know how to process the fact that a girl I loved was so seemingly unloved by her own mother. All I knew was that I had to do whatever I could for Whittley. I called her as much as I could, and on her twelfth birthday, I took a cake and some scented lotions and body splash to her at the group home. Besides candy from her sister, mine were the only presents she received.

A week before Christmas, I was talking to Whittley on the phone when I asked her if she was excited to spend the holiday with her older sister. She sighed. "I don't get to go. Something happened and—I don't know. I just don't get to go."

"Oh my gosh, I'm so sorry," I said. "Are you going to your mom's instead?"

"No," she said quietly. "I'm staying here."

"What? No!" I was furious. "There is no way you are staying at a group home by yourself on Christmas. You're coming to my house."

"Emily, they're never gonna let you do that."

Whittley didn't yet know that when I see something that has to be done, I will not take no for an answer. The next morning I called her caseworker. "I can't let this girl spend Christmas by herself. I need her to come to my house and spend Christmas with my family," I insisted.

"Emily, it's not that simple," the caseworker explained. "She can't just stay anywhere. You'd all need background checks. We'd have to do a home visit. Christmas is next week and . . ."

"We'll do whatever it takes. Come to my house. We'll do background checks and whatever else we have to do." I didn't hear her say no, so I kept going. "Please. It's Christmas."

A few days later, Whittley came to our house for Christmas. I can't even begin to explain the joy I felt on our way back home after I picked up Whittley from the group home. Knowing I was a part of helping her spend Christmas with a family was the best Christmas present I could've ever received. I couldn't wait to see her relax with my brothers and sister and open the presents my parents had bought for her. She had been around my family a few times, but I could see she was more nervous than usual. My family did everything they could to make her feel welcome. We made Christmas cookies and treats, watched movies, and played the game Apples to Apples, which had us all cracking up. She was starting to feel comfortable. But the best part came later.

The two of us were alone in my room when I handed her a box. "Go ahead, open it!" I said, not trying to hide my excitement.

Whittley pulled off the lid to reveal a scrapbook. She looked up at me, confused, then silently flipped through the brightly decorated pages. For weeks I'd taken the book to every counselor, friend, and group home staff member, asking them to write Whittley a Christmas message. Her sisters and my family all wrote notes telling her how special she is. I'd pasted various pictures of us under inspirational quotes.

She kept turning the pages without saying a word. For a moment I was worried that she didn't like it or that I'd offended her somehow. Then she looked up, and I saw the tears streaming down her face. "My heart," she said, her voice breaking, "my heart has never felt like this." We both bawled as I held her in my arms. I couldn't believe that a twelve-year-old had never felt the kind of love that a scrapbook made her feel.

The more time I spent with Whittley, the more I believed that God put me on this earth to help kids like her. Everywhere I went, I saw kids cutting themselves, kids being bullied, kids being abused. I saw kids who had nothing, while I had everything I ever wanted and the most loving family any girl could ever have. Sometimes I felt angry at God for letting these children suffer. Why should I have all these incredible privileges when other kids my age were struggling? I felt I had to do something to help others and made it my goal to do everything I possibly could to make an impact.

Sometimes making an impact meant being kind to kids at school who seemed sad or who were ignored by my classmates. I wanted them to feel included and to show them God's love. Over and over again, that kindness led to kids opening up to me about the most unbelievable, hor-rific trauma they'd lived through. Each time, I listened and helped steer them to the right person who could help. At home I wrote in my prayer journal and asked God to help them.

I took on other kids' problems without thinking about the burden I was inadvertently carrying. When I confided in my mom, she sighed. "I worry about you, Emily," she'd say. "These are some heavy issues for a girl your age to deal with. You have to take care of yourself first."

I was confused and I brushed her off. "I'm fine, Mom. These kids need me. I have to do everything I can to help them. I can handle it. Don't worry about me." I thought, *Why would I need to take care of myself when I have never gone through anything difficult?* It took me some time to realize it, but I wish I'd listened to her.

3

Three Percent Chance

▪ CHRIS ▪

I stared up at the ambulance's metal roof as it raced through the streets of my college campus, siren blaring. Try as I might, I couldn't force any part of my body below my neck to move. I tried to look down at my hand to see if anything had changed, but the neck brace made it difficult. "Don't move your head," an EMT warned.

"Okay," I said and tried to relax. Lights flashed bright through the windows, and the distinct smell of hospital disinfectant filled my nostrils. I still held out hope that the feeling in my body would come back. I waited for a tingle, a pain, anything, but nothing happened. All my life I'd been a strong, active athlete. Not even being able to wiggle my toes made me feel trapped. The looks on the faces of the two EMTs on either side of me told me I was in serious trouble. *Oh, God, help me*, I prayed.

The ambulance slowed to a stop. The EMTs jumped to their feet. "Time to go," one said. I closed my eyes as they wheeled me into Winneshiek Hospital.

I burst through the doors, still strapped to the gurney. All at once I found myself in the middle of what felt like a scene from a movie. Doctors and nurses surrounded me, shouting to one another and pelting me with questions. Someone cut off my blue, number 16 Luther College jersey while someone else sawed off my shoulder pads. They even ripped off the wristband I wore to remember my friend who was killed in a car accident that summer. I wanted to yell, Hey!, but before I could say anything, they barraged me with the same questions I was asked on the field:

"Can you make a fist?"

"Can you wiggle your toes?"

"Can you feel this?"

"Which foot am I touching?"

I was so sick of the questions that all had one of two answers—no or I don't know. I closed my eyes again. *Please, God, let me wake up from this nightmare. This can't really be happening to me.*

The sound of my mom's voice interrupted my prayers. "Chris! We're right here, baby. Everything's going to be okay. The doctors are going to take good care of you." I opened my eyes to see her standing next to me along with my dad, my sister Alex, and my grandma. I'd almost forgotten my grandmother had come out for the game. More than anything I wished she didn't have to see this. Luckily, my younger sister Katie had gone to a sleepover instead of my game. Seeing me in the hospital would have crushed her.

Once again I shut my eyes to try to close out the world, only to be interrupted by my mom's panicked voice shouting, "Stay with us, Chris!" She must have assumed I had a head injury and was fading in and out of consciousness.

"I'm awake, Mom," I reassured her. "I just can't watch all this. If I close my eyes, I can pretend none of this is happening."

My grandmother silently stroked my hand and arm, as though if she tried long enough, all the feeling would come back. "Can you feel that, Chris?" she asked hopefully.

"No, Grandma. I'm sorry."

Mom and Dad moved out of earshot to ask the doctors questions, their brows furrowed with worry. I'd spent my whole life with a ball in my hand, and every game, they were in the stands cheering me on. When I got knocked down in basketball or took a hard tackle playing football, they always gave me space. Never once did they play the part of the overly worried parents. Even when I knew they had to be dying inside, they stayed strong for me. They tried to do that now, but the look on my mom's face gave her away.

"I'm going to be okay, Mom." I tried to reassure her, but my voice didn't quite work right, like someone had turned the volume down.

The doctor examining my head immediately stopped what he was doing. "It sounds like your voice is getting pretty soft," he said. "Are you having trouble breathing? Do you need some assistance?"

"No. I'm okay," I whispered. All my life, I'm okay had been my default answer to anyone asking me if I needed help. I hated when people made a fuss over me. Being surrounded by all these doctors and nurses was almost more than I could take.

"Well, let us know right away if you don't feel like you're getting enough air," the doctor said. "We can insert a tube down your throat to help you breathe. We'd like to keep that as a last resort, though. We don't know the extent of your injury yet, and if we insert a breathing tube, there's a chance it could do further damage."

"No, I'm good." I'd already lost all the feeling in most of my body. I didn't want to find out how much worse it could get.

After an X-ray confirmed my spinal injury, they whisked me to the top floor to wait for the helicopter that would fly me to the Mayo Clinic. As I tried to process what was happening, I looked for something, anything, to pull me back to reality. I remembered that the University of Iowa played Michigan in football that day. Like my dad, I grew up an avid Hawkeyes fan. "Does anyone know the score of the Iowa game?" I asked.

Someone told me Iowa had won. *Okay. That's a good sign*, I thought. Then I heard the helicopter coming in for a landing. The blades were still loud when the EMTs started pushing me toward it. *Here we go*. Another flurry of activity erupted around me as the EMTs loaded me into the helicopter and strapped my gurney to the floor.

"Now remember, if you can't breathe, let us know and we'll intubate you," one of the EMTs said.

"Okay," I whispered.

With that last comforting tidbit, the helicopter took off. I'd been in a helicopter only once before. My dad and I had ridden in a helicopter around the island of Aruba for my thirteenth birthday during spring break. On that ride the crew gave my dad and me headsets with microphones to talk to one another over the roar of the rotors. My dad and I laughed and smiled and had a great time.

This experience was totally different.

I couldn't look around the cabin, much less out the window. Instead, I lay there, staring straight up, thinking this wasn't how my life was supposed to turn out. My mind jumped from one worst-case scenario to another. *Will I ever play football again? Will I even walk again? What kind of life am I going to have? Will I be alone for the rest of my life? What kind of woman would ever want to be with a guy who can't move?*

Suddenly, I couldn't get enough air. I tried to take a deep breath, but no air came. Trying not to panic, I then took a couple of short, rapid breaths. That didn't help. I was suffocating. For the first time since my accident, I believed I was about to die.

"Help," I wheezed, but I didn't know if I had made any noise. The roar of the helicopter drowned out every sound. If I couldn't hear myself, how could the EMTs hear me? The answer was: they couldn't. "I can't breathe!" I said, but no one moved. "Help," I called again, but neither EMT turned toward me. My only hope was to make eye contact with one of them or for one of them to see me mouthing "help." Both were looking the other way. I wanted to wave my hands to get their attention, but clearly that wasn't an option. *Surely the heart monitor will alert them that I'm struggling*, I hoped, but still no one noticed. I was on my own.

Desperate to breathe, I went into full-on panic mode. *This is it. I'm going to die in a helicopter on my way to a hospital with two EMTs right beside me because no one noticed I needed help.* I started to give up and let the inevitable happen, but I could not bring myself to do that. *No, I* thought, *I am not going down without a fight.*

I closed my eyes and went back to the ritual I used before every game to help me get in the right frame of mind. Before I took the football field, I visualized exactly where I would run, where the ball would be, where the other players might go.

That's what I did in the helicopter. I visualized myself breathing. I imagined my lungs filling with air and expelling it out. Then I counted. One breath. Two. Three. I focused on the air I was getting instead of the air I wasn't. With every positive thought, each breath got a little easier. *I'm going to make it*, I told myself. *I'm going to be fine.*

From the moment my body hit the ground after the tackle that put me in this mess, I had focused completely on what I could not do. I could not move; I could not feel; I could not breathe. The obstacles kept getting bigger and bigger until they completely overwhelmed me. Everything changed when I switched my focus to what I could do. For the first time, I realized that my attitude had the power to change my reality. I have never forgotten that lesson even though it was about to be tested more times than I could count. The first test was about to begin.

Before I knew it, we were on the ground, and I was wheeled into another sterile room full of masked doctors and nurses. They didn't waste any time cutting off my pants and socks and setting up an IV. Someone walked away with vials of my blood, but I never felt anyone drawing it. It was the most bizarre thing to be poked and prodded and feel absolutely nothing.

Then came more of the same questions. This time doctors poked different parts of my body as they asked if I could feel what they were doing. The answer was always the same until one of them asked, "Can you squeeze your butt?" *Well that's a new one*, I thought. I was about to say no when I felt a sharp jab in my butt.

"Hey! I felt that!" I'd never been so happy to be poked in the butt in my life. I expected the doctors and nurses to share my excitement, but no one said anything. To me, though, the fact that I felt something below my neck was encouraging.

After another round of X-rays, a doctor told me I needed surgery to repair a grade IV spinal dislocation. Before they could operate, the doctor wanted an MRI. But they couldn't simply slide me into the MRI tube in my present condition. First they needed to realign my neck using traction. I didn't know what that meant until I saw someone carrying a round contraption with screws on both sides. It looked like some kind of medieval torture device. My heart pounded as they placed it on my head.

I got two numbing shots in my head before the doctor said, "This is probably going to hurt." The next thing I knew, I heard a spinning sound, and a stabbing pain shot through my brain. *Great, the one part of my body I can feel is the one they have to put this torture device on*, I thought. "Uh, did you numb my head?" I asked. "It feels like someone is driving two nails into my skull." The doctor gave me more numbing medication, but the pain didn't let up. I felt something warm dripping down by my ear and to the back of my head. I didn't have to see it to know it was my blood.

But the medical staff was just getting started.

To realign my neck, the doctor had to add weight to a pulley system connected to the contraption on my head. The weights subtly pushed the bone over. The doctor added weight in five-pound increments until at forty-five pounds I heard what sounded like someone chomping into a celery stalk. My neck had snapped back into place. I sighed with relief. The worst pain I'd felt in my life was over.

They removed the head stabilizer and replaced it with a neck brace. The edge of the brace reached the middle of my head. When they laid me on the MRI cot, I felt like I was resting on the edge of a piece of metal. While it wasn't as painful as the traction, it was extremely uncomfortable. I sighed. This day just would not let up.

I was miserable as the doctor explained that I'd have to lie completely still for an hour during the MRI—which was obviously easy for me at the time. A technician switched on the machine. There was a whirring sound as the cot under me began to move. The light above me slowly disappeared as I slid into the white plastic tunnel. The tiny tube was even smaller than it looked. The ceiling was almost on top of me. Once I was completely inside the machine, the whir stopped. Instead, my ears were blasted with what sounded like a jackhammer. *This is going to be the longest hour of my life*, I thought.

Worry started rising inside me until I remembered the helicopter ride. *Don't focus on the negative*, I reminded myself. *Focus on the positive*. Trapped in an MRI tube, I wasn't sure what the positive might be, so I prayed instead. I'd been praying most of the day— "God, give me the strength to get through this." That's what my family did when life got tough. I grew up going to church most Sundays and praying before meals. I'd never doubted my belief in God. At the time, I didn't realize there was a difference between believing in God and believing God. I just knew that I needed him at that moment more than ever.

"God, can you give me a break, just this once?" I prayed. "Please, can

I just fall asleep? All I want is to escape this for just a little bit. Please let me fall asleep."

Suddenly, my eyes snapped open as my cot slid out of the machine. Despite the jackhammering and the claustrophobia, I had fallen sound asleep. How? There was only one explanation: God had answered my prayers. All day I'd asked, *God, what are you doing? Are you going to show up?* Now he reminded me that he was with me the whole time.

In that moment I felt God's presence more clearly than ever before. "God, I know you're there," I prayed. "It's going to be okay. I know you're in this with me."

Immediately after my MRI, hospital employees wheeled me into surgery. My doctor stood over me and explained what was about to happen. "The whole procedure could take six hours," he said. "Do you have any questions?"

My voice caught in my throat. "Will I ever walk again?"

I couldn't make out his expression because the doctor bowed his head. "I don't know, Chris."

My eyes filled with tears. I didn't know how to stay positive with those words ringing in my ears. Then tears welled up in the eyes of the nurses. It was hard not to notice when the only thing not covered were their eyes. Before I could process what the doctor had said, someone placed a mask over my face. The heart monitor beeped away as I faded out of consciousness.

What felt like one minute later, my eyes fluttered as nausea rose up my throat. The surgery was over. It had only lasted three hours—half of what they'd expected. I thought that had to be good news.

Still groggy from the anesthesia, I forced my eyes open while I tried not to throw up. The room was blurry and spinning around me. I had a sense that my family was in the room with me, although I kept moving in and out of consciousness. When I became more aware, all I could think was, *Why is this tube down my throat?* I wanted to reach up and yank it out. When my arms didn't cooperate, I pushed against the tube with my tongue. I heard a voice say, "Stop, Chris. You need that to breathe," but I didn't listen. I kept pushing the tube out of my mouth with my tongue until a nurse finally removed it. She replaced it with what looked like straws under my nose.

I melted with relief when I finally came to enough to see my parents and sisters Alex and Katie next to me. "Mom. Dad," I croaked. My throat was still sore from the breathing tube, and my lungs were weak from my injury.

"The surgery went great, honey," my mom said, kissing my forehead. She was using that funny voice she always has when she's trying not to cry. "The surgeon will be in any moment to give us an update."

"You did great, buddy." My dad patted my shoulder and cleared his throat. They stayed next to me in my dimly lit hospital room until the surgeon arrived.

"The surgery went much faster than we expected," he said. "We thought we'd have to operate on the front and back of your neck, but we only had to go in through the back. Basically, we took a piece of your hip bone and used it to replace a bone in your neck. You now have that bone and several screws fusing your C2, C3, and C4 vertebrae together."

The children's song about dry bones ran through my mind as the surgeon talked to me. My mind had trouble comprehending what he was saying as he told me I'd suffered a grade IV dislocation and a fractured break of my C3 and C4 vertebrae. "Based on what we've seen, and on the fact that you have no feeling below the injury site, I estimate that you have a three percent chance of recovery," the surgeon said.

"What?" I asked. "You mean, I have a three percent chance of ever walking again?"

The surgeon stared at the floor before he spoke. "No. A three percent chance of ever moving or feeling anything below the injury site."

I wanted to look around and see if he was talking to someone else. Even in my worst nightmares, I had never imagined myself trapped in a body that could not move. I was an eighteen-year-old athlete, a hard worker, the kid with a bright future. I was indestructible. This could not be my life. No, I planned to become an All-American football player, meet the girl of my dreams, graduate with a business degree and someday buy a lake house. Or even better, the girl of my dreams' family would already own a lake house. *So much for that,* I thought.

Yet even as that thought flashed in my head, a sudden urgency came over me. Maybe I was naive; maybe it was faith. I don't know what it was, but something inside me said, *No. Not me. I will not let this happen. I can't let this happen. This isn't going to be my life. I am going to beat the odds.*

I looked up at the surgeon and mustered all the strength inside me to move something, anything. Somehow, I contorted the muscles in my shoulder into a shrug. "No way," I said. "I'm going to do whatever it takes to be in that three percent. I won't be that ninety-seven percent."

The surgeon was visibly surprised that my shoulder had moved ever so slightly. "You just beat the odds right there," he said, pointing to my shoulders. "You aren't supposed to be able to move anything below your neck. That's huge, Chris."

That's just a start, I thought. *I'm going to get my life back. I'm going to walk again. Just you wait and see.*

4

"You Will Beat This!"

· CHRIS ·

One day in the winter of 2004, I slammed the front door as my dad and I came home from the worst basketball game of my life. I had missed every shot. I had turned the ball over. Each time the coach put me in the game, my team played worse. The fact that my dad was the coach made the situation even worse. I couldn't do anything right. I was frustrated. My team was frustrated. And my dad definitely was too. The ride home was even worse.

Once I was inside my house, tears rolled down my cheeks as I kicked off my shoes, stomped to the living room, and flopped on the couch. I switched on the TV and flipped mindlessly through the channels while in my mind I replayed my every missed shot and bad pass. *It's official. I'm a terrible basketball player*, I thought. What made it even worse was that I knew I was much better than how I'd played. I think that's what made me even more mad at myself. When my team needed me to rise to the occasion, I instead fell well short of my potential and cost us the game.

"Anything good on?" My dad said as he sat next to me.

I just grunted in classic middle-school-boy style and kept flipping through the channels. I expected my dad to try to make me feel better like he always did. But he didn't. Instead, he turned to me and said, "Chris, if you don't like where you are, then do something about it."

I put down the remote and stared at him, wide-eyed.

"I'm serious," my dad continued. "You know what it takes to get better, and that's practice. Don't just sit here feeling sorry for yourself. Let's get off the couch, grab your basketball, and I'll rebound for you."

Ugh. I thought. *That's the last thing I want to do. I'd rather sit here and fume. I know he's right, but the last thing I want to do is admit it!* I opened my mouth to give him some lame excuse as to why I didn't need to go outside and practice.

Then something clicked.

Wait a minute, I thought. *Why* am *I sitting here feeling sorry for myself? I have the opportunity to get better, and I'm not taking advantage of it. That's just ridiculous.* I then felt embarrassed for feeling sorry for myself. "You're right, Dad," I said. I dropped the remote, put my shoes back on, went outside, and shot baskets until my mom called us in for dinner.

My dad's words have stuck with me. Anytime I become upset or discouraged, I refuse to let myself fall into a pity party. Instead, my dad's words ring in my ears, "If you don't like where you are, do something about it. Change it."

I never needed those words as much as I did as I lay in my hospital bed in Mayo Clinic's Intensive Care Unit. Aside from my shoulders shrugging a little, nothing below my neck worked, and my doctor had just told me that this was how I was going to spend the rest of my life. I had every right to feel sorry for myself, but something inside me said, *Do something. Change your situation.* However, my determination still had to navigate reality, and right then reality according to the doctors meant up to three weeks in the ICU and an incredibly uncertain future beyond that.

My physical therapy (PT) started almost immediately while I was still in ICU. From the start, I could tell that I had a long way to go. I went from being a college athlete to having my therapist work on sitting me up in bed without my blood pressure dropping too quickly. She then worked on strengthening my neck by having me nod my head. Lori Eaton, my physical therapist, was a bright spot in my day and had lots of energy.

I was shocked that they limited me to thirty to sixty minutes of PT a day. When I complained, Lori suggested that I keep working after she left. Whatever she had me do that day, even if it was just nodding my head, I did it over and over for as long as I was physically able. I thought about the lesson I'd learned in the helicopter just a few days before. I didn't dwell on the laundry list of things I couldn't do. I focused on what I could do, even if that meant shrugging my shoulders or nodding my head over and over.

Despite the hospital being three hours away from home, my family made sure I was never alone in the ICU. My sisters, Katie and Alex, always sat by my side holding my hands, and Mom and Dad sat in the few seats available. My grandma visited regularly as well. My parents brought me a DVD player so we could watch movies together. I learned in the first few days that there's only so much daytime TV you can watch. Katie and Alex also played games in which they'd touch my feet under a blanket and have me guess which foot it was. My mind was always occupied, which helped me stay positive and optimistic . . . at least during the day.

The dark moments came at night.

Even though someone was usually sleeping in my room in case I needed help, I couldn't sleep. Whenever the lights went out, I felt like a prisoner trapped in my bed. All the doubts, all the fears that I pushed away during the day with work and distractions came flooding back. Alone with my thoughts, my optimism evaporated. My mind raced through every worst-case scenario while dark questions haunted me: Will I be stuck like this forever? Will I have to quit school and live with my parents for the rest of my life? Will I always need nursing care? How can I be happy like this? How am I ever going to meet a girl? How can anyone love me like I am right now?

The longer I lay there, the darker my fears became. I thought about how even if I got well enough to live on my own, my life would still suck. Everything I loved to do required a body that worked—playing sports, hiking, waterskiing, and tubing at the lake. How could I love a life in which everything I ever wanted to do was taken away?

One night in the ICU, the dark thoughts threw me into a panic. I thought I was about to lose it when a doctor walked briskly through the door to check my vitals. That wasn't unusual—someone stopped by every two hours to roll me on my side, adjust my pillows, and check for pressure sores. Normally they finished the job and left without saying too much. But tonight was different.

After checking my vitals, the doctor stooped down on one knee next to my bed so she could look me in the eyes. "Chris, look at me," she said. She didn't use that half-whisper everyone else did in the middle of the night. Her voice was tough and authoritative.

I looked at her, taking in her short reddish hair and glasses. She was probably in her sixties and spoke with a cowboy twang, as if she had walked straight out of a Western movie. I wondered what she could possibly want.

We locked eyes. "My name is Georgia," she said. "I'm from Wyoming. Do you know anyone from Wyoming?"

I stuttered. "No." *Where in the world is this going?* I thought. I just wanted to get back to feeling sorry for myself.

Georgia kept going. "Well, people from Wyoming don't tell lies. And I want you to know that you will beat this. You *will* beat this."

Instantly, the waterworks started. I sobbed uncontrollably as I stared at her in disbelief. I'd been lying there questioning whether all my effort and all my time was worth it. No one else on the medical team had given me much assurance. Georgia didn't have to say a word to me that night, but the fact that she took an opportunity to encourage me when I was struggling completely changed my life.

Georgia's words gave me the courage to keep fighting for what I believed to be the ultimate reward: getting my old life back. In other words, I was thinking only about *me* and how *I* could beat this and how *I* could get on with *my* life. But the first hint that God might have something else in store for me came one day when my dad opened his laptop. "Chris, you've got to hear these messages coming in," he said.

I raised my eyebrows. "What messages?"

"We had so many people asking how you were doing that Alex helped us set up a CaringBridge site for you," he explained. "We've been sharing the link, posting updates, and people can write messages in reply. They're pouring in like you wouldn't believe."

He held the laptop so I could read the replies. I expected to see a few from my college buddies or my aunts and uncles, but that wasn't the case.

Entry after entry began the same way: "Hi, Chris, you don't know me, but . . ." Some shared their own stories of injuries and rehabilitation. Many encouraged me and quoted Scripture. But the ones that really grabbed me were the ones that read:

> *"I am not really sure if you know how much God is using you to touch the lives of so many people. Your faith. Your determination. Your winning attitude."*
>
> *"You all make me want to be a better person."*
>
> *"Your bravery to keep on going to your full recovery keeps us inspired. Every encouraging note touches me deeply, I can't help but cry."*
>
> *"Chris, I don't know you, but you seem like a strong young man with the will to fight. You are an inspiration to me to stay positive for the recovery of my daughter."*

I finally looked up in tears. *I'm just a kid who got injured*, I thought. What have I done that could possibly inspire anyone? Tears began to flow.

"What's wrong?" Dad asked. "I didn't mean to make you sad."

"Not sad," I said. "Just touched, I guess."

Dad put his hand on my shoulder and smiled. "Son, you have an opportunity here to make a big impact. You can show the whole world your character and what you're made of. Everyone who reads your story will see what faith in God looks like."

I didn't know what to say. "That's a lot of pressure," I finally replied.

"I know it is," Dad agreed. "But maybe your accident will be the beginning of a new plan for you. And if I know God, it's going to be even better than anything you could have expected."

From the moment I couldn't push myself up off the football field, all I'd thought about was getting my old life back. Up until I read the CaringBridge entries, it had never occurred to me that God could use my injury for his good. For whatever reason, all these people I didn't even know were turning to God because of me. I didn't understand it, but little by little, with every CaringBridge message, I started to see the pieces of the new story he was writing.

"Maybe God has a different plan for me than I thought," I said to Dad.

He smiled at me. "I think you're exactly right."

From then on my parents read me new CaringBridge messages every day. Believe me, I needed them.

My recovery beat my doctors' expectations. I moved from ICU to the rehab floor in five days, not three weeks. But even on the rehab floor, staying positive didn't come easy. Five weeks into my recovery, I felt slight sensations throughout my body and even had some movement in my arms. All this time and effort and still nothing in my legs.

By now I'd talked to several people who'd been through injuries similar to mine. Anyone who regained use of their legs had some kind of movement by no later than five or six weeks. Now, at my five-week mark, I heard a ticking clock in my head. If I was ever going to walk again, I had to move my legs *now*!

Every night my prayer was the same. "God, please let me move something in my legs. I just need that first glimpse into walking. I need you. Please."

Then one morning, the week before Thanksgiving 2010, I woke up and realized I felt a sensation in my left big toe. It almost felt as if my toe were tingling or exposed, like a blanket had fallen off at night and you feel that brisk air on your toes. I still couldn't move my toe, but when I told my family about the new feeling, everyone was excited. I thought the doctor would be too, but when I explained this sensation to him, he didn't look up from the charts in his hands.

"I'm serious, doctor," I said. "If you'd just take off my shoe and look at my toe, maybe . . ."

The doctor sighed. "Chris, you're experiencing what we call a phantom feeling," he said. "You want to believe you can feel something in your left big toe. You tricked yourself into thinking it's real, but it's not. I'm sorry."

I frowned, trying to keep my jaw from dropping. "I'm telling you, I haven't felt anything like this until today. I know something is different," I insisted.

"This happens all time with people who have spinal cord injuries," the doctor said. "But at the end of the day, the fact is, you're not going to be able to move anything in your legs ever again." And with those lovely parting words, he nonchalantly walked out of the room.

To say I was crushed would be putting it mildly. He had cast aside everything I had been working toward and praying for as if it were all for nothing. I'd never worked harder for anything in my life, and this doctor had just shut the door on my hope of moving anything soon. My dad, who was with me during that pleasant exchange, grabbed my hand. Tears welled in his eyes as his voice broke, "Chris, do not let anyone tell you what you can or cannot do."

That was the first time I ever saw my dad cry. I teared up too as I promised him, "I never will."

I now had a new goal: prove that doctor wrong. Over the next week, I worked up to three hours of therapy a day. That still wasn't enough for me. I asked for a fourth hour, which, I was told, no one had ever asked for before. Eventually they gave it to me, but they drew the line at a fifth hour. Undeterred, I asked my physical and occupational therapists to write up workouts I could do on my own, outside of my scheduled therapy time.

After a week of nonstop work, I woke up on Thanksgiving morning and felt a new, even stronger sensation in my left big toe. My physical therapist, Megan Gill, had barely walked into my room for our therapy when I blurted out, "My big toe! I think I can move it!"

She pulled back the covers, and there it was: my big toe twitching on command. Seeing that toe jerk to life felt better than every Christmas morning and football win I'd ever experienced in my life, put together. I yelled for Katie and Alex to come see.

"Look at this!" I yelled. My sisters screamed when they saw me wiggle my toe.

"Chris!" Alex burst into tears. "It happened! You did it!"

"We have to get Mom and Dad back here," Katie said. They had stayed in a hotel the night before and hadn't come to the hospital yet. They were in for quite a surprise.

When my parents arrived, I told Dad I needed help. "Can you give my feet a pep talk?" I asked. Every once in a while, my dad would stoop down by my feet and scream in a sarcastic motivational voice as if he could inspire them enough to move. "I feel like they need it today."

My dad laughed, pulled back the covers, and took his usual position at the foot of the bed. "Move!" he screamed in that voice. When my toe wiggled, Dad's eyes popped wide open as if he'd seen a ghost.

"Did you just do that?" my mom cried. She broke down in tears when she saw me do it again as if it were nothing. Finally she took a break from sobbing to smack me playfully. "You knew you could do this and never told us?"

I'd never been so thankful for a moving toe in my life. I was downright giddy. "Someone bring that doctor, Dr. Phantom, in here, and you tell him to phantom this," I asked everyone who came into my room that day. It's probably for the best that he was gone that day.

The movement in my toe aside, over the next few months, it became increasingly obvious that walking out of the hospital unassisted—my definition of "beating this"—wasn't going to happen in the time frame I had set for myself. Throughout those months, I clung to God as if my life depended on it. Rather than dwell on the fact that I was not going to walk unassisted any time soon, I chose to forget about what I couldn't do and instead focused on what I could do and the progress I was making. By God's grace I grew to believe that my injury would not define or limit me. I was a realist, which meant I accepted where I was but held out hope that I could go much, much further.

But I didn't feel completely comfortable with my new identity until March 20, 2011. It was my nineteenth birthday, and I was home for a weekend visit—we started going home once a week that month. About ten of my friends planned to take me to Buffalo Wild Wings to watch college basketball. We were running late, and when my friend transferred me to the front seat of his car, he accidentally hit the lock button on the car door. Before we realized what had happened, he slammed the door shut. I looked and saw his keys sitting on the seat next to me.

He turned to my buddies in disbelief. "Oh my gosh. I just locked Chris in the car." My friends called to me, "Chris, just hit the unlock button. It's right next to you." But I couldn't do it. By this point I'd regained limited movement in my arms, but there was no way I could reach up and hit the button to unlock the doors. I did not have the strength. My eyes stung with embarrassment as my friends kept asking me to unlock the door. I felt completely helpless.

I was just about to lose it and start crying when one of my best friends, Richie, leaned forward and fogged up the window next to me. He rubbed off the fog and put his hands dramatically over his eyes, as if he was peering in with binoculars. "Chris, conserve your oxygen!" he yelled in a fake panic. "You have five minutes to live! I need you to breathe slowly!"

My other friends stared at him in shock. Making fun of the situation seemed like a terrible thing to do, but for me it was the best thing he could have done. I burst out laughing as he took me through mock breathing exercises, as if I were running out of oxygen, as the other guys ran to their house to get spare keys. The forty-minute experience could have made for an awful night, but the whole thing was turned around by a little laughter. Right then I realized that being in a wheelchair, with limited physical ability, meant that life might not always be smooth. And that was okay. In fact, it wasn't a big deal at all.

About seven months after my injury, my family and I decided it was time for me to move home.[1] But I didn't stay there permanently. That fall I returned to Luther College. My sister Alex got an apartment less than a mile from campus so she could get me to my classes, take me to therapy appointments, and help me with homework when I needed it. On campus I lived in a cluster, with a big common room and six double rooms around it. That meant I had ten friends nearby who could help out. And everyone did. That support system gave me the confidence to pursue my education and not give up.

Before classes started I was terrified that the whole college experiment was doomed to fail. But my friends showed me that I could live a pretty normal life. I could get back to how I used to be, but now from a wheelchair. The week before classes started, they even convinced me to go with them to float down a nearby river on inner tubes. "There's no way I can do that," I'd told them when they first asked. "That sounds way too scary."

My friends refused to take no for an answer. "You can do it. Let's just go," they said. Finally, they convinced me to suck up my fears and let them bring me along. They gave me a raft that wouldn't tip and had a backrest. We bought rope to tie my raft with theirs so they could be close by. We left my chair in the vehicle, and two guys carried me to

---

1 You can read a more in-depth account of my recovery in the book I wrote with my dad, *The Power of Faith When Tragedy Strikes*.

the riverbank, one under my shoulders and the other under my knees. Floating freely in the river turned out to be one of the best experiences I'd had since my injury. I looked and, more importantly, felt like everyone else having a good time floating down the river. For the first time since my accident, I felt "normal."

While the accident impacted nearly every area of my life, one aspect it thankfully didn't affect was my family's finances. Because I was injured in an NCAA game, I was covered by their Catastrophic Insurance Program, which, combined with my mom's great health insurance policy through her employer, paid for everything I needed. Even after I got out of the hospital, I didn't have to worry about the cost of physical therapy or the specialized equipment I needed. I could even pay for friends and caregivers to help me get up in the morning or drive me to physical therapy. I soon discovered that my situation was the exception, not the rule, for people who suffer injuries like mine.

On a trip back to Mayo about a year after my injury, I ran into a friend I'd met during my hospital stay. He'd fallen off his tree stand while deer hunting and stayed just one room away from me at Mayo. Both of us were from Iowa, and we bonded during our time there. "What are you doing here?" I asked as we greeted each other in the hall of Mayo Clinic's rehab center. I was surprised to see him because he had to travel two hours each way to get there.

"Physical therapy, man," he said. "There are no clinics back home that have this kind of technology. Plus I can use their bike afterward." Mayo had an RT300 leg and arm therapeutic bike that stimulates your muscles and is great for people with spinal cord injuries and strokes.

My friend wheeled back and gave me the once over. "You're looking strong. I bet you'll be walking again in no time."

"I don't know if I'm there yet," I said. "But my therapy has helped a ton."

My friend didn't say anything, but I could see pain behind his smile. I knew he wondered how I could afford all the therapy and equipment I had. I realized how unfair the system is. To me, it's not right that money limits how far good, hard-working people, like my friend, can go in their recovery. To this day, it makes me uncomfortable how fortunate my circumstance is compared to him or anyone else going through this.

I had all this in my mind when I was invited to speak at the Lynch Family Foundation's annual banquet. This foundation was created to support those who find themselves in financial need, especially need created by health problems. They had heard my story and wanted me to share it.

"Something you should consider is that people get paid to speak," they mentioned. "As you recover, this could be a career for you. There will be a few speakers in the audience who will speak before you. They might be able to help you get started."

I'd never spoken anywhere, except in class, but I thought it sounded amazing. I knew I had a powerful story to tell, and who knows, maybe it could help someone.

Despite being extremely nervous, that first time speaking in front of an audience was unbelievable. I shared about making the tackle, my life being flipped upside down because of my spinal cord injury, and the highs and lows of my recovery process. Here and there I saw some nods, some sparks of connection. So I kept going. I emphasized how your circumstances do not determine your future. Your responses to your circumstances do. Even though I felt I didn't deliver a very good speech, everyone was entranced. The audience laughed and cried, and when I was finished, they gave me a standing ovation. *Okay, that was fun*, I thought. *I want to do that again*.

Afterward, the person who'd booked me came to shake my hand. "If you ever want to do anything to help other people or host a fundraiser to pay for anything you need, let us know," he said. "We can help you out."

I opened my mouth to say I didn't need anything, then it hit me. Maybe I didn't need anything, but I knew plenty of people who did. What if I could help others suffering from spinal injuries with equipment and recovery options they couldn't afford? That thought prompted me to approach my dad with the idea of starting our own foundation. I knew we could fill a void for people without the kind of insurance I had. My cousin helped me design a website, and we called every family friend who was an accountant or lawyer that we could think of to help us get started.

Within six months we formed a nonprofit and raised thirty-five thousand dollars with our first fundraiser. That was enough to purchase a therapeutic bike like the one my friend used at Mayo, only this one went to Winneshiek Medical Center in Decorah, Iowa, the first place I was taken by ambulance after my accident. I wanted those who couldn't go to an elite medical center to still have access to top-notch equipment. To raise the funds, my sister Alex and I went door-to-door to different businesses in town to ask for their support in our mission. Today the Chris Norton Foundation has raised close to one million dollars. We've helped patients get treatment they couldn't otherwise afford, sent people to camps for spinal cord injuries, and even started our own camp.

As my foundation evolved, so did my recovery. For far too long, I was convinced that I needed my physical abilities to be happy. My foundation helped me realize that life is about giving yourself to others and helping people. I began to see how I could have a richer life than I ever imagined, even if I never took another step as long as I lived. It also gave me contentment in the present while still having hope for a recovery.

5

Not What I Expected

· EMILY ·

Dear God,

About four months ago I met the most amazing person. I was planning on being single for a while, but that completely changed when I met Chris. There was something different about him, and I knew I had to give it a chance. This is so crazy to say since we have only been dating for a few months, but I am going to marry him and spend the rest of my life with him.

He has made me feel something that I haven't ever felt for any other guy. He has already changed the way I look at life. He has helped me appreciate the small things I used to take for granted. He has helped me not stress out over things that don't matter in the big picture. He has shown me that with hard work, anything is possible. I now believe that I can achieve my dreams and goals in life. He has helped me to be more positive and not complain. Chris and I had an immediate connection. After hanging out a few times, I just felt so comfortable around him and I felt like I had known him my whole life. I truly believe that you brought us

*together, and I am so thankful for that. I love having him in my
life, and I don't want that to ever change.*

I could hardly believe the words I'd just written in my journal. A few
months earlier I'd have bet you any amount of money that I'd never
be in a relationship that I was pretty sure was going to lead to marriage.

I felt called by God to help girls like Whittley as a vocation. The
demands of college had kept me from working with girls as hands-on as I
had in high school. But I wanted to change that. Whittley and I still talked
on a regular basis, but I missed being close enough to spend quality time
with her. On top of that, when I broke up with my old boyfriend, I had told
all my friends that I was through with relationships for a while. I needed to
take care of myself and refocus my energy on what mattered most to me,
and that's what I planned to do the summer after my junior year of college.

My friend Danielle didn't buy it. "Come on, Emily," she said when
I told her I wanted to take a break from dating. "You've been with the
same guy since you were what, fifteen?" She shook her head. "You need
to see what else is out there."

"I'm serious!" I protested. "We just broke up. The last thing I need
is another relationship."

"Who said anything about relationships? I'm talking about dating
around, having fun."

I laughed. "Oh, please. No way am I going out picking up guys. That
sounds awful."

"You really have been out of the dating scene awhile." Danielle pulled
out her phone and opened an app I'd never seen before. "There's this
website where you can meet guys in your area. You just look through the
ones that come up, and if you think he's cute, you can get matched up
and start talking."

I watched as she swiped through picture after picture. The idea that
you would start talking to some stranger because you saw his picture was
weird to me. "So you really do this? You've talked to guys from the app
and gone out with them?" I asked.

"I have a few times!" She paused on an attractive photo. "It's not like
I'm trying to meet my soul mate or anything. It's just a good distraction.
That's what you need."

I wasn't convinced, but the next thing I knew, Danielle had me downloading the app and entering my information. She even helped me pick out a photo to use in my profile.

"That's it!" she said. "You're all set up!" We swiped through a few pictures together as she gave me advice on red flags to look out for. I picked a few guys I thought were cute and set my phone down.

"You know I'm not going to actually meet up with some random person, right?" I told her. "This is just for fun."

I didn't think about the dating app again until my phone buzzed with a notification a few days later. I glanced down and saw, "Congratulations! You have a new match!"

I sighed. *Ugh, I forgot to turn off the notifications.* Before I could change my settings, a message popped up from a guy named Chris Norton. "Hey, what's up?" it said.

Wow, I thought. *That's your big opening line? What's up?* I mentally blamed Danielle for talking me into signing up for this stupid app.

I couldn't help but notice that this Chris Norton guy was wearing a cross necklace in his pictures, which made me think he might be a Christian. This was important to me. Even though I had attended church sporadically since moving off to college, my faith was still important to me. In my last relationship, my longtime boyfriend didn't have a strong faith in Christ. It wasn't a priority, and I wanted to make sure that my next boyfriend not only had a strong faith but was living out his faith.

I hoped this Chris Norton guy did. There was a link to his website in his profile, so I decided to check it out before I replied to his message. I couldn't believe the professional-looking website that popped up. Another picture of the same guy appeared, but this picture showed him in a wheelchair. I read about his injury, how he recovered and went back to school, and how he was using his story to help people with spinal cord injuries who can't afford the treatment and equipment they need.

I'd never met anyone with a spinal cord injury. I'm not sure I even knew what exactly that meant.

Chris's injury sounded as if it must have been a big deal, and I was curious to find out more. I did a Google search on his name, and I went down an internet rabbit hole, reading article after article. With every article I was struck that Chris seemed devoted to doing what he could for others. Just like that, I went from not being sure if this guy was worth the time to feeling a very strong attraction to him. He was already doing exactly what I wanted to do with my life. I never expected to find someone like him through a dating app.

As I read more about Chris and his foundation, never once did I think, *Oh, he's in a wheelchair, I don't want to deal with that.* More than anything, I was amazed at the way he didn't let his condition hold him back. I love getting to know people who are different than me and learning how they deal with difficult situations. I still wasn't thinking about dating Chris or even meeting him just yet, but I was dying to hear more about his experience. And he was very attractive.

By the time I finally closed my browser, I was thinking, *Okay, now I'm curious. I need to respond to his message.* I knew I wanted to get to know him, but I didn't want him to think I was a stalker, so I decided not to mention that I'd researched his story. I typed a quick message saying that I was visiting my Grandma Max and asked what he was doing. There. No big deal.

I anxiously waited for him to respond. But he didn't. I stared at my phone, annoyed that I cared. *You're the one who messaged me in the first place*, I thought, *and now you don't answer me?*

I checked my phone a couple of times throughout the evening. Nothing. I got a little mad at myself for letting this dating app distract me from Grandma Max. My grandma lived two hours away, but I tried to visit her as much as I could. She was the most special person in my life. I always felt so connected to her, and I admired the strong faith she had. She was a fighter, and I strived to be like her. Every moment I had with her was precious because she had a lot of health issues. Life had never been easy for her. She was a single mom to seven after she and my grandpa divorced. She continued to fight through every situation with so much strength, trust for God, and love. She was one of the most amazing people I knew. *Who is this guy who's distracting me from her? I don't care if he replies to me or not*, I told myself.

But late the next morning, there it was—a message. "Ha ha oh nice. I'm just getting ready for the day."

Seriously? You waited until today to text me that? I should have ignored him, but I couldn't. I messaged him back. Then he replied. And I replied. We went back and forth messaging through the dating app with the usual small talk conversation you have a million times in college: "What school do you go to? What's your major?" He told me he was a student at Luther College, majoring in business management and communications.

I told him a little about me and asked him if he knew what he wanted to do with his degree. His answer was exactly what I had hoped: "To run my nonprofit and do public speaking," he said.

Although I already knew the answer, I asked him, "How'd you decide to start that?"

"Because I got a neck injury in a college football game," he responded.

"I just checked out your foundation," I messaged him. Again, I didn't want to creep him out that I knew his entire story and had read every article about him. "That is seriously so awesome, Chris! You are such an inspiring person. I think it's amazing that you were able to make something positive out of a hard situation."

Now we were messaging back and forth on the dating app in real time, no waiting between responses. I really wanted to ask him about his recovery, but I didn't know if it was okay to ask someone with a spinal cord injury that question. I decided to go for it.

"How's everything going with your recovery, if you don't mind me asking?"

"I don't mind at all," he typed back. "It's going really well. I've been doing some walking in a walker and on crutches. My goal is to walk across the stage for graduation."

I couldn't put down my phone; I was so fascinated. "That's so awesome! I have a very good feeling you will make that happen. From reading your story online, you seem extremely motivated and determined." *Hope he doesn't mind that I just internet stalked him,* I thought as I typed out the message.

"What's helped you get through this and allowed you to be so strong?" I asked him. I realized my questions weren't your usual dating app questions, but I was too engrossed in his story to hold back. I wanted to find out everything I could about this guy who seemed almost superhuman.

My question didn't seem to faze him. "Well, my faith, family, and friends helped me," he said. "I'm also a pretty optimistic person. I knew feeling sorry for myself wouldn't do me any good, so I just concentrated on getting better every day."

So he is a Christian. Wow. This seems almost too good to be true, I thought. When I thought about the kind of guy I'd be interested in dating, a deep faith in God was at the top of my list. Like many students, my relationship with God during my college years wasn't quite what it was when I was in high school. I had always felt very connected to God as I prayed, and I listened to him as he directed me to help other kids at school. I never felt closer to him than when I was following my purpose in life. In college I let myself get so busy with classes and homework that I never made the effort to find a church. My relationship with God suffered as a result, but my faith in God was still foundational to my life. I always knew that my future husband had to be a Christian. Hearing this about Chris drew me to him even more.

We messaged back and forth throughout the next two days. Sometimes we simply talked about what we were doing throughout the day, but other times we dove into some deeply personal topics. I told him about Whittley and why I wanted to help teenage girls someday. Then on the third day, he messaged me again. "Hey, this app really drains my battery. If you want to keep talking, text me!" And there it was—his phone number.

I had never planned on talking to anyone from this app, but I knew I didn't want the conversation to end. So I texted. *Here goes nothing,* I thought before texting, "Hey, it's Emily! Here's my phone number so you have it!"

He replied quickly. Our text conversation continued over the next couple of days. Sometimes I had a text waiting for me when I woke up in the morning, and I never went more than a few hours without hearing from Chris. We never said hello or goodbye—it was like a conversation that never stopped. And I certainly didn't want it to.

Eventually I mentioned that I was moving back to college that weekend.

"No way!" he said. "I'm visiting my high school friend at Iowa State this weekend too! I'd love to meet up with you."

I froze. I was definitely drawn to him, but the idea of meeting a stranger made me nervous. Sure, we'd texted, but we had never even spoken on the phone. Was this crazy? But Chris was clearly a positive, amazing guy who had the qualities I'd always been looking for in a lifelong partner. What could it hurt to meet?

I must have typed and deleted my response five times before I finally texted back, "Absolutely, I'd love that."

We agreed to hang out that weekend but didn't make a solid plan for what we would do. Our plans were pretty noncommittal, but that didn't bother me. I wasn't ready to call this a date anyway. This was just two new friends meeting for the first time. Our first few attempts to get together didn't work out. Finally, we decided to meet at the Campustown Square near the Iowa State campus at 8:00 p.m. on Saturday.

A short time before I needed to leave to meet Chris, I caught a glimpse of myself in the mirror. I'd just spent the day unpacking boxes and it showed. I'm definitely not a high heels, full face of makeup kind of girl, but for this night I wanted to wear something nice. Even though I didn't want to admit it to myself, I cared way more about what I looked like than I usually do.

A knot formed in my stomach as I drove to the Campustown Square. What was I thinking meeting a guy I'd never even talked to on the phone? This could be the most awkward night ever.

I parked across the street from the hot dog stand where we'd agreed to meet and strained to see if he was already there. Sure enough, I saw a guy in a wheelchair with a few other college-age guys. My heart beat faster as I walked toward him. Mistake or not, it was too late to turn back now.

"Emily! You made it!" Chris said. His smile was so warm and friendly that my nerves melted away almost instantly.

"It's so good to meet you!" I said. I noticed his arms reaching up, so I met him halfway and knelt to hug him. Seeing him in person was surreal and yet the most natural thing in the world.

"So are you all moved in?" he asked after introducing me to his friends.

"Yep. Finally. Move-in day is the worst," I said, laughing.

"Oh, I know. It's brutal. Did your brothers help you? You have two of them, right?"

I was impressed he remembered so many details I had told him and that he took the lead in steering the conversation. He didn't wait for me to ask him questions but jumped right in, wanting to know more about me. The conversation flowed, and we kept talking long after his friends wandered over to a few benches far enough away to give us some privacy.

The next few minutes were a blur. I can't remember most of what we talked about. I only remember looking into his eyes and seeing this light and energy that emanated from him. I went into this night thinking there was no way he could be as positive and upbeat as he seemed in his texts. Yet here he was, smiling and laughing when he had every reason to be mad at the world. I found myself feeling more drawn to him every minute.

I felt so comfortable that when he asked if I wanted to head over to his friend's house with him, I didn't hesitate. I noticed as we walked to the house that Chris could get himself around in his manual wheelchair that had power assisted wheels, but any time we crossed gravel, grass, or went uphill, he needed a friend to push him. I was naively surprised that he needed any help at all. *Huh, I guess I have a lot to learn*, I thought.

Once we were in the house, Chris's friend Cory said, "Okay, who wants to play cards?"

"Me!" I turned to Chris. "Want to play me?"

He grinned. "You're on."

For the next few hours, we played cards and talked as if we would never run out of things to say. I looked for red flags or signs that his app persona wasn't real, but everything checked out. I thought for sure I was going to see cracks in what I thought might be a facade when he reached for his drink next to him, and his hand awkwardly knocked it over. Sprite spilled all over the plastic end table and onto the shag carpet below. My eyes jerked from the mess to Chris, waiting for the anger and embarrassment I was sure would follow. I listened for a shout, a curse word, anything. But he just laughed and shook his head. "Well I really missed that, didn't I? Whoops."

I burst out laughing. Not only was he not embarrassed that he spilled his drink, he was also so confident that he could make fun of himself. *He's the real deal*, I thought. *You can't fake that kind of reaction.* "Let me help you with that," I said, jumping up to find a roll of paper towels. I finished wiping up the soda and looked up to see him smiling at me with this indescribable look in his eyes. Butterflies fluttered in my stomach, and I smiled back nervously.

"Thank you," he said. "I really appreciate your help."

"Oh, of course!" The noise of a dozen other conversations filled the room, but I didn't even notice. My eyes were locked on his.

Suddenly, my vibrating phone woke me out of my daze. I picked it up to see a text from one of my roommates. "Just checking to make sure you're okay!" she said. Then I realized what time it was.

"Oh, man, it's getting really late. I should probably get back."

"Already?" Chris's face fell. "That went by fast."

"It really did." I pulled out my keys. Normally this is the part where a guy asks if he can walk me to my car, but since this wasn't exactly a normal situation, I wasn't sure what to expect. Maybe he'd have a friend go along with us in case he needed help getting back.

"Well, this was fun. I'm glad we did this," he said.

"Me too," I said. I played with my keys, waiting. Finally, I realized the walk to my car wasn't going to happen, and I was slightly disappointed. My dad would have warned me that this was a bad sign. I told myself that in this particular circumstance, it was alright to let it slide.

I bent down to hug him. I noticed that we lingered a little longer than when we first hugged when we met.

"We'll talk soon," he grinned as I turned to leave.

As I walked to my car, I had a feeling he was right. This wasn't love at first sight, although I definitely thought he was cute. And I wasn't thrilled about trudging down the dark neighborhood street and past the Campustown Square by myself in the middle of the night. Still, my lips couldn't help but curl into a smile as I replayed bits of our conversations over and over in my head.

I didn't know exactly what role I wanted Chris to play in my life, but I already knew I wanted him to be a part of it.

6

Finding Emily

· CHRIS ·

When I arrived at Luther College as a freshman, I wondered if the girl for me might be in one of my classes or cheering for me at football games. Before I could even think about trying to meet her, *boom*, I mistimed a tackle, broke my neck, and life as I knew it changed in an instant. Suddenly, all the things I thought girls cared about—my athleticism, my strength, my ability to protect them—the things I thought made me attractive, were gone. The way I saw it, everyone just thought of me as the guy in the wheelchair.

I thought that because there were days when that was how I felt about myself. My injury changed a lot about me, but it did not change my desire to find love. But deep down I wondered if it was ever going to happen for me. Late at night when I had trouble sleeping, the same worries with which I wrestled in the hospital right after my accident came back to haunt me. Lying in the dark, I wondered how any girl could ever love me in my condition. Let's face it, anyone who decided to be with me was signing up for helping me shower, get dressed, and even use the bathroom for the rest of her life. What kind of person would be willing to do that?

Over time I slowly learned that physical abilities weren't at the top of every girl's priority list. The more people I met and got to know, the more I realized that people cared more about who I was and who I was trying to become than my chair. I started to accept that someone could like me for my personality and what I did for others. Still, I had trouble getting past my physical limitations and dependence on others. In the early days after my accident, I struggled to fully accept myself. My unspoken question was: Even if I could fully accept myself, could anyone else? These feelings were driven home every time a doctor recommended that my parents install a ramp at their house or that I buy a handicap-accessible van. *Why would we do that when I'm not going to need them forever?* I thought. I tried to convince myself that my condition was temporary, even though I knew it wasn't. I felt as if I needed to walk again to truly be myself and have the life I'd always wanted.

All of this swirled around in my head as I eased back into college life post-accident. I had my eyes open for a girl who sparked my interest while also wondering if my limitations might scare that girl away. My standards for the girl of my dreams were pretty high. I always told myself I would never date a girl I couldn't see myself marrying. Setting the bar that high, plus my own insecurities, combined with the fact that Luther College is pretty small, meant that a year after returning to campus, I was still single.

I was thinking about all this late one night while hanging out with my buddy A.P., watching Jimmy Kimmel. The two of us weren't talking too much, just watching the show, which gave me time to think. I looked around and it hit me: *I have eight or more friends who all pitch in to help me at school, but once I graduate, will one person be able to handle all the responsibilities? And where am I going to meet that "one person"? I certainly don't have any prospects now. Once I go out into the real world, it will be even harder to meet someone. Time is ticking, but I also don't want to force anything.*

Thankfully the TV show distracted me enough to pull me out of that dark place. The person Kimmel was interviewing told a funny story about her friend who signed up for a dating website that rated you on whether you're beautiful or not before you could get into the site. A.P. snorted with laughter. "Oh my gosh. That's a real thing? That website probably crushes a lot of people's confidence. If you lack self-esteem, that might not be a good dating site."

"I wonder how harsh they really are," I said. "Like, how depressing would it be to think you're a ten and get rejected from a beautiful people website?"

"You know what we should do? We should make a profile and see if they vote us in."

"Yes!" I could always count on A.P. to come up with something hilarious. He was already pulling up the website on his phone when another guy from the cluster wandered out of his room.

"You know, it's not really the same thing, but a lot of people are using this other app to meet girls," our friend said. He'd clearly overheard what we were talking about. "It pulls up people who live within a certain distance from you. If you think a girl is cute and she thinks you're cute, you match up and start a conversation."

My ears perked up. I'd just been complaining that the dating pool at Luther College was too shallow. Maybe this app was the answer.

We all created profiles. It didn't take long for me to match up with girls, and I was so excited that I didn't waste any time before starting conversations with them.

But the results were disappointing.

Every conversation sputtered and died after exchanging a few messages. My "matches" and I never even shared phone numbers, much less actually met. I decided the whole thing was a waste of time. I still checked the dating app from time to time when I was bored, and I messaged matches here and there, but overall, I was discouraged.

A few months later, I happened to see the profile of a girl named Emily Summers. She was absolutely beautiful. But I didn't let myself get too excited since every other so-called match had ended poorly. Even though I knew nothing was going to happen, I decided to go ahead and send her a halfhearted, "Hey, what's up?" message. *Who knows? Maybe she'll respond*, I thought, then went back to hanging out with my friends.

I was halfway through my morning the next day when I finally got around to checking the app to see if she had replied. She had, but with a noncommittal, "What are you doing?" *Oh, that was quick*, I thought. I replied with something about getting ready for the day, then hit send.

Like I said, I had no faith in this app and zero expectations that these casual texts might develop into an actual conversation.

We exchanged a few more small-talk messages, nothing memorable, until I mentioned my foundation. I was getting ready for an event, which is why I brought it up. I didn't think much of it until Emily asked why I started the foundation. I told her I had a neck injury. I kept my answers short. I figured if she really wanted to know more, she could Google me.

And that's exactly what she did.

My first sign of hope came when Emily told me she was passionate about helping people too. I could tell she wasn't just saying this, because her passion radiated from her enthusiastic messages. Now my interest was piqued. She didn't sound like any other girl I'd talked to.

She sent me a message asking about my foundation and my story. She said lots of nice things about me, but that's what everyone does. Since my accident, multiple girls had seemed interested in me, but I came to find out most found me inspiring but had no interest in me romantically. I figured this was just more of the same.

Then she asked me something that caught me off guard: "How's your recovery going, if you don't mind me asking?"

Believe it or not, no one outside of my closest friends and family ever asked me anything like that. Most people are too scared to broach the subject. They don't know what language to use or how to be sensitive, so more often than not, I found they simply steered clear altogether. I don't know if people think I'll be embarrassed or hurt if they draw attention to my injury, but it's usually a taboo subject.

Not for Emily.

She straight-up asked the question, and I was glad. I appreciated that she wanted to know. I told her I'd been doing some walking with help from equipment. I even shared my goal of walking across the stage for graduation, something that drove me more than I let on to most people.

She asked about my accident and how I got through it. Her question took our conversation to a whole new level. I tried not to let the conversation be all about me. I asked her questions too and genuinely cared about what she said. But she kept coming back to my situation. Then she asked me something no girl had ever asked me before. "I'm just wondering," Emily wrote, "do you think everything happens for a reason?"

Whoa, I thought. In the months I'd used this app, I'd only had surface-level conversations. I figured that's what the app was for until Emily and I started talking. I would have been scared to ask a stranger such a personal question. Emily just went right for it after only talking for a few hours. To me, her questions revealed Emily as a selfless girl who was actually interested in me and who I was. I felt more drawn to her with every message she sent and every question she asked. There is something comforting about addressing an insecurity.

Emily and I continued messaging back and forth through the dating app, but I wanted more. After a few days of talking, I took a deep breath and put myself out there. "Well hey, this app really drains my phone's battery. If you want to talk more, text me!"

And I gave her my number.

I worried that it was too soon or that I would never hear from her again. Relief flooded over me when my phone vibrated with a text from a number I didn't recognize. "This is Emily!" it said.

A week later I knew I had to meet this girl. At first I'd messaged her because I thought she was beautiful. Now I knew she was even more beautiful on the inside. Her heart and her passion made her irresistible. She seemed like the real deal, like the kind of girl I'd always hoped to find. I hoped this could lead to something serious.

I didn't want to seem overeager, so I decided to delay my messages instead of responding instantly. In my mind, girls want you more when you play it cool. I also wanted her to know I had a life and had things going on other than staring at my phone all day. Maybe that explains why I was still single. I didn't know much about girls or how to be romantic.

"What are you up to this weekend?" I asked her, trying not to sound as desperate to know as I actually was.

"I'm moving back into school!" she said. "I can't wait to get back, but it's going to be so hot. I'm not looking forward to carrying all my stuff up and down all those stairs!"

She's moving in at Iowa State, my mind raced. *I have friends who go there. Surely I can come up with a reason to be there too, so we can finally meet.* Suddenly, I came up with a brilliant idea. I shot a text to my friend at Iowa State, and within a few minutes, I had made plans to visit him and convinced a friend to drive me the three hours to get there.

I texted Emily. "No way, I'm visiting my high school friend at Iowa State this weekend too!" Yep, total coincidence. "I'd love to meet up with you."

I felt nauseated as I waited for her to respond. *Why did I do that?* I thought. *This was a huge mistake. She's going to be totally freaked out by my pushing to meet so soon and never talk to me again. Stupid, stupid, stupid.*

When I saw her response, it was all I could do not to shout, "Yes!" She said she'd love to see me! Not only had I not scared her off, we were going to meet face-to-face.

We didn't make solid plans, but I thought I would see her that Friday night or Saturday. However, she was still moving into her apartment that Friday night and couldn't come. The following day when I asked her to come to my friend's house, she said she wasn't comfortable going to someone's house she didn't know when she didn't have a friend who could come with her. Looking back, I completely understand. But that day I was consumed with worry. Here I thought we'd made plans when really she was just being nice. Now that it was time to actually meet, she was going to find every excuse in the book to back out. *Don't get your hopes up. It's not going to work out,* I told myself.

But then again . . . maybe she wasn't making excuses. I just needed to come up with a better plan on where to meet.

Then I read her next text. "Where does your friend live?" she said. "I could pick you up and we could grab something to eat."

At first I laughed. Not only would my chair not fit in her car, but she also had no idea of all it took to get me in and out of vehicles. Then a knot formed in my stomach. She really didn't know what she was getting herself into by meeting me. I'd never tried to hide my condition, but I hadn't made it super obvious in my app profile either. *Maybe she thinks I'm pretty much recovered,* I thought. *She doesn't understand that I can hardly move my arms, let alone my legs. She has no concept of how much help I need to get around. When she sees me, she's going to be out the door.* Since having her pick me up was not an option, I scrambled to come up with something better.

"Tell her to meet you in at Campustown Square," my friend said. "There are always a ton of people there. Tell her you'll bring your friends too so she's not alone with you. We can go to Superdog. I'm up for a hot dog anyway."

Yes. Perfect. I threw out the suggestion to her and was relieved when she agreed.

I realized it was too late to back out now. If my condition scared her off, then this relationship was never meant to be. We agreed to meet at Superdog, and I was a nervous wreck. I wanted everything to be perfect. Then an hour before I was supposed to meet her, we were at the Campustown student apartments when a friend's hand slipped as he held up my cup for me to take a drink. Pop spilled all over my shirt, leaving not just a huge wet mark but also a distinct smell.

"I am so sorry, man," my friend said.

"No, it's my fault." I was so mad at myself. "This is going to be so embarrassing. I don't think she's going to be interested anyway. And now I'm a mess."

"Come on, it'll dry," he said. "Let's go outside and wait. It's going to be fine."

I hoped he was right. When he and another friend went with me to Superdog, I told them to sit on a bench close by so if I got shot down, I could get out of there quickly.

Then I waited.

And waited.

I checked my phone constantly, wondering if she was really going to show up. I squinted into the distance, trying to make her appear.

Then I saw her walking across the street, coming straight toward me. Immediately, my heart pounded. My jaw dropped. She was even more beautiful in person than I had anticipated. I'd seen her profile picture and photos on Facebook, but her smile, her eyes, everything was even more striking in person. Seeing a woman this gorgeous walking toward me gave me butterflies.

"Hey!" Emily greeted me. I wasn't sure what I should do, but a handshake didn't seem quite right. I took a risk and lifted my arms for a hug. Luckily, she reciprocated. Her long brown hair tickled my neck as she leaned in.

"It's so nice to meet you," I said, meaning it way more than she knew.

"Wow, I can't believe it's really you!" she said. Her smile was downright electric. I had to take a deep breath to collect myself enough to form whole sentences.

"So, are you all moved in?" I asked, which started the small talk of catching up. The whole time, her eyes never darted to my hands or legs. If she looked at the chair, I didn't notice. She was looking me right in the eyes, like there was nothing wrong with me. I was blown away.

After hanging out at Superdog for a while, I finally felt confident enough to ask her to come to my friend's house to hang out.

"Yeah, that sounds great," she said.

While I was relieved, I wondered if she could possibly keep seeing me and not my wheelchair. As the night went on, I braced myself for her to make up a reason to leave early. But she came to my friend's house. She met my friends. She was a natural conversationalist with everyone she met and had an incredible energy.

When my friend suggested a card game, Emily jumped in and challenged me. "You might not know this, but I am a good card player," she bragged.

"Oh, really?" I laughed. "You're setting the bar pretty high there."

"I'm pretty confident you won't be disappointed." She winked. "I am a very competitive person. I hate losing."

I couldn't believe how well this was going. I kept waiting for her to be scared off or for something embarrassing to happen. I had told my friends to stay nearby to stave off disaster. One fun fact about being paralyzed from the shoulders down is that I have to use a urinary leg bag, which basically means I am attached to a portable toilet at all times. To make life even more interesting, I was not strong enough to empty it myself. Someone else had to do it for me. I needed a friend with me in case I needed my leg bag emptied that night. Not only that, my upper body was still super weak. I had wanted my friend there to push me so I didn't look helpless or make her feel like she had to help me. I even had him suggest a simple game in which you guess if someone's card is higher or lower, so I never had to worry about holding a single card.

But aside from me knocking over a drink, the night went smoothly. I couldn't believe the two of us were actually hanging out. I was floating on cloud nine. Emily was way out of my league. She was so beautiful, with such a huge heart. She was way too good for me. Yet she wasn't running.

She wasn't staring at my chair. And she seemed genuinely interested in me.

When we hugged goodbye, I knew it wouldn't be the last time. I had a feeling that this night was a great start to something special.

Looking back, I now know I had a lot to learn. It didn't even occur to me to suggest that I accompany her to her car or at least text her and ask if she made it home safely. I hadn't yet learned how to think of another person's needs before my own. Thankfully, Emily looked past my thoughtlessness. I didn't know how to be in a relationship, but I would soon find out.

7

Falling for Each Other

· EMILY ·

After meeting face-to-face for the first time, I could feel myself falling for Chris. But I also had some reservations that had nothing to do with him. When I first told my parents about Chris, before the meeting at Campustown, my dad had warned me that there are a lot of crazy people out there and that I should be extra cautious of someone I met online. He also told me to make it clear to Chris that I just wanted to be friends. I told my dad I would, but after meeting Chris, I knew I wanted more. That made me feel guilty because I had specifically told my ex when I broke up with him that I was not interested in dating anyone else. How would it look to everyone if I jumped right into a relationship with another guy?

A few days after our first meeting, Chris invited me to visit him, this time to go to a high school football game where they were honoring his foundation in Des Moines. Des Moines is only about thirty minutes from Ames, which made this a very low commitment-level meeting. The football game itself turned out to be huge. Over ten thousand people were there. At halftime Chris wheeled out to the middle of the field to share his story and to raise money for his foundation. He wanted me to hang out on the sidelines with him during the game. While I really wanted to see him again, I hesitated when he told me that his parents would be there. Meeting the parents is a big step. I sidestepped it by asking if my sister, Marisa, and her boyfriend, Brooks, could come along. I don't know why, but I thought if I brought other people with me, then I'd appear to be nothing more than a friend rather than a potential girlfriend. My sister and her boyfriend were coming up from Muscatine to visit me anyway. It didn't take much to convince them to come with me.

▪ CHRIS ▪

It was still light out that warm Friday night when Emily and her guests walked over to me in the stadium end zone. I introduced my parents to "my friend Emily." I braced myself and waited for my parents to say something embarrassing, but to my surprise, they kept their cool. Not once did they mention how much I'd talked about this amazing girl. Emily was true to form and was as engaging, articulate, and polite as always. She was all the things you want a girl to be when introducing her to your parents.

For my parents, meeting Emily was a huge deal. I'd never introduced them to a girl since my injury. They'd never said anything to me, but I knew they were worried I'd never find someone. That's why I was eager to tell them I was talking to this wonderful girl, albeit via text. They reacted like I knew they would. The two of them tried to contain their excitement, but they weren't too good at it. I didn't mind. Now that they'd finally gotten to meet this mystery woman, their excitement hit a new level.

Mine did too, although I tried to keep it under control. I kept looking for red flags that might mean Emily didn't want to be anything more than friends. Instead, I saw good signs—a flirty laugh here, a hand on my shoulder there. I didn't want to read too much into anything, but I could tell she was into me. At least I hoped she was.

I'd be lying if I said I wasn't trying to impress Emily that night. There we were at a major high school football game, holding a fundraiser for a nonprofit I started, and I was being recognized on the field in front of thousands of people. That's got to look pretty good, right?

After the game, Emily and I went back to my parents' house in Altoona, about half an hour away, along with the rest of my family and our friends. We played board games and chatted until everyone decided they wanted ice cream. I didn't really want to go because it's clumsy and difficult for me to get loaded in and out of a vehicle.

"I'm going to stay here," I said. "Could you pick up some ice cream for me?" This didn't surprise my family, so they all stood up to leave.

Emily looked around and moved toward me. "I'll stay here too. I don't mind."

This was definitely a good sign.

· EMILY ·

After Chris's family left to get ice cream, we were alone for the first time. I sat down on the love seat in their living room, across from Chris in his chair. "Are you sure you don't want to go?" he asked me. "You said you loved ice cream."

I laughed nervously. "I'd rather be here," I said. Then I did something I had never done with a guy. Instead of waiting for Chris to hold my hand for the first time, I reached over and took hold of his. I didn't know what was going to happen next, but I knew what I hoped he'd do.

Chris and I sat there like that for a moment, looking at each other, not really saying anything. Then he asked what I'd hoped he'd ask. "Can I have a kiss?" he said. I didn't answer. Instead, I leaned over to him, and we shared our first kiss.

His family soon returned. A little while later, his dad transferred Chris from his chair to the couch, next to me, where the two of us could watch a movie together. Once Chris was situated, his dad left the room. I was glad. I wanted to be alone with him. At first I sat a little ways apart from Chris, but I soon scooted close to him. Normally, he should have made the move over to me, but Chris couldn't move his body that way. I knew he wouldn't mind if I made the move instead.

We'd been watching the movie for a while when my phone buzzed. I answered the text and didn't think anything of it. But I noticed a change in the way Chris was acting, as though he was suddenly all nervous or something. I could not imagine why. Finally, he asked, "Oh, who is that on your phone?"

"That's my brother David," I said.

"Oh, great," he said with a relieved tone. I laughed. He must have thought it was my ex or some other guy I was interested in, especially since my brother's photo popped up on the screen when he texted me. Chris must have seen it and jumped to all kinds of crazy conclusions. Thankfully it didn't last long. I snuggled over next to him as the movie played. I can't even remember what we watched because my mind wasn't really on the movie.

About halfway through the movie, Chris asked, "Can I put my arm around you?"

I sort of smiled and said, "Yeah."

I sat there waiting for a moment before Chris finally said, "Well, can you help me put it around you?"

"Oh, yeah," I said. We both laughed as I picked up his hand and gently draped his arm around my shoulders. Later he kissed me again. The night was pretty much perfect.

▪ CHRIS ▪

I am not the kind of guy to fall fast for a girl, but with Emily I couldn't help myself. She was everything I'd ever dreamed of. I liked her so much that I was afraid I might push her away. No girl wants a guy who comes across as desperate. Still, I wanted to see her the very next weekend. I can't drive because of my injury, so if we were going to see each other, it was on her to visit me. I hated that and felt insecure that I couldn't do typical things I'd always thought I should do in a relationship. A couple of days passed. We talked via FaceTime, which only made me want to see her more. When I couldn't take it anymore, I swallowed my insecurities and asked her to come visit me at Luther.

I'd mostly kept quiet about Emily around my friends, but that week I slowly started mentioning her. But I played it cool. "Yeah, I'm talking to this girl, Emily. It sounds like she might come up this weekend. You guys can meet her if you're around."

My act didn't work. All my friends knew this was a *huge* deal, and they were excited for me. "Wow, we're going to meet a girl you're talking to?" they said. "Must be serious."

I could hardly wait for Friday to get there. But when the day came, Emily texted me with bad news. "I don't think I'm going to be able to come," she said. "My grandma is sick, and I have to visit her in Dubuque. I'm so sorry."

I was crushed. A sick grandma is the oldest excuse in the book for blowing someone off. I thought, *Maybe she's making this up because she doesn't want to come. She's getting cold feet. She's not really into me after all.* I wondered what I would tell my friends.

I replayed our conversations in my head, looking for a sign I'd missed, but nothing added up. I had no doubt that our feelings were mutual. Why would she make up an excuse not to come? Perhaps she didn't want things to get too serious. Just like in my hospital bed all those months ago, I found myself in that dark place, with all my deepest insecurities running through my mind. One setback and my worst fears came bubbling up again.

My thoughts were spiraling downward when she texted me again. "I really want to see you," she said. "Is it okay if I drive up tonight? I know it will be late, but I don't want to miss our visit."

A wave of relief. The fact that she made it work was the best sign I could have hoped for. As it turned out, her grandmother really was sick, but she got better, which is why Emily drove on up to see me.

• EMILY •

About a month after we first met, I was visiting Chris at Luther and sitting on his lap in his dorm. We sit like that a lot so we can be close to one another without having to worry about transferring him to a sofa or love seat. We were having a normal conversation when it hit me that his positive mind-set was the most amazing gift anyone could have. He'd pushed himself to get through the most difficult things I could imagine. My eyes filled with tears as I gazed at him. I realized that as long as I had Chris in my life, everything was going to be okay. No matter what I would go through, I knew we'd get through it together. For the first time, I thought, *I want to marry this guy someday.*

▪ CHRIS ▪

As Emily and I grew closer, my insecurities didn't go away. Everything was going too well. Something had to be wrong, I just knew it.

Several weeks after we met, I texted her around 9:00 on a Tuesday night. "Hey, what are you doing?" I asked her.

She responded, "I'm just chilling at a park."

Her text caught me off guard. It was a cold night, not exactly your ideal park weather. I asked her why she was there, and I felt like she was hedging. She said, "I'm just in my car hanging out."

Instantly, my mind flashed with all my worst fears. *Oh no,* I thought. *She's with someone else.* I thought I was past the insecurity and was done trying to guard myself. Guess not. Immediately, I called her. When she picked up the phone, I could tell she'd been crying. "Are you okay?" I asked.

"I'm fine," she said, but her voice sounded hoarse.

"Come on, Emily. You can tell me. What's wrong?"

She sighed. "I'm just thinking about all these kids out there who are hurting. This is something I think about often. I feel like I'm not doing as much as I could be doing. Before I moved to college, I mentored kids, taught Christian education classes, even ran a program called Girl Talk for middle school girls. I felt like I was making a huge impact for so many kids. But now . . . I feel like I've dropped the ball. There are hurting kids in Ames that I could help, but I've done nothing to even find out where I might be needed. I still talk to so many of the kids I mentored back home, especially Whittley . . . but I feel like there is more I could be doing." Her voice broke as she started crying again.

Emily had spoken to me about her passion to help kids who have been placed in the foster care system. She was studying family services for that exact reason. I knew about her special relationship with Whittley, whom she loved. I did not doubt that the empathy she felt for children was real. But to be this randomly upset without a specific trigger? I didn't buy it.

I proceeded carefully. "Really? That's why you're crying?" I hesitated, then continued. "Have you talked to your ex?"

"No," she insisted. "I'm so done with that. All I've been thinking about is wanting to make a difference in the lives of kids who are hurting. I just want to know what I'm meant to do and how I can make the biggest impact."

I was stunned. Her heart, her desire to make a difference was unreal. I'd certainly never felt that way. I've never seen anyone else cry because they didn't think they were doing enough to help others. I realized how much she felt for others, and that made me admire her even more. Over time I've realized that because I've gone through a spinal cord injury, I'm not as empathetic as I once was. When you go through a traumatic experience, other things don't rattle you as much. So to see Emily reveal her heart in this way made her even more attractive to me. Once again I saw what I'd known since the first night I met her—no matter how beautiful she was on the outside, her true beauty came from within.

▪ EMILY ▪

I wanted my family to be just as excited about Chris as I was. He was the best person I'd ever met and had the greatest attitude. At first, though, my parents and family couldn't understand it. They thought I wasn't thinking through what it would be like to be with someone who's a quadriplegic. I knew they trusted me and thought he was a great guy and an incredible person, but they were worried I was caught up in the moment and not thinking through the logistics and the future. Plus, they knew my history of helping kids who were in trouble. I'm sure they thought I was doing the same thing with Chris.

I dreaded the whole meet-the-parents scenario because my mom and dad had not been shy about expressing their concerns. But after a few weeks of dating, Chris told me he and his friends were going to pass through Muscatine on their way to Ohio State. Chris had met Urban Meyer, the coach of the school's football team, and gottten tickets to a game. "What would you think about me stopping by to meet your parents?" Chris asked.

"Definitely!" I said. "That would be great!" Inside, though, I was super nervous. Would my mom and dad be able to look past the wheel-chair and see Chris for who he really was? What were they going to think of him? Our relationship was pretty low-key at this point, but I could already picture a future with Chris. The fact that I really liked him raised the stakes of this first meeting.

It turned out I didn't have to worry. That Friday night my parents greeted Chris with hugs and genuine smiles. "We're so glad to meet you, Chris," my mom said as she helped him inside.

Dad carried Chris's bag and shook his friends' hands. "Emily has told us so much about you."

It was late, but we all sat around the kitchen table talking and eating chocolate chip cookies my mom had baked. My concerns melted away as I watched them all in the dim kitchen, laughing and smiling. True, it was mostly small talk, and I could tell they weren't completely hooked yet, but it looked like they were on their way to seeing Chris the way I saw him.

"Well, he seems like a nice young man," my mom said the next morning. It wasn't the raving endorsement I'd hoped for, but I'd take it.

· CHRIS ·

After a month, Emily and I were talking constantly and seeing each other every weekend. I tried to play it cool, but I knew I was in love with her. I also knew it was too early to say it. The last thing I wanted was to scare her away. One night Emily told me "I heart you," which was pretty close to the real thing in my mind, so I started saying it to her after that. I know it sounds cheesy now, but she thought it was cute, and it was special to both of us.

There was no doubt in my mind that I wanted her to be my girlfriend. With all the time we spent together, it felt like she already was, but noth-ing was official. In early October, several weeks after we started talking, I got up the courage to ask her as she drove me in my van to Iowa City.

"What would you think if we made it official? Like, boyfriend and girlfriend?" I asked. I'll fully admit that I'm not a romantic guy. I was doing my best, though.

I thought for sure she would smile and say yes. Instead, she was quiet. "I just don't know if I'm ready for that," she finally said. "It's not that I don't like you, but I just got out of a relationship, and it would look bad if I jumped right into something else. It's too soon. I just don't feel right about it yet."

I played it off as if everything were fine and we could wait as long as she wanted, but inside I was crushed. I wondered if maybe she was embarrassed to be with me. We were obviously so close; what could be holding her back?

A couple of weeks later, I tried again. My foundation was having a fundraiser with at least two hundred people, and Emily was coming with me. We were in my dorm as I ironed out a few last-minute details.

"Are you about ready to go?" she asked, checking the time. I nodded and smiled at her. She looked so pretty standing there in her dress, her straight brown hair flowing down her back. *I can't believe I get to sit next to her tonight*, I thought. I knew it was the right moment to ask the question I'd been dying to ask—again.

"There are going to be a lot of people at this thing," I said. "So, when I introduce you to people . . . could I introduce you as my girlfriend?" I held my breath as I waited for her answer. She'd said no before. Would she say it again tonight?

To my relief, Emily just said, "Yeah, you can."

It doesn't exactly rank up there with the most romantic moments of all time. Emily still ribs me from time to time that I never really asked her to be my girlfriend. I got in on a technicality. That night, though, I didn't care. My chest puffed with pride, and I fought back a grin every time I said, "This is my girlfriend, Emily."

▪ EMILY ▪

I was definitely ready for Chris to ask me to be his girlfriend. We'd spent so much time together, and I was crazy about him. However, the way he asked still makes me laugh. He never actually said the words, "Will you be my girlfriend?" But I was into him enough that I let it slide.

Even though it already seemed like we were dating, I felt good knowing we were finally official. He must have introduced me as his girlfriend at least a dozen times that night at the foundation fundraiser. And every time I heard it, it felt so right.

That night was also a chance for me to see Chris in his element. I was blown away by the scale of that fundraiser. I'd never been to a foundation event, much less known someone who put the whole thing together. He was so determined to help people, and the fact that he was doing it successfully as a college student showed me that he's not the kind of guy who's all talk. If he wants something, he goes after it.

At this point we were still just saying "I heart you," but in my heart it was much deeper than a cute saying. I loved his drive and passion, his positive attitude, and his dedication to helping others. I loved the way his eyes lit up when we saw one another. And I hated saying goodbye at the end of each visit. I wasn't quite ready to name my feelings yet, but I knew they were stronger than anything I'd ever experienced.

8

Up to the Challenge

· CHRIS ·

Once Emily and I finally became "official," all my insecurities melted away. I stopped watching for signs that she didn't want to be with me. At long last I could let my guard down and accept that this incredible woman, who was so beautiful inside and out, was into me.

But I still had one last hill to climb: I had not told her I loved her, even though I really wanted to. I'd never felt this way about anyone before. I was completely head over heels for her, and my feelings only grew stronger each time we were together. I could have told her I was falling in love with her two weeks after we first met. But telling a girl you are falling in love with her two weeks into a relationship is not usually a good move. If I blurted the words out too soon, I was sure I'd scare her away.

So I waited.

And waited.

And waited.

Even though I could not wait to tell Emily that I loved her, part of me could not bring myself to do it. I'd never said these words to a girl before. I took them too seriously to blurt them out to just anyone. When I told a girl I loved her, I wanted that girl to be "the one." How could I know that

Emily was the one after only eight weeks, much less two weeks? Before I met her, I'd have told you that the very idea was crazy. Now I only knew I was crazy about her, and I wanted to tell her how I felt. I didn't know exactly what the right timing was, so I kept the words to myself week after week until the words were bubbling up inside me. I didn't think I could hold them in much longer.

That weekend, Emily came to Luther College to hang out with me like she did most weekends. We went out with some of my friends that Saturday night, then came back to my dorm cluster (which is like a living room connected to six rooms) to watch a movie or talk or something. It kept getting later and later, but neither of us wanted to call it a night. Everyone else went to their rooms and were now sound asleep. I couldn't think of sleep. When we got back to the dorm, a friend had transferred me to the couch and reclined the seat back. So Emily and I sat back together, my arm around her, her head on my shoulder. For hours we just sat and talked. By now it was 3:00 a.m. The words "I love you," kept bouncing around in my head, but I told myself that the timing was all wrong. It was too late at night and too early in our relationship to make a big declaration. But my heart wouldn't listen. It told me this was the moment I'd been waiting for.

My heart pounded as I cleared my throat. I had no idea if she felt the same way about me that I did about her. There was a good chance she didn't, not yet at least. I knew she'd say something back. Emily is so honest that she'll tell you exactly what she thinks. I didn't know what I would say if she rejected me. I also didn't know how I could keep these words to myself.

"I know this is crazy," I whispered. "It's probably way too early to say this, and you may not be quite there yet, but . . . I love you."

▪ EMILY ▪

Chris's words hung in the air. I could not speak. I wanted to answer him and not leave him hanging, but I didn't know how to respond. I knew what was in my heart, but how could I put that into words? Were my feelings truly love?

This would not be my first time saying I love you. I had told myself I wouldn't say it again until I was sure that it was true love. But we'd only known each other for two months. Is that really enough time to know if you love someone? Chris sure seemed to know. Did I?

I sat there, not saying a word, as all these thoughts ran through my head. Silence is not what a guy expects when he says I love you. I had to say something before this became even more awkward.

"Honestly," I said, then paused. ". . . I'm just not sure how to respond." Okay, so that probably didn't help, but I couldn't take the silence any-more. "So, I'm definitely falling for you," I reassured him. "You're the strongest, most positive person I've ever met. I feel like you've already made me a better person just from my being around you."

Chris didn't say anything. He was probably wondering where I was going with this. I was kind of wondering the same thing. I'm a verbal processor, so I had to talk this out to figure it out. That's not the most romantic way to answer someone who had just poured their heart out to you, but it's what I needed.

"I miss you when I'm not with you," I continued, "and I never want to leave when it's time for me to go home. I can picture our future together, and I know that as long as I have you, everything's going to be okay no matter what happens."

Then it hit me. Whatever I've said to anyone else, and how early it was in our relationship—none of that mattered. My voice caught in my throat as I realized that everything I wanted was right there with me.

"You know what, Chris? I love you too."

His face was a mixture of relief and joy. "You do?"

"I really do."

He didn't have to ask me to kiss him this time. I drew him close to me and pressed his lips against mine. This was exactly how I wanted to spend every moment for the rest of my life.

And then I had to drive three hours back to Iowa State. After Chris and I declared our love for one another, the drive seemed longer than ever. *I don't know how much longer I can keep this up. It's just too far.* Then it hit me: what if I transferred to Luther College so we could be together all the time? People transfer from one school to another all the time. It couldn't be that big of a deal.

When I arrived back at my apartment, I quickly hopped on Luther College's website, looking for a major that was close to my current major of family services. I'd spent a lot of time and gone through a lot of majors—journalism, psychology and adult, child and family services—before I found one that was exactly right for me. I wanted something that would lead to helping teenagers in a group home or foster care setting, but not every college has that. As it turned out, Luther College was one of those colleges. They didn't offer anything even close.

I was disappointed, but I wasn't ready to give up. Being closer to Chris was so appealing that I continued my search. I wanted to find another state school close to Decorah that also happened to offer the perfect major.

On a whim I Googled the first state school I thought of—The University of Northern Iowa. At an hour and a half away from Luther College, it wasn't exactly right next door, but I'd only have to drive half as far as I did from Iowa State. I scrolled through their list of majors and found one in family services. *Perfect*, I thought. But before I could click on it, I noticed something in a completely different field that was intriguing to me. If I went to UNI, I'd have the chance to also major in video production. I'd always been interested in capturing people's stories on camera and sharing them with others who could relate or learn from what the person went through. That summer I'd even done a talk show through school, helping people share their stories.

The more I researched UNI, the more I realized that this was the perfect solution to my problem. It was close enough to make visiting Chris a lot easier, without me giving up on any of my dreams or callings I knew God had on my life. I called the school, and an admissions counselor helped me go through my credits to figure out what would transfer and how far behind I would be. It turned out I had more than enough credits to put me on track for early graduation. I'd be done after just a spring semester and summer internship—or if I wanted to pursue the video production double major, I'd have to take classes the following fall semester as well.

Chris was obviously ecstatic that I was looking into transferring, and once my parents understood that transferring wouldn't mean adding extra semesters and tuition payments, they were totally on board. The thought of leaving Iowa State was hard, but any sadness I felt evaporated as soon as I talked to Chris. I couldn't wait to be closer to him.

▪ CHRIS ▪

I was so excited when Emily told me she was thinking of transferring to UNI, though it wouldn't necessarily mean we would get to see each other more often. I knew it was still a hike to get from Cedar Falls to Decorah, but the thought of easing the burden on Emily was a huge relief to me.

I hated that I could never drive to see her or drive her around. In my mind, that's something a guy should do for his girlfriend. It wasn't fair that she had to drive so much for us to see each other.

Emily ended up deciding to take the leap and transfer that spring semester. It turned out to be even better than I thought. My buddy Tanner's girlfriend, Taisha, went to UNI too, so she and Emily became roommates. Not only did that give her an instant friend, but it also took the pressure off Emily to constantly drive to Luther. When Tanner drove down to visit Taisha, I'd ride with him, and Emily and Taisha carpooled up to Luther as often as they could.

While that was one worry taken off my plate, I still struggled to let Emily see how much help I actually needed. Getting emotionally vulnerable with her was hard enough. My injury meant I had a whole other level of vulnerability that most people never experience. I didn't want to ask her for help with all the little things that most people can easily do for themselves, like sitting on the couch or changing my shirt or putting on deodorant. Then there was the issue of my urinary leg bag. The idea of asking this girl who I found incredibly attractive to drain my leg bag terrified me. What if she realized how much work I was and decided it was too much?

The more Emily came around, the more she tried to put my fears at ease. Whenever I needed help with something, I usually asked one of my friends, but Emily always jumped at the chance to learn how to help me.

"You don't know what you're volunteering for," I said. "You have no idea how much help I need for the smallest things."

"I honestly don't care about that," she told me. "Just tell me how I can help. If you want me to ask one of your friends, I will, but I really do want to help you."

▪ EMILY ▪

Before I transferred to UNI, I had this crazy dream of getting Chris on *The Ellen DeGeneres Show*, a show we both love. The next best thing was going to see a taping of the show in person. Deep down I hoped that if we could get into the studio, one of the producers might ask us about Chris's story and we'd go from being a part of the audience to appearing on her show. I know it was a crazy dream, but I've always dreamed big.

I applied to get tickets to the show, and Chris loved the idea. But I did not breathe a word to him about trying to get him on the show. I secretly made a video for Ellen with the story of Chris's injury and how he'd used his experience to help other people. The video included interviews I did with his parents and friends. I then sent the video off to the show's producers, brought extra copies to secretly give to someone on the show at the taping, and prayed the right people would see it.

▪ CHRIS ▪

I couldn't believe we actually got tickets to *The Ellen DeGeneres Show*. We were both such big fans. The person who called me said we'd see Ellen on February 4 and that they were ready and able to accommodate my wheelchair.

The show tapes in Los Angeles, which obviously meant we'd have to travel there. At first I couldn't wait. A trip to California when it's the dead of winter in Iowa? Sign me up.

Then it hit me.

Everything I was afraid to let Emily do—the transfers, getting me ready, draining my leg bag—I would have no choice but to have her help me with all of it, because there would be no one else to do it. Taking a trip together is a big step in any relationship. For us it would be a giant leap.

Getting ready for the trip meant tons of planning. We had to call the airline and let them know we needed assistance. Once we arrived we would have to arrange for a wheelchair-accessible vehicle to pick us up at Los Angeles International Airport and take us to our hotel. We also found an app that allowed us to reserve a wheelchair-accessible vehicle whenever we needed to get around the city. These were the easy arrangements to make. Emily also had to take a crash course on how to do all the things for me that I couldn't do for myself. For better or worse, we were about to find out what it would really be like to handle life together.

• EMILY •

I wasn't nervous about helping Chris and being responsible for everything. What terrified me was transferring him in and out of his chair. Up until now Chris had had his friends do it for him, since they were already around. I had no idea how to lift him out of his wheelchair and move him to a stationary seat or a car until literally right before we left. A couple of his friends showed me how to lean his shoulders against mine and position my hands around his hips so I could lift him out of his chair.

"You guys, I don't know if I can do this," I said as I tried it the first time. My heart pounded as I realized I didn't have a choice. No one else was coming with us to L.A. Everything was on me. "What if I make him fall? I'm going to hurt him! This is going to be awful," I said to his friends.

His friends assured me I would be fine, but my stomach was in knots as we drove to the airport. What if this whole trip was a huge mistake? I prepared myself for disaster.

I took a deep breath as we made our way into the airport. After checking in I pushed Chris over to the security line. Getting through security is never pleasant, and when I saw a TSA agent approach us, I thought for sure we were in trouble. Instead, he said, "You two can head up to the front of the line." He led us past the line of travelers snaking through the terminal, and within seconds we were at the front and going through security. *Wow*, I thought. *This is already going better than I thought.*

Chris looked up at me as we walked past coffee shops and bookstores. "It's going to be fine, Em. They do this every day."

We checked in with the gate agent and learned we could board early. I thought for sure I'd have to transfer him to his seat, but instead, airport attendants transferred him to a small chair that easily fit down the plane aisle and then lifted him into his seat. I'd been so nervous, but the whole morning went pretty smoothly.

I breathed a sigh of relief as our plane roared down the runway and lifted into the air. I took Chris's hand. "We did it!" I said with a grin. "I can't believe we really get to do this."

"I'm so excited to go to L.A. with you," he smiled back.

Once we'd reached our cruising altitude, a flight attendant rolled the beverage cart up to us. "Would you like a beverage, ma'am?"

"Oh, sure, I'll take a water," I said.

"What about him?" The flight attendant gestured at Chris and looked at me. "Can he have something to drink?"

I nearly lost it. I could not believe that someone in this day and age who is allegedly trained to work with people could be so dismissive of someone simply because of his disability. "He can talk, you know. You can just ask him yourself," I snapped at her.

"Oh, I'm so sorry. I didn't mean to—"

"You can't automatically assume that he can't speak just because he's in a wheelchair." I could feel my face getting red as I sputtered in anger. Chris raised his hand to stop me, but I kept going. "There's nothing wrong with his mind. Just because someone's in a wheelchair doesn't mean they're not mentally all there."

"Of course. Of course. You're right. I'm so sorry," the flight attendant apologized. She couldn't get away from us fast enough. Chris turned his head toward me when she was gone.

"Emily, it's not a big deal," he said. "People make assumptions, but you can't get upset about it. I learned a long time ago to just let it go. It's okay."

But I couldn't let it go. I talked for the rest of the flight about how ridiculous the flight attendant's actions were. I was so upset that I forgot to be nervous about getting through LAX and finding an accessible taxi to get to our hotel.

Aside from the rude flight attendant, the rest of our trip was amazing. Watching the live taping of *The Ellen DeGeneres Show* was so much fun. At the beginning of each show, she dances up and down the aisles with the audience. That day, she came right up to Chris and danced with him. I did hand one of the tapes I'd made to her staff worker on the set. We got a casting interview the next week but nothing else came of it. While Chris may not have shared his story on her show, it was a trip we will always remember.

The wheelchair-accessible van app made it easy for us to get around L.A., and we took full advantage. We ate dinner at a trendy restaurant and talked for hours. But when our phones died and we couldn't use the app to get picked up, we walked a mile to a gas station to buy a charger. We enjoyed the adventure. Our hotel had an outdoor fire pit, where we stayed together under the stars, talking about life and our future.

Helping Chris with his day-to-day needs was a lot easier than either of us anticipated. I know he was nervous about letting me drain his leg bag or getting him ready in the morning, but I loved him so much that it didn't bother me. Thankfully, I never once dropped him while transferring him in and out of his wheelchair. We realized not only that we could travel together but also that we could do anything as long as we had each other. Those days in L.A. gave us confidence that the chair couldn't hold us back from anything, and "anything" was about to get much bigger than either of us could have ever dreamed.

9

Chasing Something
Bigger than Ourselves

▪ EMILY ▪

From the start of our relationship, Chris talked about his goal to walk across the stage at his college graduation. When he first mentioned it, I was blown away. He planned to do the impossible, but in his mind, walking again was not impossible at all. And I had no doubt he'd find a way to make it happen. After we started dating, we talked a lot about his goal. It didn't take long for me to decide I didn't want to just stand on the sidelines and watch. I wanted to jump in there and do everything I possibly could to help him reach it.

Unfortunately, since we only saw one another on weekends, there wasn't a lot I could do. He did physical therapy during the week, which meant I never got to go with him. But Chris never confined his workouts to his PT sessions. He had a Rifton walker, which is a large green rolling frame with a Velcro brace that supports his waist and hips. During my weekend visits, we'd often go to the gym and either one of his friends or I would help strap him into the walker and walk behind him to hold him steady.

After a workout one day in the spring of his junior year, we went back to his dorm cluster to relax. I told him how impressed I was with all the progress he'd made in just the last few months and how much steadier he was in the walker. Chris didn't reply. He just sat there, thinking. Finally he said, "You know, graduation is about a year away."

"Yeah," I said.

"I know I'm capable of doing this, but I feel like if I make my goal public somehow, I'll definitely stick to it."

I laughed. "Chris, you're going to stick to it anyway. It's not like you're slacking here."

"I know, but I could work harder. If I put it out there to everyone, I think that would push me to work as hard as I can."

He had a point. Chris will do anything he can to avoid letting anyone down. "What were you thinking of doing? Putting up a Facebook post?" I asked.

"I thought maybe I'd blog about it," Chris replied. At the time, Chris's foundation website had a blog where he regularly posted stories about grants he'd given out as well as updates on his recovery. "Blogging about it will give me more space to explain my goal than a regular Facebook post."

"I completely agree. I think it would be great and maybe even inspire others to go for their goals too," I said.

Chris wrote the blog right there. He read me bits and pieces of it before posting it online and then sharing a link to it on Facebook. We thought it might get some buzz around campus since Chris had such a huge community supporting him at Luther. We didn't expect anyone else to see it.

Boy, were we wrong.

We did hear back from his friends, but things really took off when the *Des Moines Register* called. The paper had covered Chris's injury from the start and featured regular updates on how he was doing. Someone in the newsroom must have followed him on Facebook, because they called not long after Chris posted the link. A few days later, a reporter drove up from Des Moines to interview Chris. All of a sudden, Chris was plastered on the front page of the paper, along with the story of his goal of walking across the stage at his graduation.

"Well, you wanted it to be public," I said.

"No pressure or anything," Chris laughed. "I guess we need to make this happen, huh?"

I grinned. "You got this."

• CHRIS •

When I set a goal of walking at graduation, I did not mean having some friends haul a huge contraption on stage, stopping the ceremony while I got strapped in, then slowly trudging across the stage. For me, walking meant walking on my own two feet, without the aid of any kind of equipment. I thought if I could pull this off, it might inspire others never to give up. At the same time, I didn't want to annoy everyone else by taking too much time to get across the stage. A giant green walker would have the opposite effect.

Walking without extra equipment was only one issue. Before my accident I may not have been the greatest athlete, but I prided myself on pushing myself and trying to outwork everyone else. I spent extra time in the weight room and ran extra laps just to get an edge. But now a short walk in my walker left me completely spent. That had to change. My physical therapy had already taken me light-years beyond anything doctors had said was possible, but I was ready to kick it up a notch.

Emily knew my frustrations and decided to do something about it. She researched different therapies and places that might get me to my goal. Emily had never been one to sit back and wait for someone else to act. When Emily set her mind to something, she made it happen. After some intense Googling, she thought she might have found the answer. "Have you ever heard of Barwis Methods?" she asked me in a text.

I racked my brain, trying to remember. I'm around a lot more people with spinal injuries than the average person, so if there was a foolproof method out there, it seemed like I would have heard of it. As it turns out, Mike Barwis didn't just do "physical training." He had devised a whole new method for restarting the neurological system. I even found a story where he'd helped someone with a serious spinal cord injury walk again. *This is it,* I thought. *Mike Barwis is the guy who can help me walk again.*

"We have to go see him," I texted Emily. "I have a really good feeling about this."

A few weeks later, Emily and I drove up to Mike's gym in Plymouth, Michigan, for what was supposed to be an hour-long workout. The giant physical therapy center looked more like a sports training center, with its turf field, weight room, and stadium-height ceilings. Music blared from the speakers as people in wheelchairs worked out alongside Jack Johnson, a professional hockey player I recognized. Just being in this place made me feel like an athlete again, and that felt good. I didn't realize how much I missed it until I experienced it again.

A man walked toward us that I immediately recognized from his online pictures as Mike Barwis. "Chris?" Mike said in his deep, raspy voice as he shook my hand. "Good to meet you. Let's get going and see what you've got."

I had never met someone as intense as Mike. As he helped me lie on the mat, every movement had a purpose behind it. "Good," he said as he pulled my legs inward. "See right there? Your muscles are tight. That's not gonna help. Let's stretch you out and get you moving."

I don't know if it was the way he positioned me or just his huge personality, but my legs moved in ways they hadn't in years. My one-hour session turned into a four-hour workout. Mike got so excited about what I was able to do that he kept pushing me to do more. He stood right by me, barking, "Come on, Chris! You got it! Push it! Push it!" My body shook as I grunted and scrunched my face, pushing my legs against the press with all my might. Emily got right in there too, joining Mike in cheering for me.

Suddenly, I heard a voice I didn't recognize. "You can do it! Come on, man!" I turned my head to see Jack Johnson, now standing with Mike and Emily. Adrenaline coursed through my veins as I pushed for one more rep. I'm a hard worker, but somehow Mike and his trainers pushed me beyond even what I thought I was capable of. Before I left, Mike even told me, "If you were in this program for five or six weeks, you'd be a changed man." I could not wait to find out how great that change could be!

• EMILY •

I didn't know Chris in his days as an athlete. I had seen pictures and heard stories from his parents about how long and hard he worked in every practice and beyond, stories that were pretty easy to believe because he was so intense in the workouts I helped him with at Luther. Seeing him working out at Barwis Methods for the first time, though, went beyond anything I'd seen in Chris before. He lit up in a new way, as though he was finally back in his element. Chris was having fun, but he was also being pushed outside his comfort zone. I'm not a trainer, but even I could see that something good was happening here.

These are the people who are going to get Chris to walk across the stage at his gradation, I thought as I watched him with a smile. *We have to get him here.*

When the evaluation workout ended and we left Barwis Methods, Chris and I looked at one another and had one of those moments where you can practically read each other's minds. I knew he was thinking what I was thinking.

"We're moving here," I said. "You have to work out with these people."

Chris just grinned.

Of course this meant we had a lot of things to figure out.

• CHRIS •

Before meeting Mike and trying Barwis Methods, I was starting to believe that walking on my own was a long way off or wouldn't happen without a scientific breakthrough. After that initial workout, both Emily and I could see me walking again in a matter of months, no longer than a year. I felt I had come this far, sacrificed and worked harder than ever before, and now I was so close. I just had to figure out how to move to Michigan. The biggest thing stopping me was finding someone to move there with me. I can't live on my own, can't afford to live on my own, and would need someone to completely sacrifice five months of their life for me.

Who would do that?

The only person who offered was Emily, and frankly there was no one else in the world I would rather have with me for the journey. Neither of us had planned on living together before marriage. But on a pragmatic level, the move to Michigan would only work if I had in-home care. Plus, my insurance would be able to pay Emily for this full-time care. So we talked to our parents, made our plans, and starting getting ready for the big move.

• EMILY •

Before he could move to Plymouth, Chris first had to finish his course-work at Luther. He was on schedule to finish all his classes that fall, then officially graduate the following May. We planned to move to Michigan in January so Chris could spend the spring semester working out with Mike and getting in peak condition to walk across the stage.

However, moving to Michigan meant putting my goals on hold to help Chris pursue his. I had graduated from UNI the year before Chris was scheduled to graduate. My whole family, plus Whittley and Chris, came to my graduation. It was the first time Chris and Whittley offi-cially met. On paper I was ready to start my career in helping kids like I had always dreamed of. Earlier that year I finished my last semester of classes and found an internship at a group home in Waverly, Iowa. It was exactly the kind of place where I had imagined myself working. When I landed the internship, I hoped it might lead to a full-time job. I had always been drawn to teenagers and could not wait to help change their lives for the better.

But my experience at the group home quickly showed me how far the reality could be from the dream. I will never forget walking into the group home for the first time. So many girls had scars covering their bodies from self-harming. There was one girl I was instantly drawn to—Sophia. Her body was covered in scars. I mean scars on top of scars. "Hate" was carved on her leg, covering her entire thigh. It was harrowing to see the kind of pain these girls lived with every day.

I had yet to learn that the surface scars did not go nearly as deep as the emotional ones. Instead of trusting God to heal these kids' hearts and teaching the kids to lean on him, I took on the responsibility of changing their lives myself. I had no idea how to handle and cope with the most terrible things you could ever imagine. I felt it in a way that shattered my heart and got me so down. Not only was I so sad that kids had gone through these situations, but I began to feel more and more anger toward the people who did such awful things to their children.

While working at the group home, I met kids who had survived sexual abuse, gang violence, and crazy situations that I could not even fathom. There were so many times I witnessed girls jumping on top of one another in all-out fights and screaming at the staff, threatening to kill them. Once a girl actually attempted to choke one of the staff members. There were many times I caught girls cutting themselves, no matter how vigilant we were at trying to keep them away from anything that could hurt them. One girl I was especially close with found a piece of glass and sliced her wrist so deep that I saw parts of her that only a doctor should see. I can still smell the sickening metallic scent of blood as it soaked the sweatshirt she used to cover up her arm and dripped onto the floor.

Suicide attempts were common among the girls living at the group home. I came in the morning after staff members caught Sophia, the girl covered in scars, jumping off the gym roof trying to kill herself. Another time I rode to the hospital with a girl who had swallowed batteries. There was another situation in which a girl had taken the string out of her hoodie and was trying to choke herself. I was the one who found her and had to scream for the staff to help get it off her.

None of the girls ever seemed to get better. Previously, I had this God-given ability to get through to people on a deep level and could see progress right away. I felt God called me to this line of work. Now I felt as though I was making small impacts to get the girls through their days but not having breakthroughs. I imagined myself getting these girls to experience breakthrough after breakthrough and changing the trajectory of their lives. I began to feel hopeless and didn't know how to process it. Every day when I went into work, I braced myself for new levels of bad. *What are you doing, God?* I thought. *I know you want me to help these kids, and I want to do it, but it's not working. I literally can't do anything to help these girls.*

Even as I became frustrated by how ill-equipped I felt to actually make a difference in any of these girls' lives, I still loved the one-on-one moments with them. There were many times when I successfully calmed one of them down or talked runaway girls into coming back to the group home. As I thought about what these girls had seen and experienced, I wondered what kind of lives they could possibly have beyond this place. Before I started working there, I thought that if I could just get through to these kids, then they could go on to live perfectly normal lives. After a few months, I realized how laughably naïve I'd been. These kids were never going to magically get better and be free from their emotional scars. How could they when they had been through so much trauma? They had scars that were so deep. No one could come out of that and be the same person. For the first time, I wondered if I could make a real difference, or if I could even handle the trauma and chaos of working with troubled kids.

After my internship ended, I moved home instead of applying for a full-time job. I told everyone I needed some time to figure things out, but deep down I knew something had changed inside me. Where I once felt so much empathy and compassion, I was becoming numb and disconnected. My mind-set only got worse when I received an unexpected phone call while I was visiting my grandparents in Wisconsin.

"Emily?" My heart skipped as I recognized the voice. I could tell she was in tears, but she barely spoke.

"Whittley, is that you? Where are you?"

"I'm outside of a gas station." She paused. "For now."

A knot formed in my stomach. "What happened? Tell me. What are you going to do?"

Whittley didn't say a word for what felt like forever before finally uttering a short, "Nothing."

"Come on, Whittley. I need you to tell me what's going on."

She sighed. "I stole some pills, okay?"

"Whittley, did you take any of those pills? Whittley, please don't do it. You have no idea what I would do if I lost you. I love you more than you could *ever* imagine. You are so special, and God has such a great life planned for you. I know it's so hard right now, but Whittley, we will get through this together. I will do anything for you. Whittley, please, I beg you, don't give up!!"

I heard her sniffle on the other end of the phone. "I have to go. I love you, Emily," she whispered.

"Whittley!" I yelled. My heart pounded as I immediately called the main number of the group home where she was staying. "I think Whittley is trying to hurt herself. She just told me she stole some pills, and I know she has a history of suicide attempts."

One of the staff members confirmed my worst fears. Whittley had run away earlier in the day, and they just received a call that she was in an ambulance on the way to the hospital. Someone at the gas station had noticed something was wrong with her and called the police. They told me they were taking her to the Dubuque Hospital. I raced to meet her there. I was on my way when I got another call telling me she'd been transferred to the University of Iowa Hospital. Her condition was more severe than they thought.

I tried to focus on the road as tears streamed down my cheeks. *All this time I've spent with her, all the effort I poured into her, and she still ended up right here, in the hospital from a suicide attempt.*

By the time I arrived at the hospital, Whittley showed signs of improvement. However, they still transferred her from the emergency room to the intensive care unit. When they let me see her, she looked like a ghost. Her skin was so pale in the fluorescent lighting, and the room was silent except for the beeping of the machines tracking her vitals. Doctors had given her charcoal to help her get rid of the toxins from the pills, but she clearly was not well. She wouldn't even look at me.

I felt numb as I drove home that night. Whittley had been in my life for six years. I had been there for her when no one else was. Even after I moved off to college, the two of us stayed in touch. It just wasn't enough. I couldn't save Whittley or any of the kids from the group home. What was the point of even trying? My dream, the thing I had worked for my whole life, was crashing down around me. In that moment I began to build a wall around myself. *What if caring so much about others is just going to hurt me? What if Whittley had succeeded in killing herself?*

For the first time in my life, I questioned whether the pain of pouring myself into others was worth it. I asked God why he chose me to care this much. Why did everyone around me seem to have a normal life, worrying more about themselves than others. Their lives seemed so much easier. I was always putting others' needs in front of my own and internalizing their pain. Now I felt weighed down by their problems and mentally paralyzed. Another layer of the wall around my heart went up.

I had to have that wall. It protected me from the pain, but it also left me empty. I didn't know who I was any longer. One night I poured my heart out in my journal:

> I have absolutely no idea what I want to do with my life. I'm so lost and so confused. I feel depressed and like I'm not the same person. I've honestly been going through the hardest time in my life, and I don't know why. I push you away, God, when I need you more than I have ever needed you. I need help. I need guidance. I feel like I'm starting to lose my purpose, and that's who I am. I feel like I don't care as much. I feel so alone, and I think I've felt that way my whole life. I've always been the one who does everything for other people. I've always been a very strong person, so people just automatically assume that I'm okay. I'm also a very closed person and keep everything inside. It's a horrible way to be, because I'm not okay, and nobody knows it.

Then came the opportunity to help Chris reach his goal of walking at graduation. I jumped at it. Sure, I had to put my life on hold so I could help Chris, but I didn't even know what my life was supposed to be about any longer. Moving to Michigan was a welcome distraction. Someday I needed to figure out what to do with my life, but that could wait. Right now I had to find an apartment, shop for furniture, pick out decorations to make a bland apartment feel more like home, and figure out Chris's training schedule. I had too much to do to worry about my own future. I threw myself into the move because, honestly, that was all I had.

▪ CHRIS ▪

I could tell something seemed off about Emily when she moved home after she graduated from UNI. She stopped running, which she had always loved doing, and she seemed tired all the time. Little incidents set her off more than they used to. I chalked up most of this to the normal letdown of graduating from college and not having a job right away. Some of my friends went through it. Plus, Whittley was struggling, and I knew it affected Emily more than she let on. She avoided talking about it because it was too upsetting and stressful for her. When Emily blew up at me over something small, I told myself it was her way of dealing with everything else going on in her life.

But I couldn't explain away the biggest change I saw in her. Her spark of passion was missing. Emily makes things happen. I figured when she moved home she would start a blog or run a business making videos of people's family stories, an idea she had mentioned to me before. She did end up making a video for her grandparents, but the project stopped there. She also wasn't looking for opportunities to help others like she used to. I knew she had sent a message to an alternative school asking about volunteering, but when they didn't get back to her right away, she gave up. It seemed like she was in a holding pattern until we moved to Michigan. While that seemed like something most people might do in her situation, Emily wasn't most people. This wasn't the girl I'd fallen in love with. And I was worried.

I didn't say anything to her about my concerns because I didn't want to be pushy. I tried to gently ask questions here and there to see if she was getting back to her old self, but I backed off pretty quickly so as not to irritate her. Every once in a while, she'd say she didn't feel like herself. She couldn't put her finger on why or what could be going on, though. She told me one day that she was going to get her thyroid levels checked out. Her mom and sister both have thyroid problems, and Emily thought that might explain why she had felt more annoyed than usual. But all her tests came back normal.

Although Emily was having more moments of frustration, she was still the girl I'd fallen in love with. During a weekend stay together at Emily's parents' house during the time we were talking about moving to Michigan, Emily got a look in her eyes I knew all too well. It meant she was up to something.

"Hey," she said with a sly smile. "Let's take a step."

"No, let's not," I said with a laugh. "We're in the kitchen. It's not a good idea."

Emily wasn't giving up. I could see her slipping into coach mode. "Come on," she said. "Take a step. Just try. Just this once."

"I don't know. We've never been able to do it before."

"I've got you!" she said, her voice getting louder. "I promise. I've got you. Just take a step."

When Emily slips into coach mode, you listen. So Emily pulled me up out of the chair to a stand. Emily stood in front of me, her hands on my midsection. I took a step. Then another. I wobbled slightly and felt her hands keeping me balanced. But we did it.

We walked all the way into the piano room and collapsed with laughter on the couch. "I can't believe we just did that," I said, breathing a sigh of relief.

I told myself we'd have a lot more moments like this after we moved to Michigan. She seemed just as committed to getting me walking as I was, and she seemed excited about making a fresh start in a new place. *We just have to make it to January,* I thought. Everything would be fine once we got to Michigan.

In some ways that was true. But in other ways, all we did was delay the inevitable.

10

Olympic-Level Training

· EMILY ·

Chris and I didn't celebrate the New Year with brunch and mimosas. We didn't spend the day watching college football championships. Bright and early that morning, we were on our way to start the next chapter of our lives in Michigan.

I had found an apartment for us online after a seemingly endless search. Finding a place that could accommodate Chris's wheelchair was a much bigger challenge than I had anticipated. It should not be that hard to find an apartment that's accessible to people with physical disabilities, but apparently it is. I was on the phone for hours, asking apartment managers about their door frame widths or whether there was an open spot under the bathroom sink. We never did find a place with a roll-in shower, but there were so few options that Chris decided he could make do with a bathtub. When I found an apartment that came close to what we were looking for, I jumped on it. But we didn't see it until the day we moved in. We took a leap of faith and hoped our trust would pay off.

Bright and early on New Year's Day, Chris and his friend Brock pulled up in front of my parents' house in his van, while his parents followed in a U-Haul. Chris supervised while the rest of us loaded the moving truck with the new furniture and decorations I had picked out over the past couple of months. It didn't bother me that Chris couldn't help. My parents raised me to be extremely independent and take care of myself. I didn't mind carrying boxes and lifting furniture, and I certainly didn't need him doing everything for me. Actually, if he did that, it would drive me nuts.

The temperature barely hit double digits that day, which meant my face and hands were freezing while I was sweating under my parka. Winters in the upper Midwest are brutal, but it wasn't like we could wait until the weather warmed up to move. Chris was scheduled to start his workouts at Barwis Methods on January 4. We didn't have any time to waste.

▪ CHRIS ▪

Moving day should have been exciting, and it was. But it was tough for me to sit back while everyone else did all the work. Emily didn't mind, but I did. In spite of my injury, I still thought I should be the heavy lifter like my dad was. Growing up, my dad always manned the steering wheel for long car rides. He fixed loose floorboards and leaky faucets. If there was a problem, he took care of it. He was right there in the middle of our move as well. Even though he was well into his fifties, he still grabbed the heaviest boxes and the biggest pieces of furniture, and Emily was always right there with him. She is fearless and always wants to do the most difficult task. While I find that trait quite endearing, I worry about her getting hurt. That didn't stop her from jumping in with my dad to carry a large dresser, couch, or mattress. Watching them, I couldn't help but think that it should be me, not them. I understand that I had no choice in the matter, but it still ate at me and made me that much more motivated to do everything in my power to regain as much mobility as I could.

Once we arrived in Plymouth, Michigan, we had three days to unpack and get settled into our new apartment before my first training session. Those days are a blur to me because I was so excited about getting started with Mike. The night before my first workout, I could barely sleep. My mind kept replaying the tape of my previous workout with Mike Barwis. Mike had such a charismatic, commanding presence that might have intimidated me under other circumstances. That day in

August, though, he got my legs to move in a way they hadn't since my injury. I saw Mike as my great hope, my answer to prayer.

The next morning, I felt butterflies in my stomach as Emily drove us to Barwis Methods. *This is it*, I thought. *A few months here and I'm not only going to crush the graduation walk, I'm going to get the chance to walk independently. Mike is going to break me out of my chair.* Emily looked over at me and smiled. She was as excited as I was.

But my excitement died when I arrived at the gym and discovered that Mike Barwis was not going to be my trainer. Instead, I had to settle for a trainer who was so new to the team that he still had someone watching over his shoulder.

After my first session with the new guy, Emily and I went to the front desk to schedule some times to work with Mike, even though we understood he couldn't be my everyday trainer, due to demand. "Oh, I'm so sorry, Chris," the front desk staffer said. "Mike's not going to be at the gym until February. Even then, he's going to be in and out before he goes to Florida in March. He helps the Mets with their spring training, so he's going to be there a while. We can't schedule anyone with him due to his fluctuating schedule.

Oh, wow. I knew coming in that Mike was a busy guy and in high demand, but I assumed he would at least be in the building. Emily and I had just moved ten and a half hours from home to work with him, and now they were telling me he wasn't going to be around for months? My rock-solid optimism started to crack.

I didn't say a word during the whole drive home. Emily tried to coax me out of my shell. "I know your trainer is not the person you thought you'd work with, but I'm sure he will still be great," she said. "We're definitely in the right place. We're supposed to be here."

I could barely muster a nod. "Yeah. Maybe you're right," I lied.

▪ EMILY ▪

I had never seen Chris so down, and it scared me. He's always so positive and able to see the bright side, so to see him completely defeated after his second day of therapy threw me for a loop.

He practically spoke in grunts during dinner and was silent as we watched TV afterward. "I think I'm ready to head to bed," he finally said. "I'm just tired. It's been a rough day."

I could not stand the thought of Chris going to sleep without talking through his feelings. I needed to find a way to make him feel better about the situation. So, of course, I had to talk to him about how he was feeling.

To transfer Chris to bed, I help him up and he does a standing pivot, but when I helped Chris stand up, I held him up before he could crash down into bed. I said, "Let's work on your standing balance." Some nights Chris and I would practice balancing, where he would find a spot he was balanced and hold it for as long as he could by himself.

"Emily, just let me go to bed. I've had a long day already."

"Let's see how long you can hold it."

He balanced for a few seconds before he started toppling over, then I grabbed him back to an upright position.

"Emily, that's enough. I can't balance today. Let me go to bed."

Okay, I thought. *This definitely isn't like him. He never gives up. Ever.*

"Okay, what's going on?" I said in frustration. I sat him back in his chair. I crawled onto his lap. He was not going to bed this upset.

He wouldn't look at me but instead just stared at the floor. Chris hates showing his feelings. "I think this whole move was a huge mistake," he said with his voice cracking. He was trying so hard not to cry.

I looked Chris in the eye. I had seen him tear up maybe once before, but never anything like this. Tears started to run down his face. "I'm never going to walk at my graduation," he continued. "I'm not where I need to be physically. I uprooted you from everything, and I never should have done that. What if we are wasting our time here and now there is no turning back?"

My heart melted as I wiped the tears from his eyes. "Chris, we are not wasting our time!" I cried, tears in my eyes too. "This is going to work. I have a gut feeling. I know God has us here for a reason."

Chris shook his head as he tried to stop crying but couldn't quite do it. "I hope you're right."

By now I was done crying. I could see he was spiraling downward, and I had to stop it. My tears were replaced by a different but very familiar feeling—sheer stubborn determination. I knew it came from God. I hopped off Chris's lap and said, "That's it. We're going to walk." I didn't wait for him to say yes before I pushed his wheelchair down the hallway, past the bathroom, and into the kitchen. "We're walking you to bed," I said firmly.

"What are you doing?" Chris sputtered. "We've never walked that far. If we get going and get stuck in the hallway, that's it. We don't have anyone who can help us. This is insane."

I didn't let him sway me. "Well you better make it to the bed then," I said. "Just trust me."

We assumed the position—Chris's hands on my arms, my hands on his waist. Both of us stared at our feet. We easily made it out of the kitchen, and I held my breath as we stepped into the hallway. This was the tricky part where if we fell, I wasn't exactly sure how I would get him back on his feet.

But we kept moving. Step. Step. Shuffle. Step. Slowly, we pushed past the last corner of the hallway and through the doorframe. Playfully I pushed Chris into bed as we both took a moment to realize what we had done.

"You and I can do this together," I said. "We're an unstoppable force. It doesn't matter who's training you. I know it's going to work because we're together."

▪ CHRIS ▪

Emily pushing me that January night when I was at my lowest point was exactly what I needed to pull me out of a dark place. When we walked that night, I went from doubting whether we'd made the right choice in moving to Michigan to thinking that maybe this was going to work after all.

The next day of therapy was a little better. And the day after that. And the day after that. My trainer, Mike Rhoades, may have been new, but he by no means took it easy on me. He pushed me harder than I had ever pushed myself. Each day I felt a little stronger than I had the day before. Seeing tangible progress made me that much more eager to get back to work the next day. My workouts soon had a regular pattern. Every day Emily and I drove together to Barwis Methods in time for Rhoades to set me up in the walker by 10:00 a.m. Emily stayed during my training to help with transfers and extra support. Each movement was a victory—keeping my body upright and balanced, picking up my feet and moving them forward. Emily was right there behind me in case I lost my footing as I walked five to ten yards.

Once I was warmed up, it was time for the mat table. Rhoades laid me down and we started with stretches—quads, hamstrings, calves, ankles, every muscle in my lower body. Rhoades didn't stop until I was loosened up and ready for some strength training. I tuned out the clank of weights being dropped and the grunts of someone straining for one more rep as I focused every ounce of energy on movement—driving out my bent knee to the other side of my hips, driving my knee to my chest. We worked my core with sit-ups, bicycle crunches, and twists.

All the exercises were designed to get me closer to my goal. It was important that every muscle in my legs became as strong as it could in order to support walking. When one muscle group fatigues, that means another muscle group has to do more. When a muscle group has to do more, it causes more strain and imbalance in my body, making it very difficult to take a step. For example, if I am trying to take a step forward with my right leg but my right ankle can't lift my foot up, that means my hip flexor, which picks up my knee, has to lift higher for my right foot to move forward without dragging on the ground. Or if my left leg glute and quad aren't strong enough to support most of my body weight in order for my right leg to step forward, that means my right leg will lock up to compensate for the instability in my left leg. Therefore, it is important that every muscle group can carry its own weight.

I loved the intensity of my workouts. I always smiled when we headed to the squat rack. True, it wasn't like the squat rack of my football days. This one had an air suspension system in which I stood in a harness, and a hydraulic system off-weighted me so I could squat down and up. Each set, Rhoades decreased the amount of assistance I was getting. Seventy pounds. Sixty-five pounds. Sixty-pounds. Over time, I didn't need the help anymore and even wore a weighted vest for squats. Once I was out of the squat rack, Rhoades would lay me back on the floor as I drove my legs into his hands. The two of us were completely in sync. We knew exactly what we needed to do to help me progress.

On paper the three-hour workouts didn't compare to my long hours in football camp or college practices. But those hours I spent at Barwis Methods were hands down the most taxing thing I have done because it was so mentally challenging. By the time Emily and I left at 1:00 p.m., I was mentally drained. It is exhausting to focus on each muscle required to activate a single movement. Then when it doesn't work, frustration builds and makes it difficult to continue focusing.

I wasn't finished for the day, though. After lunch I was ready to get back at it. At our apartment we had an RT300 therapy bike set up in our family room. I pushed right up to it in my chair, and Emily set my feet in the pedals and strapped the electrodes to my hamstrings, calves, ankles, and abs. As I pushed my feet, the electrodes would fire and would activate my muscles so I could pedal. I normally watched a TV show as I biked seven or eight miles. It also had the option to use it as an arm bike so I could keep my upper body strong.

In the evenings we'd have dinner or go out to eat. My insurance from the NCAA paid Emily to be my full-time caregiver, which helped cover our expenses. We would play cards or watch a movie together. Sometimes we'd just talk. And always we walked together one last time before I went to bed. For some reason I was at my physical best at night. Those walks not only helped me train but also gave me a big confidence boost.

▪ EMILY ▪

Before Chris and I moved to Michigan, I had always lived with roommates who helped take the garbage out and empty the dishwasher. Now everything fell on my shoulders. If it had to be done, I did it—grocery shopping, cooking, cleaning, laundry, everything. On top of that, I was Chris's full-time caregiver. I filled his water bottle, emptied his leg bag, set him up on his bike, stayed nearby in case he fell, and helped him get ready each morning and night. And that's not counting the time I spent at his therapy sessions.

It was a lot, but honestly, it didn't feel like work. I loved Chris and I wanted to help him. Helping others is what I love to do; it's what makes me feel most alive. And most of the time, he genuinely seemed like he appreciated everything I was doing.

But sometimes I'd make a nice dinner and he wouldn't say thank you. Or instead of asking nicely for what he wanted, he'd just tell me he needed more water or he was ready to get out of his bike. I knew he didn't mean anything by it, but it was hard not to feel like he was taking me for granted in those moments.

I still didn't know what I wanted to do with my life anymore, but I wasn't ready to let go of the idea of helping kids, not completely. At this point it wasn't feasible for me to look for a job, not when I was so busy helping Chris with therapy. But Chris was determined to help me find a volunteer opportunity or something where I could use my gifts.

"You're the most intelligent, passionate girl I've ever met, and you're putting your life on hold for me," he said. "You can't just take care of me. You have to fulfill your potential."

"I would love that too," I said. "But I don't even know what that would be."

One day I went with Chris to talk to Mike Barwis about his foundation that helps with spinal cord injuries. He described the foundation's mission and how Chris's foundation could potentially partner with it. When I heard him mention a program for at-risk kids called Athletic Angels, my ears immediately perked up.

"Wait, what?" I interrupted. "I love working with at-risk kids. Is that something I could help with?" I had to physically keep myself in my seat as he described how they had just partnered with a local group home and were starting a program to mentor the kids and let them work out at Barwis Methods. A few questions turned into a three-hour conversation, and before I knew it, Mike had me leading a new mentoring program for Athletic Angels. It was only a weekly commitment—perfect for our schedule. As part of Athletic Angels, I helped to create the mentoring and athletic program for a local group home. I went every week and worked on life skills with the kids, created relationships with them, and helped with the workouts. A trainer from Barwis led the workouts; I just helped. I could tell Chris was relieved that I was once again doing something I was passionate about.

Overall, we were happy, but the wall I had built up that previous summer wasn't going away. Everything was not all sunshine and roses in my life. My phone constantly buzzed with texts from Whittley and Sophia. Whittley tried killing herself within weeks of our move, and for the first time, I couldn't rush to the hospital and sit by her side. A pit grew in my stomach as I worried that one day she would finally succeed.

Then that March my phone buzzed with a single text from Sophia as I was just about to fall asleep. My heart beat faster as I read just two words: "Love you." *Something is definitely wrong*, I thought. I was so tired. It had been a long day, and I just wanted to go to sleep. I thought, *Someone else will help. Maybe it's nothing and she just wants me to know she loves me. But what if no one helps?* I knew Sophia struggled with depression and other mental health issues. Her body was already covered in scars from self-harm and past suicide attempts. I had a terrible feeling as I dialed her number and waited breathlessly for her to pick up.

Miraculously, she answered the phone, but it was as bad as I had feared. I got her to admit that she was walking along the interstate, carrying pills and a razor blade. I listened in horror as she told me she planned to walk to a secluded place, take a fatal dose of pills, and carve her body with the word "worthless" and other names her mother and people in her life had called her. I thought back to when Whittley called me in a very similar situation. Feeling like you are the only person responsible for whether someone will live or end their life is the most terrifying feeling. My heart was racing, but I went into action and was ready to do everything possible to stop her from going through with it.

"Sophia, listen to me. Stay where you are. I'm going to stay on the phone with you." My voice shook as I spoke.

"I'm here," she said. "You don't have to stay on the phone. I just wanted you to know that I love you and it's not your fault."

I woke Chris and rapidly scratched out a note telling him what Sophia planned to do and where she was. I shoved it in his hands. He stared at me in horror as I mouthed, now! I dialed 9-1-1 on his phone and handed it to him.

"I love you too, Sophia." I listened as Chris spoke in hushed tones to the police in the still-dark room. "Don't do this. You don't want to do this."

Please let the police get there soon! I thought. I said anything and everything to keep Sophia on the phone and distracted, which I successfully did for nearly thirty minutes. I wondered how I would know when the police had arrived. But when Sophia started screaming a few minutes later, I knew what had happened.

"How could you, Emily?" she screamed into the phone. "I can't believe you would do this to me! I trusted you!" Tears rolled down my cheeks as she shouted, "I hate you!"

I knew I did the right thing. I knew I had saved her life. At the same time, I thought, *How long can I keep doing this? What would I have done if she killed herself right there on the phone? What would I have done if I didn't call and just went to bed? How could I move on?*

It's so easy for each of us to think someone else will help. But so many times they don't, and then what? Terrible things happen. We all have to step up and do what we can for others who are hurting. I knew that, but I wondered how long I could keep that mind-set. I wrote out prayers to God in my journal about this. I knew I couldn't keep this up without his strength.

The close call with Sophia left me drained. I forced a smile in the days that followed and threw myself into Chris's therapy and care. After all, he was the only stable force in my life, and I needed him. I needed us to meet our goal. I needed to succeed. But something was happening under the surface that even I didn't understand yet.

▪ CHRIS ▪

About three months into my training, I came to the conclusion that my training at Barwis Methods plus all the extra work I was putting in wasn't the magic bullet I had hoped it might be. Yes, I was making real progress, but it was slower than I had hoped. I wanted to walk across the stage completely on my own, unassisted by anyone or anything. By the end of March, I knew that was not going to happen. I had to have some help. At first I thought, *Okay, I'll use crutches.* Walking with crutches got easier, but it was always clumsy. I simply couldn't see myself walking on a graduation stage with them. Using the walker also wasn't a real option.

As I thought about how I could possibly show everyone how hard

I'd worked and how far I'd come, I slowly turned to Emily. I was more confident walking with her than with any crutch or walker. What could be more natural than walking across the stage with the woman I loved? She loved the idea. Our nightly walks to bed became practice runs for the graduation walk. By April, Emily and I were ready to go.

But in May disaster struck. Suddenly, the therapy exercises that were challenging before became impossible. Eventually, I couldn't even lift my foot to take one step, Emily or no Emily.

When I couldn't walk in therapy, I broke down in tears. "Are you kidding me?" I shouted in frustration. "My graduation is in a month. I've wasted the last five months working toward this, and now I'm going to fail."

I finally decided to call Mike Barwis. I'm sure he could tell I was a wreck. "Why don't you take a few days off?" he said. "You never take breaks. You even skipped your spring break. Maybe this is your body telling you to slow down."

For the first time since moving to Michigan, I stayed home and rested for three days. But when I came back to therapy, I hadn't improved. If anything, I'd gotten worse. Mike Barwis, who had come for that session to check on me, folded his arms as he watched me struggle to move my legs. "Has anything changed about your routine? Something's got to be different," he said.

In May I had started taking a nighttime supplement to help my body relax and go to sleep, so I said, "Just the nighttime supplement. But I didn't think it had any side effects."

"That's got to be it," Mike said. "Throw out the rest. Don't take another pill. Then we'll see how you do."

Thankfully, Mike was right. My strength came back, and I was able to take steps again. *Okay, Em and I are going to make this happen*, I thought. *I'm back to myself again.*

11

The Graduation Walk

· CHRIS ·

"You ready?" Emily said.

I nodded.

She helped move my feet from the footrests to the floor. I placed my hands on the sides of my seat cushion, leaned forward, and pushed to my feet. Emily held out her arms, and I rested my hands on her elbows. We stared at the floor, trying not to tangle our legs. Slowly, we moved together. Step. Step. Shuffle. Step. I looked at Emily and grinned. "We're doing this."

But I looked up too soon. Emily tried to step backward but couldn't move. My foot was resting squarely on her long skirt. "Whoops," I laughed. "Sorry."

"It's okay. Just pick up your foot."

"Uh. I can't." We both cracked up as Emily knelt down to pick up my foot and move it off her coral skirt.

"Note to self: get my skirt hemmed," Emily laughed. "Tomorrow let's try it with a shorter dress."

A few weeks out from graduation, we faced crunch time. We had the walking part down. Now we had to control for the variables that came with walking in dress clothes in front of an audience. In addition to my regular therapy and biking, Emily and I had a dress rehearsal in our apartment every night. I borrowed Emily's brother's graduation gown and put on the shoes I planned to wear for the actual walk—sturdy shoes that would support my ankles instead of your typical flimsy dress shoes. Emily tried different dresses and searched for shoes that would allow her to walk backward without slipping. I stepped on her sandal a few times, and her shoe fell off. Sometimes I stepped on her skirt. We kept pushing through. As Memorial Day weekend crept closer, we brought our graduation gear to Barwis Methods and doubled up on practices.

"I think we're ready," Em said one night after yet another dress rehearsal. We were on a hot streak. Multiple nights in a row, we had gotten through the walk without one hiccup.

I nodded slowly. "I think you're right. I just wish we could practice with a cap." It was the one piece of the graduation outfit we didn't have.

"I don't think that's going to be a problem." Emily was confident. "It's not going to affect your feet. And I think I finally have the right skirt length and shoes. Your shoes are perfect. We've got this."

"Yeah." I was confident too, but I couldn't shake my nerves. The truth was, I had something else on my mind. The graduation walk wasn't the only major life event I had planned for Memorial Day weekend.

· EMILY ·

The time finally came for Chris and me to drive down to Decorah. We had talked about graduation and practiced for this moment for so long that I couldn't believe it was finally here.

Chris had agreed to speak to a group of graduating senior athletes Saturday morning, which seemed crazy to me. I thought it was insane to add one more thing to his already busy schedule, but he was insistent. Afterward, we stopped at Culver's to get some lunch. I devoured my sandwich, but when I looked at Chris, he hadn't touched his burger. "What are you doing, Chris?" I was dumbfounded. "Tomorrow is one of the biggest days of your life, and you're not going to eat? You've been training for years for this moment!"

He shrugged and looked away. "I guess I'm just not hungry."

"But you know it matters what you eat the day before. You need to get some good food in you!"

"I promise I'll eat dinner tonight."

"Oh my gosh. You always eat and eat! This doesn't make sense."

I knew better than to keep pushing, but it was so unlike him not to fuel his body before a big day. He finally ate a few cheese curds to make me happy. *Wow,* I thought, *he must be more nervous about the graduation walk than I thought.*

Back at our dorm room, Chris's mom and sisters told us they were about to go shopping.

"I think I'll go too," his dad said.

I stared at him. "Terry, why are you going shopping? You hate shopping."

He looked around nervously. "Oh, sometimes I like it. It's a nice day; it might be fun to walk around."

"Okay . . ." I said. *This graduation walk must be getting to everyone, because no one is acting like themselves,* I thought.

Chris told me someone was coming to interview us at Luther before dinner. "It's going to be on camera, so you might want to dress up."

"No problem. I brought an extra dress anyway." I put on makeup and straightened my hair before helping Chris put on his tie.

"Is it okay if we stop by my friend's restaurant first?" he asked. "She told me she has a graduation gift for me. We just have to pick it up."

"Sounds good. Just tell me where to go."

Chris barely said a word as we drove to the restaurant. Given how nervous he'd seemed all day, I didn't push him.

The restaurant was closed when we pulled up, and the owner met us out front. She hadn't opened yet, so the main dining room was still dark. "I have your present in the banquet room back here," she said, motioning for us to follow her.

When I walked through the doorway, my jaw dropped. Our song— "All of Me" by John Legend—was playing softly in a dimly lit room. *What? Could this be what I think it is?*

I tried to wrap my head around what was happening. I looked around the room. A sign hung from the ceiling and was decorated in sparkling letters that read "All of me loves all of you." Tables draped in black tablecloths were sprinkled with rose petals and twinkling candles. Photographs of Chris and me were everywhere. My heart raced. This could only mean one thing. And then I saw the final touch: rose petals and candles had been strategically arranged in the middle of the room, spelling out the words, "Will you marry me?"

My hand flew to my mouth as I laughed in surprise. When I turned to Chris, he had a velvet jewelry box sitting in his lap. I could see tears shining in his eyes. Never in a million years did I expect this. For the past four months, we'd spent every day focusing on Chris's graduation walk, and now he had pulled off the surprise of a lifetime! I knew I wanted to marry Chris, but I wasn't thinking about that now. To my great surprise, this amazing man who had never been the most romantic guy in the world, had now hit one out of the park.

"I want to spend the rest of my life with you," he said, taking my hand. "There's no doubt in my mind." His voice was thick with emotion. I knew he meant every word.

"You're the most amazing person I've ever met. Will you marry me and share the rest of our lives together?"

I didn't hesitate. "Yes!" I cried. He grinned and opened the box to reveal the most beautiful ring I had ever seen. He lifted the box up, and I knew that was my cue to take it and put it on my finger. I sobbed as I slipped it on my left ring finger.

"I love you so much," I managed to choke out between sobs. Bending over, I held his face in my hands as I kissed him. I had known for so long that I always wanted him by my side. Now it was official.

Suddenly, our parents and siblings came rushing out of a supply closet down the hall, where they had apparently been hiding. Even my grandparents were there. I was shocked—I thought they weren't coming until Sunday because my little brother David had a state track meet in Des Moines. "What! What are you doing here?" I cried in disbelief. One by one, they greeted us with hugs and congratulations. I noticed both of our moms wipe away tears. I had never seen so much joy in one room. All the anxiety and depression about my future that I'd dealt with over the previous six months seemed like a lifetime ago. I was happier than I'd ever been in my life. I'd always told Chris that I wanted a memorable proposal. He exceeded my wildest dreams. Oh, I could not wait to marry this man!

▪ CHRIS ▪

We celebrated our engagement with our families at dinner, but I called it a night early. I needed as much rest as possible to make this walk happen. On our way back to the dorms where we were staying, I checked my phone and noticed an alert. "Hey, they're moving the graduation inside," I said. "It's supposed to rain all day, so they can't have it on the football field anymore."

"Oh nice, what a blessing!" Emily said. She was right. I had worried for weeks about how well I would be able to walk on a hot day. Since my injury, my body has trouble regulating my internal temperature. I can't sweat anymore. I have no way to keep my body cool when I overheat. Instead, my body shuts down and doesn't respond. Even if the gym got hot, it would be better than sitting outside with the sun beating down on me.

Back at the dorm, we set our alarms for 4:00 a.m. Obviously, graduation didn't start that early. But most days my body didn't respond nearly as well first thing in the morning as it did after I'd been up for several hours. I wanted to make sure I had plenty of time to wake up my muscles and get my body ready so I had the best chance for success.

But sleep was hard to find. My mind raced back to everything that had just happened. I had asked the woman I loved to marry me. Emily wasn't going to walk across the stage with me as my girlfriend anymore. She was walking with me as my fiancée. I couldn't have imagined a better scenario. Now the graduation wasn't just a symbol of my hard work or how far I had come. It was our celebration. These few steps would be the beginning of our journey together, a plan only God could have created.

And that journey was going to start very early the next morning.

▪ EMILY ▪

I am definitely not a morning person. Normally I would pull the covers over my head if my alarm went off at 4:00 a.m. On graduation day, however, I was awake long before the alarm went off. I was too excited to sleep. This was it. This was the day we had waited for.

"How are you feeling?" I asked Chris. "Muscles feeling good?" Chris's body still wasn't back to one hundred percent after that supplement had set him back a few weeks before, and I couldn't help but feel a little scared. *Did we get up early enough?* I wondered. *Did we give ourselves enough time?*

Chris nodded, without a trace of grogginess on his face. "I feel great," he said. "I'm ready."

After getting Chris up and dressed, we got ready for the graduation walk with some stretching. I pulled Chris's knees into his chest and straightened them out, over and over, then rolled his ankles and helped him lift his feet and toes. After standing for a bit and catching his balance, we took a few steps together. We had to be careful not to overdo it, though. He needed to warm up and get ready, but we did not want him to tire out before the walk.

"I think you're in good shape," I said. "Why don't we take a break and eat breakfast?"

Over the next few hours, other friends staying in the dorm cluster woke up and came out into the family room. They kept Chris occupied as I fixed my hair and makeup. My stomach churned, and my hand shook slightly as I brushed on eye shadow and mascara. More than anything, I simply wanted this day to go smoothly. *Please, God, let this work,* I prayed. *Chris has put so much into this moment. Don't let our nerves get the best of us today.*

▪ CHRIS ▪

The gym was already packed when we arrived well before the 10:00 a.m. ceremony. Emily helped me find my spot as a professor lined us up two-by-two in alphabetical order.

"Wow, good thing your last name doesn't start with Z," she whispered in my ear, which made me laugh. Just having Emily there helped me breathe and push away the nerves.

I looked at the huge line of students all waiting to graduate that day. Every single one of them would be able to glide across the stage with no issue and quickly grab their diplomas. My walk would take at least ten times longer than anyone else's. *I'm going to stick out like a sore thumb,* I thought. *Are people going to be mad? This ceremony is already going to be so long, and now I'm going to make it even longer.*

"Hey." Emily interrupted my thoughts. "Don't worry. Everyone is going to be so excited for you. I promise."

I nodded, trying to believe it. "You're right. I know you're right."

One of my classmates who also had a last name that started with N planned to push me to my spot in the gym, which allowed Emily to take her place with my family at the front. We had told the school about our plan, so they reserved a spot for my family near the podium. "I'll see you out there," she said.

"See you out there."

A few minutes later, I heard the opening notes to "Pomp and Circumstance." Game time. I felt exactly like I had before a football game all those years before. I was an athlete about to take the field. Now I just needed all that practice to translate into a good performance.

My classmate pushed me into the gym, and I scanned the crowd, looking for my family. There were no empty seats. This was not some huge arena like major colleges have. Luther College played its basketball games in an honest-to-goodness gym, and it was packed like a sold-out game. I felt my heart beat faster, and I took a deep breath. *You can do this*, I told myself.

We took our spots in the middle of a long row of seats—a chair had been moved out of the way so my wheelchair would fit. I locked in on the graduation stage and looked at the ramp leading up to the platform and podium. *Time to visualize.* I closed my eyes and imagined myself wheeling up the ramp, pushing out of my chair, and taking that first step with Emily. *I hope this works.*

I wondered if I would be able to enjoy the ceremony at all. Luckily, our speaker, Mike Danforth, was a welcome distraction. He was a 1995 Luther graduate who was now a senior producer on National Public Radio's "Wait, Wait . . . Don't Tell Me!" He was funny and entertaining and before I knew it, my shoulders dropped and I relaxed. Mike talked about how it's okay not to have a plan for your future. Everyone laughed as he described his poor grades and his lack of plans for after graduation. His words resonated with me because the plan I had for my life when I started at Luther College had drastically changed over the past four years. I loved how Mike told us not to panic but to keep working.

Then, just like that, Mike was done, and the first row of graduates stood and made their way to the podium. I listened as the announcer read each student's first, middle, and last name. *Here we go*, I thought.

Getting through all the graduates was a long process. I could see people checking their watches and fanning themselves as the ceremony dragged on. The body heat from thousands of people canceled out the gym's air conditioning. *Everyone is going to be so annoyed by how long I take. What if this is a mistake?*

I watched the next row stand up. Then the next. They were getting closer and closer. Then it was our turn. I tried to slow my breathing as my classmate pushed me down the row and off to the side while I waited to hear my name. Finally, it came. "Christopher . . . Anderson . . . Norton." My heart pounded in my ears as one of my best friends, Tanner, pushed me up the ramp. Emily stepped up to the stage and stood in front of me, moving my feet out of the footrests and onto the stage floor.

"Are you ready?" she asked, grinning.

"Let's do this," I said.

Just like we had practiced so many times, I placed my hands on the sides of my seat cushion and tried to push myself out of the chair. I wanted to do as much by myself as I could. But today, my hands shook uncontrollably. Maybe it was nerves, maybe it was the heat, maybe it was just one of those days. But whatever it was, I quickly realized it wasn't going to work.

I looked up at Emily. "Can you help me up?"

"Are you sure? Don't you want to do it yourself?"

I shook my head. "I need help."

Emily bent down, and I leaned into her shoulders as she gripped me under my arms. We hadn't practiced this part, and I could feel the tassel on my cap whacking both of us in the face. But within a few seconds, I was on my feet. *Okay*, I thought. *Now I can do this.*

We took the position—her arms out, my hands on her elbows. Step. Step. Shuffle. I stared at the floor. *Don't step on her feet*, I thought. With a few more steps behind us, I smiled. I knew I had momentum now. People had begun to cheer as soon as I stood out of my chair. Now the crowd was so loud that I began to hear the gasps and cheers as I kept moving. But I was completely focused on my walk.

I was still moving, but my steps weren't as big as I needed them to be. "Can you put your hands on my hips?" I asked Emily. With a little extra help to stabilize my core, I was able to focus on my legs.

Step. Step. Step. I tried to look up every so often. This was the moment I had waited for. I wanted to remember it.

Finally, we reached the college president. Emily shifted me to her side, and I leaned against her as I stuck out my hand to shake the president's hand. When the place erupted in cheers, I jumped, startled. For the first time, I looked around and realized that everyone was on their feet. Applause echoed off the wood floor and into the rafters. Some people I had never met were openly crying. Energy built to a crescendo as I pumped my fist and took my diploma.

Emily and I grinned at one another. We didn't have to say a word. We both knew what the other was thinking—*We did it.*

Emily helped me back into my chair. When Tanner wheeled me off the stage, I exhaled as a huge weight lifted off my shoulders. It was over. I did what I wanted to do, and by the grace of God, I succeeded. I thought about all the workouts, the roughly 4,500-plus hours of dedication to one goal, to one moment. So many times I had asked myself, *What am I doing?* I never had an answer, but I kept going anyway. Now I knew the answer. This moment would forever be something I'm proud of.

The cheers hadn't died down as other graduates hugged me and wiped their eyes. I was blown away by their emotional response. I had always known that the Luther College community supported me, but I had no idea how invested they were in my story or how much they cared.

Five years before, doctors had told me I had a three percent chance of ever moving anything below my shoulders. I wondered how I could ever go back to school and get my degree. I worried that no one would see past my injury and love me for who I am. That graduation Sunday, I shattered those odds. I shattered those doubts. True, I didn't have the life I had imagined. This one was even better.

My graduation walk felt like the kind of moment where the curtain goes down or the movie screen goes dark. But that always signals an end. This was not the end but a beginning—one I could not wait to dive into.

I'm making a diving tackle for my high school football team, Bondurant-Farrar, in 2009 in the first round of high school playoffs. I'm in blue.

My family attended and supported every activity I was in. Here I am with my dad, Terry Norton, and my mom, Deb Norton, on senior night of fall 2009.

My high school graduation with longtime friend Logan Hamm, class of 2010, Bondurant-Farrar High School.

After a home football game at Luther College with teammates Richie Vickers (#17) and Shawn Burrows (#19), fall 2010. Richie was also my college roommate.

Here I am on a gurney, being taken off the helicopter by EMTs during a film reenactment of October 16, 2010, for my documentary film *7 Yards: The Chris Norton Story.*

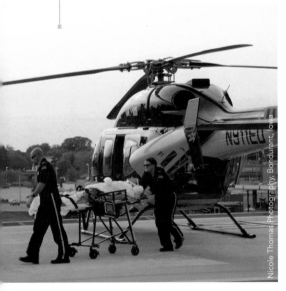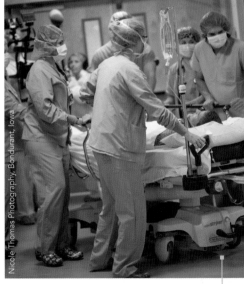

I am being transported through the hospital to get prepped for surgery, during a film reenactment of October 16, 2010, for my documentary film *7 Yards: The Chris Norton Story.*

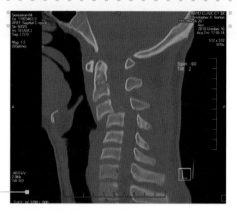

X-ray taken of my neck fracture at Winneshiek Medical Center before being flown to Mayo Clinic, October 16, 2010.

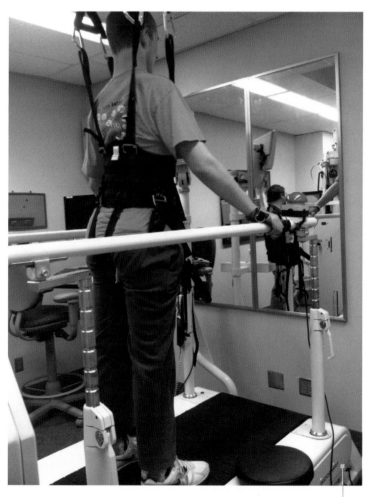

Standing on the Lokomat machine at Mayo Clinic, fully weight bearing and balancing on my legs, during a physical therapy session, fall 2011.

Our family celebrated Christmas in the hospital of Mayo Clinic. *From left*: Aunt Ginger Palmer; Uncle Gary Palmer; my sister Alex McManus (formerly Norton); me; my sister Katie Norton; Grandma Virginia; my dad, Terry Norton; and my mom, Deb Norton.

My college friends and teammates brought ugly Christmas sweaters for a Christmas card, winter 2010. They visited me a lot when I was in the hospital and were great company. *From left*: Zac Pearson, Shawn Burrows, me, Richie Vickers, Eric Essendrup, Tanner Douglas.

My old dorm room and my first visit there since my injury. We had our football banquet that night, February 2011. I am with my college buddies plus our floor's RA. *From left*: Tim (RA), Eric Essendrup, Rich Vickers, Shawn Burrows, Tanner Douglas, Spencer Bruess.

My sisters, Alex and Katie, in my hospital room at Mayo Clinic, fall 2010. They were by my side constantly while I was in the hospital. Every weekend they were there, driving six hours round trip.

Our very first photo together, taken the first night Emily and I met at Iowa State University, August 2013.

Tyler Rinken

I surprised Emily with a proposal the day before my graduation, May 2015. Emily read "Will you marry me?" when we came into the room of the restaurant. Her expression in the picture says it all.

After the proposal my family and friends celebrated with us. My college friends came and greeted us. *From left:* Richie Vickers, Alex Peterson (a.k.a. A.P.), me, Rich Holton, Emily, Zac Pearson, Tanner Douglas.

Tyler Rinken

Emily graduated from the University of Northern Iowa in 2014, and we celebrated with her family and with Whittley.

Emily and I at Barwis Methods, practicing walking in the dress shoes I used for my college graduation, May 2015.

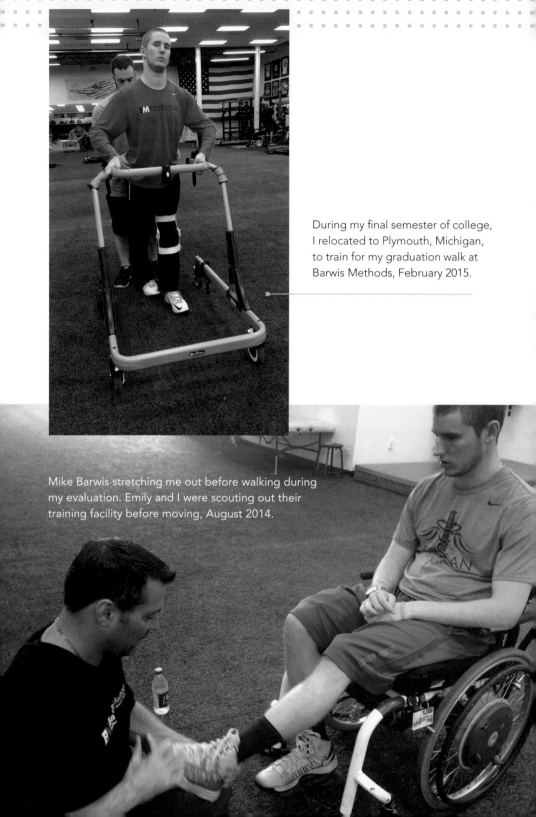

During my final semester of college, I relocated to Plymouth, Michigan, to train for my graduation walk at Barwis Methods, February 2015.

Mike Barwis stretching me out before walking during my evaluation. Emily and I were scouting out their training facility before moving, August 2014.

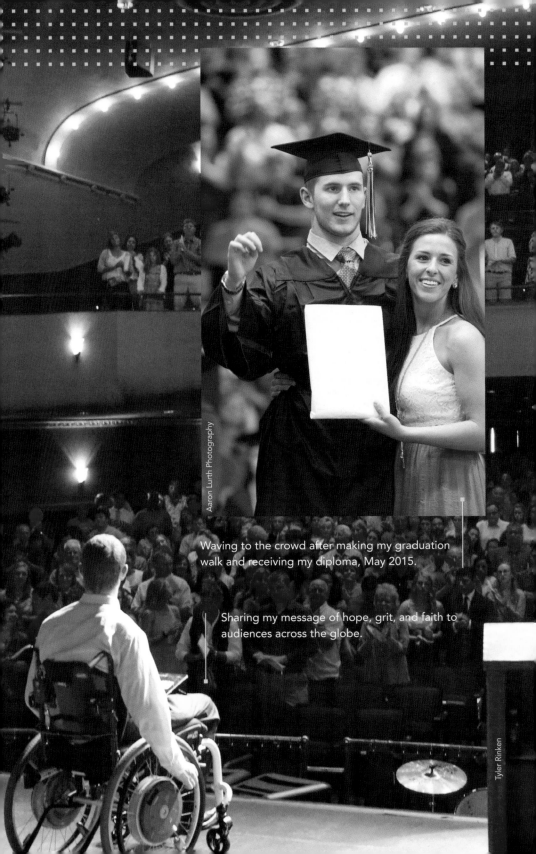

Aaron Lurth Photography

Waving to the crowd after making my graduation walk and receiving my diploma, May 2015.

Sharing my message of hope, grit, and faith to audiences across the globe.

Tyler Rinken

Before I graduated from college, I started sharing my story at schools to inspire students to overcome their challenges, which gave my pain a purpose.

The Summers family has been extremely supportive of us. We came back for the high school graduation of Emily's younger brother, May 2017. *From left*: Michael (older brother), Tim (Dad), David (younger brother), Kelly (Mom), me, Emily, Marisa (younger sister).

My family during the Chris Norton Foundation's Fundraiser dinner, February 2017. *From left*: Emily, Deb (Mom), Terry (Dad), Bill (brother-in-law), Alex (older sister), Katie (younger sister).

We celebrated Emily's twenty-fourth birthday in our apartment in Florida with Whittley, whom we were fostering at the time, December 2016.

Emily and I with Robin Roberts on the set of *Good Morning America* after being interviewed about our wedding walk, April 2018.

Emily and I in Times Square. We were there for the filming of *Say Yes to the Dress*, October 2017.

Emily and I saying our vows, April 21, 2018.

Emily and I share a moment during communion at our wedding, April 21, 2018.

Emily and I share our first kiss as a married couple, April 21, 2018.

Sarah Kata, Photographer

Emily with Whittley before Whittley's freshman year homecoming, fall 2012.

Emily and I with the five children we were fostering, July 2018.

Emily and I and our five girls outside the courthouse before we legally adopted Whittley, December 11, 2018.

Michale Crumly of Mississippi Pearl Photography

12

Media Frenzy

· EMILY ·

With the graduation walk behind us, Chris and I were riding an unbelievable high. Not only had we accomplished the goal we'd worked so hard to achieve, we were also getting married. I couldn't stop holding out my hand and admiring the diamond sparkling on my finger. I wondered how people ever got anything done with an engagement ring on their hand. I didn't know if I'd ever stop staring at it. My heart felt so full that it was hard for me to remember how I'd put walls up around it before our move to Michigan.

No media outlets covered the graduation as we had once hoped they would, but we still had a video of the moment, thanks to a friend of Chris who's also a videographer. Chris posted the video on YouTube and then shared the link on his Facebook page. We hoped it might inspire a few people. Right away the post got hundreds of shares and comments. A local TV station also ended up doing a story the next morning with a blurry clip that someone who was at the graduation had sent them. Chris and I were both thrilled that word was getting out. This was exactly what we had hoped would happen.

The day after graduation was Memorial Day. Chris and I were at his parents' house hanging out with friends and catching up when Chris noticed he had a voice mail. "I have no idea who this is," he said. "Hold on, let me listen to it."

I watched his face go white as he held the phone to his ear. "Em?" he said after hanging up. "Uh, that was *Fox & Friends*."

"Shut up." I thought he was joking. "*Fox & Friends* seriously called you? Why?"

"Apparently they saw the graduation video and want to interview us. Tomorrow."

My jaw practically hit the floor. We thought the graduation walk might get some local coverage from the Iowa outlets that had followed his story since his accident, but never in our wildest dreams did we think it would become a national story. "Do they want us to come to New York City?" I asked.

"No, no. We have to go to one of their local affiliates, and they'll do a satellite interview."

"But . . . I have nothing to wear!" were the first words out of my mouth. "I need to go shopping!" I think I was in shock.

Chris's sisters jumped in. "You can borrow something from us!" Katie said. "Don't worry! You're welcome to anything in our closets." Thankfully, both his sisters were about my size. Chris still had some dress clothes at his parents' house, so he was set.

The producer who contacted Chris told us where to go and said we had to be at the studio by 6:00 a.m. Tuesday. It was our second ridiculously early morning in four days, but once again we were so excited that we didn't mind.

When we arrived at the studio, though, my excitement gave way to nerves. I gulped as a producer led us into a room stocked with breakfast pastries and coffee. A TV played in the corner, and we were each given earpieces to listen to the interviewer. I looked at Chris to see if he was as jittery as I was, but I should have known better. He seemed unbelievably calm and relaxed.

▪ CHRIS ▪

I had a lot of experience doing interviews, but the live TV thing freaked me out a little, especially when the *Fox & Friends* producer said we wouldn't be able to see Elizabeth Hasselbeck, who was interviewing us that day. We had to look into the camera, pretend we could see her, and rely on the earpiece to know when to respond. What could possibly go wrong?

Emily and I took our places in the studio. Both of us kept grinning with excitement. Then a producer told us we'd be on in five minutes. All I could think was: *Don't say something stupid!* Thankfully I didn't, at least not that I can remember. Looking back, the interview itself is a blur. Emily and I both thought we did a pretty good job of telling our story. However, neither of us had any idea how big of a difference this walk could make, so we weren't intentional about adding value to other people's lives. Instead, we focused on simply answering the questions and not messing up on national television. The more interviews we did, the less our nerves got the best of us.

After doing the interview, we met up with some of my family at a diner over in Prairie Meadows for breakfast. We were enjoying our meal and coffee when I heard a TV announcer say my name. I looked up expecting to see a replay of the *Fox & Friends* interview but was instead shocked to see our graduation video playing on CNN.

"Wow. Do you think anyone else will pick it up?" I asked Emily.

The answer to my question was a resounding yes! The *Fox & Friends* interview immediately went viral, which made my email explode with media requests. I fielded inquiries from an Australian newspaper, a Brazilian newspaper, even media outlets in China and Norway. Since we were still living out of suitcases, Emily drove to Von Maur and Express to buy dresses for more interviews. She got four dresses just in case, never imagining she would end up wearing all of them.

I scheduled phone interviews, and Emily and I sat down with the *Des Moines Register* and the *CBS Evening News*. The *Des Moines Register* article ended up running in *USA Today*.

And that was only our Tuesday. Every once in a while during that long crazy day, Emily and I would look at one another and say, "Holy cow. This is crazy."

By Tuesday night we thought the madness was over, but when we woke up Wednesday morning, I had two missed calls and two voice mails from *NBC Nightly News*. I was excited to call them back.

"We saw your story, and we'd really like to get you on our broadcast tonight," the producer said when I returned the call. "Are you available for us to send out a news crew in a couple of hours?"

I looked at the clock. It was only 7:30 a.m. Neither of us had showered yet, and the house was cluttered from yesterday's chaos. But I answered, "Sure, that would be great!"

I had just finished telling Emily about the NBC interview when my phone rang again. And again. And again. A few local stations wanted to come and do interviews too. My answer was always the same: "Sure!"

For the next several hours, my parents' living room became a television studio filled with cameras, cables, and news crews. At one point we had three different crews at our house. When those interviews were finished, we dashed over to a local radio station for another. Before I could catch my breath, I checked my phone and noticed I had another voice mail. "Em?" I said after listening. "It's *Good Morning America*. They want us to come to New York."

Emily smacked my arm. "Stop it. Seriously?"

"I have to call him back and work out the details."

The producer I called picked up after just one ring. "Hey, we want you guys to do an exclusive in-studio interview with Robin Roberts tomorrow morning," the producer said. "Can you do it?"

I looked at Emily and mouthed, "Can we go to New York?" She nodded so hard I thought she would give herself a headache.

"Yeah, we can do it," I answered.

"Great. We'll book a flight. Your parents can come too. We'll pay for their trip. What I need you to do is stop whatever you're doing. Go home. Pack your bags and head to the airport. We'll figure out the flights while you drive."

My dad floored it down the highway while I filled Emily and my mom in on the details.

My phone rang again. "There is a flight leaving in an hour and a half," the producer said. "Can you make it?"

We still weren't home. We still needed to pack, plus my parents' house is a good twenty-five minutes from the Des Moines airport. But I said, "Absolutely. We'll be there."

· EMILY ·

My heart pounded, and I checked the time every two seconds as we raced back to Chris's parents' house. *Thank God I bought all those dresses,* I thought.

Chris's parents don't have a wheelchair-accessible car, so we had transferred Chris from his chair into the vehicle. When we finally got home, Chris and I exchanged glances. "There's no time for a transfer, right?" I said.

Chris shook his head. "I'll wait here. Go!"

His mom and dad and I dashed into the house like that scene from *Home Alone* when they oversleep and try to make their flight. I tossed my dress and Chris's suit into a suitcase like a madwoman. Even Chris's mom, who is notorious for traveling with the biggest suitcase known to man, got her things packed really quickly. Within minutes we were back in the car and on our way to the airport.

All of us could barely contain our excitement. "We're going to New York City!" I squealed. I had never been there before and couldn't wait to see Time's Square, eat at good restaurants, and do some shopping.

Part of me felt panicked because we didn't have the plane tickets yet, and I desperately wanted this to work. *How amazing would it be to share Chris's story on* Good Morning America? I thought.

Chris's dad got us to the airport in record time—I don't even want to know how fast he was driving. We parked, and Terry transferred Chris out of the car while Deb and I unloaded the suitcases. I checked my watch as we made our way to the ticket counter. We made it in time. This was going to work.

After a few minutes of waiting, we still didn't have the tickets, but I was confident we would get on a plane soon. We were already at the airport. What other obstacle could there possibly be?

Then Chris's phone rang. "Hey, we're so sorry, but it's not going to work," the producer said. "We couldn't get you on the plane. Every flight is booked."

Chris held the phone away from his face and told us what happened. When we heard the news, Deb's face fell. "Oh no, really? But we came so close."

Terry was already starting to gather up the bags when I grabbed Chris's phone. If there was a way to make this work, I was going to find it.

"Hi, this is Emily, Chris's fiancée. Could we try another airport? Omaha isn't too far from here, or Cedar Rapids. We will go anywhere. Can you just check those airports? We would love to be able to do the interview. This is such a great opportunity, and we really want to do it."

I heard the producer type on a computer keyboard. "Let me work on it and call you back. We want you here. Let me see what I can do."

I shrugged when I hung up. "Well, we'll see what happens."

"It's probably not going to work out," Chris said, ever the realist. "And if it doesn't, that's okay."

"I know," I sighed. "But I really want it to!"

Minutes ticked by as we sat around the airport waiting for a call. We found a booth at a Pizza Hut and scarfed down pizza and breadsticks. Normally, I don't have much of an appetite when I'm discouraged, but we'd done so many interviews that morning that we hadn't had time to eat lunch.

We all jumped when Chris's phone rang. Chris put it on speaker so we could listen. "Okay, it looks like there might be a flight out of Cedar Rapids that I could get you on," he said. "How long does it take you to get there, and can you leave now?" We were already standing up to leave.

"Yep. We're on our way," Chris said.

During the hour-and-forty-five-minute drive to Cedar Rapids, the producer found us first-class tickets with a layover in Chicago—it was all that was left. No flights were available going into New York, or even Newark, New Jersey. Our final flight would land in Hartford, Connecticut, which meant we'd have to take a car service from there to our hotel. None of us cared at this point. We just wanted to get there.

We made it to our gate just in time, and within five minutes they started boarding. Someone who worked at the show messaged Chris. "Are you guys on the plane? We wanted to make sure you made it." They were relieved to know we had.

Our plane landed in Chicago right on time, which was perfect because our layover was only forty-five minutes. Then I heard the ding of the loudspeaker. "Folks, we're having some trouble connecting the gate bridge to the plane. Sit tight a few minutes, and we'll let you know when it's time to deplane."

I groaned. "You have got to be kidding me!"

Chris laughed. "Em, there's nothing we can do. They'll get it figured out. We'll be okay."

At least ten minutes went by without any updates. I jiggled my knee in frustration and jerked my head around, looking for a flight attendant. "I'm going to say something," I said as I stood up. I heard Deb laughing as I confronted the first flight attendant I saw. She and the rest of their family are more go-with-the-flow people. All I could think was, *We did not come all the way to Chicago to just turn around and go home. I'm going to put some pressure on and see if I can get something to happen.*

"Okay, so here's the thing. We're supposed to be on *Good Morning America* in the morning," I said firmly. "We've gotta go. If we miss our flight, there is no other plane. We will not be on the show. How can we get off this plane and make our flight?"

The flight attendant furrowed her brow and nodded. "Let me talk to the pilot."

The captain announced that he would lower the outdoor steps and let us exit on the ground. Normally, anyone with special needs has to wait for everyone else to deplane first before they can get off the plane. But since we were in first class and the flight attendant knew our situation, the crew made everyone else wait for us to get off before they could leave.

But there was one more problem. How the heck were we going to get Chris down those steep, narrow stairs? I looked at Terry, my jaw clenched in determination. "Alright. We're just going to have to carry him. You get his arms. I'll grab his legs."

I was ready to do it too. Thankfully, another passenger heard our plan and stepped in. "You don't need to do that," he said. "Let me help."

The crew had Chris's chair waiting for him on the ground as our volunteer and Terry hoisted Chris down the stairs. Each step was so skinny that nearly half of Terry's foot hung off the front of the step. Two other people walked behind him, holding his shoulders to keep him balanced and make sure he didn't fall forward. My heart raced as I waited for them at the bottom. If I wasn't so stressed, I would have laughed at the sight of Chris being carried down airplane stairs, but we didn't have time for laughter.

With Chris safely in his chair, an airport employee directed us to an elevator under the airport that was clearly a restricted area. Once we made it inside, he pushed Chris's wheelchair as we sprinted through the terminal.

"Where are you going anyway?" he panted.

"We're going to be on *Good Morning America* tomorrow!" I cried. "We've got to make our flight."

"What? We need to get you there!" Somehow, this man dug deep and found a whole new level of speed. I checked my phone as we ran. *We're never going to make it*, I thought. A flight attendant had radioed the gate to let them know we were coming, and they delayed the flight a few minutes, but I knew they wouldn't wait forever.

Somehow, miraculously, we made it. We were the last people on the flight, and our plane took off within what seemed like seconds of us being seated.

Chris checked his phone and saw a text from someone at *Good Morning America*. "You guys are on the plane, right? We can't wait to have you here."

I dissolved into laughter—at this point I was probably delirious. "Oh my gosh," I said. "That lady has no idea what's going on right now."

▪ CHRIS ▪

Once we finally made it to our hotel, I think Emily and I got maybe an hour of sleep before we had to get up and get ready to go to the *GMA* studio. I didn't have time to be nervous thinking about the interview. I was busy making sure we were downstairs waiting for our car service to get to the studio on time.

The car drove a whole block and a half, which in Times Square takes about ten minutes. We were let in a door on a side street and led past multiple security guards. The producer was there to greet us. We took the elevator up, and he quickly led us past the cameras filming the current segment. Then we arrived in the green room, which was like a small meeting room with coffee and a television set. Another producer came in and asked, "Could you two walk into the set to start the show?"

My eyes widened and my jaw dropped. I wasn't anticipating this. Logistically, it would take too much time, it would be cumbersome, and we would need someone to push my chair up afterward. I told him it wouldn't work. He understood, then asked, "What if you start out standing for the show and after Robin greets you, you sit down?" I said I could do that, and to save time I could just leave my feet on the floor instead of Emily bending over to place them on the foot pedals, which with the lack of sleep could set my legs into a spasm anyway. I'm honestly glad they told me twenty minutes before going live instead of the night before, because I would have been way too anxious. The stand and sit went well! But doing it live on national television was nerve-racking!

The whole twenty-four-hour period was such a crazy rush that when we actually sat across from Robin Roberts, it wasn't remotely stressful. As I looked around the sea of cameras surrounding us and out the glass wall into Times Square, all I could feel was relief. Once again Emily and I had put our minds to something, and we did it. Our crazy adventure to reach New York was further proof that we were unstoppable. I knew that with Emily by my side we could accomplish anything we set our minds to. I even announced my next big goal on *GMA*: to walk with Emily back up the aisle at our wedding. We'd worked a very long time to make the graduation walk a reality. I could not wait to start working toward the wedding walk.

13

A Fog Descends

· CHRIS ·

I fully expected an emotional letdown after graduation and the whirlwind that followed. We had spent the last five months pouring all our time and energy into one goal. We had not only accomplished what we set out to do but also saw our story reach a much wider audience than we ever imagined. Anyone would have a hard time finding their groove again and getting back to real life.

At first everything between Emily and me seemed fantastic. Looking back, I guess that might be because we didn't get back to real life, at least not right away.

Before we headed back to Michigan, we stopped by Emily's hometown of Muscatine to pick up Whittley. She'd tried killing herself again. Thankfully she survived. Her sister had her come live with her, but she clearly needed a change, even if only for a couple of weeks. Emily was pretty insistent Whittley come and stay with us for a while, and I went along with it even though I was extremely nervous about it. I had met Whittley a few times, but it had been for only a few hours at a time, so I still didn't know her very well, no matter how much Emily talked about her. Unfortunately, due to Whittley's recent events, what I had been hearing wasn't encouraging, especially when I have no way to protect Emily or myself if Whittley were to be set off and lash out at us. On top of all that, I knew absolutely nothing about sixteen-year-old girls in general, and Whittley wasn't your typical teenage girl.

Even so, when Emily asked if Whittley could come stay with us for a while, I said yes. I trusted Emily. If she thought we could do this and help Whittley, I was willing to go along with her. Emily has a way of getting through to people, plus she was extremely close to Whittley. More than that, I knew that if we didn't step up and do something to help her, no one else would.

▪ EMILY ▪

Having Whittley in our apartment in Michigan for those two weeks lifted a weight of worry off my shoulders. As soon as the media frenzy after the graduation walk died down, I felt anxious again about what I was supposed to do with my life. Whittley reminded me of the answer I'd always held on to. She also always had a way of getting through to me. Being so far away from her was the hardest part of living in Michigan. Since I first met Whittley when she was in grade school, I had always tried to be there for her, whether it was taking birthday presents to her in the group home or sitting with her at the hospital after a suicide attempt. It hurt me to hear that she was struggling when I lived too far away to do anything. That's why I was so excited about having the chance to spend some time with her in a safe environment. If I could have found a way to make it happen, she would have moved in with us permanently.

Whittley and I spent the first few days we were back together laughing, talking, playing Wii, and going to the gym. The light mood changed during a trip to the gym. She suddenly burst into tears. When I asked her why, she told me that one of her friends had texted her to break the news that her boyfriend back in Iowa had cheated on her. I took her outside, and we sat on the steps together, her head on my shoulder as she sobbed, my hand patting her in reassurance.

"You are so much better off without him," I told her. "You are an amazing girl, and any guy who would do this to you obviously isn't the right one."

"But I love him!" she cried. "Why would he do this to me?"

I wiped the tears from her face and stroked her hair. "I don't know," I said. "Sometimes people just do awful things and we don't know why. But it's better for you to know now what kind of guy he is before you waste any more time on him." All I could think as I comforted her was, *This is the last thing she needs right now.*

That night I lay awake in my bed, worrying about what Whittley might do. Since I couldn't sleep, I mindlessly checked the Facebook app on my phone. What I saw made me sit straight up. "No!" I said. I marched right into the spare room where Whittley was sleeping on an air mattress and flipped on the lights. "Whittley, what is going on?"

I held out my phone with her post on the screen, which read, "I just want my life to be over."

"What do you mean by this?" I asked.

Whittley stared at the sheets and toyed with her hair. "I didn't mean it," she said softly. "I just—I don't know why I wrote that."

I stared at her. "You have to be honest here. Were you thinking about hurting yourself?"

"No," she said, still not looking at me.

I tried to talk it out with her, but I still didn't feel much better when I left her room. I hid all our kitchen knives before I went to bed.

The next few days were rough. Whittley was devastated over her boyfriend. One night Chris and I were both in her room as she broke down in tears yet again. "Alright, that's enough," I said suddenly, hopping to my feet. "We're going out. We're getting frozen yogurt, and we're not going to talk about this jerk anymore."

To my surprise, Whittley went with it. The night seemed to turn her around, at least a little bit. Over the next few days, I saw her relax and act more like herself. It helped that she didn't have her usual negative influences around her as she did back home. No one recognized her in public or made assumptions about her. Michigan was good for her. It was a fresh start.

When the time came for Chris and me to take her back to Iowa, Whittley and I cried and clung to each other. I knew she didn't want to leave, and I didn't want to say goodbye either. If it were up to me, we would have become her foster parents and kept her with us for good right then and there. I even talked to her caseworker about it once, but the conversation didn't go anywhere. The family court system works to keep kids with their families until it becomes impossible. Since a family member was still in the picture, her coming to live with Chris and me wasn't a possibility.

Driving home from Iowa, I felt a terrifying loss of control. I had no idea what Whittley would do now that she was out of my sight. *How would I go on if something happened to her?* The fears inside kept growing until I knew I had to do something to protect my heart before I got hurt so deeply that I'd never recover.

· CHRIS ·

After Whittley went home, I assumed we'd pour all our energy into planning our dream wedding. I couldn't wait to marry Emily and wanted to set a date as soon as possible. I'd already started training for the wedding walk, which, to me, was going to be so much more special than graduation, because these would be our first steps into an unbelievable future.

We knew we wanted to get married in Iowa near all our family and friends, so we checked out venues online. We brainstormed a guest list to help us figure out how much seating we needed. Emily ran color schemes by me. A few weeks went by and even though we hadn't set a firm date, we knew we wanted to tie the knot the following summer.

Emily loved weddings, and I thought she would be thrilled to be planning one of her own, but that didn't happen. Something seemed off. Emily seemed . . . different. The two of us came out of graduation on cloud nine. We had just accomplished this unbelievable goal. Life was great. We had become an unstoppable force, and we were going to do amazing things. But instead of being happy, Emily suddenly seemed to resent me.

I told myself that Emily was simply feeling a little lost now that she didn't have a goal to work toward. I knew her internship at the group home had been hard on her and that she felt uncertain of what to do with her life. *Maybe she just needs time to figure everything out*, I thought.

Later that summer we took a vacation to Florida that I hoped would rejuvenate her, or at least distract her from whatever was bothering her. While we were on the trip, our property manager called out of the blue to inform us that they had never received our rent from two months ago. She threatened legal action if she didn't receive payment in forty-eight hours. I could tell the manager was trying to scare me, but I didn't blink. I distinctly remembered paying the rent—Emily and I were with Whittley when we dropped off a check. We had the check stub to prove it. They obviously had lost it.

"Whoa, whoa, whoa. Slow down," I said calmly. "We paid our rent. There must be some mistake. I'd be happy to send you a picture of the stub if you'd like."

Emily's eyes bulged as she listened to my end of the conversation. "Chris, what's going on? Is everything okay?"

I moved my phone away from my face. "It's fine. There was just a mix-up with our rent check."

"Wait, what? We paid our rent."

"I know we did. Someone must have lost it, and now they're saying they're going to take us to court or something."

"What? No. Give me the phone."

Under normal circumstances Emily would have firmly explained that we paid our rent and asked how we might fix the situation. Emily gets things done. But when I handed her the phone and she started speaking, she was furious. After a few minutes of making no headway, she almost immediately burst into tears. This was no stray tear or two. This was a full-blown meltdown. She could barely manage a word between sobs as she gasped for breath. I stared at her in shock. I knew it wasn't an ideal situation, but a lost rent check wasn't anything we couldn't work out.

I finally took back the phone. "We'll have to call you back."

I had never seen Emily react that way to even a major crisis, much less a landlord spat. For the first time, I knew something was actually wrong.

▪ EMILY ▪

It's not like my life was drastically different after Whittley left. I still spent most of my time taking care of Chris and handling all the household jobs. I remained heavily involved in the Athletic Angels, where once a week boys from a group home came to Barwis Methods, and I led them through a workout, a life skills lesson, and a snack. For a couple of weeks, I also flipped through bridal magazines and Googled DJs and wedding cake designs.

But for reasons I couldn't explain, everything I did felt empty, meaningless. My life had no purpose. My old dream of helping at-risk teenagers had died. My internship at the group home had killed it once and for all. I thought I could help everyone no matter what they went through, but after that experience I felt helpless. For as long as I can remember, every time I heard a story of a child that had been abused or a child struggling with mental health and suicidal thoughts, I took it all in and it broke me. It had been taking a toll on me for many years. I was at a point where it hurt so much that I was shutting down and burying it all. I couldn't take the pain and responsibility of other people's well-being anymore.

Sometimes I toyed with the idea of finding a job someplace less traumatic, but I didn't get serious about finding a full-time job. We didn't know how long we would stay in Michigan, and the last thing a kid in a group home needs is to get close to an adult who will leave them like everyone else does. Besides, I was Chris's full-time caregiver. I even received payment through Chris's insurance, which let me put off finding my full-time calling, something I started to doubt even existed.

Over the next few weeks, I felt more and more lost. I didn't feel good about myself anymore. I was living with a wall between me and the rest of the world, and I didn't understand why it was there or how to make it go away. It was as if a fog had descended over my life. Everything that used to be sunny and bright was now cloudy and gray.

When we first moved to Michigan, I was happy to help Chris. I jumped at the chance to fill up his water bottle or transfer him to the couch. Now every little task felt like work. Life felt so hard. The little things became stressful and overwhelming. Each time Chris needed me to set him up in his bike or drain his leg bag, irritation bubbled up inside me, and I let it out. I'd tell Chris in no uncertain terms that I felt unappreciated and taken for granted. One night I had spent half the day grocery shopping and cooking one of his favorite meals—homemade enchiladas, rice, and a salad. I plunked his plate in front of him and waited for him to gush with thanks for the amazing meal I had slaved away to prepare especially for him. Instead, he started eating without saying a thing.

"Well, thanks a lot for the 'thank you,'" I exploded. "I spent so much time on this meal. I had to go out and buy groceries. I had to cook all this food. When we're done, I'm the one who has to clean all these dishes. I don't feel like you appreciate any of the stuff I'm doing for you."

Chris stopped midbite and put his fork down. "I was going to say thank you, but you didn't give me enough time to say it," he said, defending himself. "You know I appreciate it, even if I don't say it right away."

"All you care about is yourself!" I snapped back. "You don't care about me." I grew angrier by the second. "You're so rude and selfish, and all you think about is yourself in your own little world. I'm trying to do nice things for you, and I don't feel appreciated at all."

All I wanted was for him to say he loved me—though even that probably wouldn't have been enough. He didn't take the bait. "Where is this coming from?" he demanded. "You completely blew up at me for no reason."

I tried to stop myself from taking it up a notch, but I couldn't. Every time we fought, I wanted him to get emotional or do something, anything, to show me he cared. I got nastier and nastier, trying to get a reaction from the human thermostat who never got too hot or cold. It was a mental battle that I usually lost.

"You are such a jerk!" I was yelling now. "I don't even know why we're together anymore. You don't love me."

"You're crazy!" Chris finally lost his cool. "Of course I love you! You're being crazy!"

"I am not crazy!" I screamed, tears rolling down my cheeks. Hearing him say the very thing I worried about deep down was too much. "I'm out of here. I am done talking to you." I stormed out of the apartment and stomped to my car. As I turned the key in the ignition, I heard my phone buzzing. It was Chris. I pushed my finger down on the power button as hard as I could to turn it off. I didn't want to talk to him, or anyone. Instead, I just drove around, with no destination in mind. I was burning up inside, angry and empty, and it hit me that I didn't have a destination in mind—not tonight, not in life.

I didn't want to be here. I didn't want to be alive.

"God, please just let this other car hit me," I prayed. "Just take my life. I can't do this anymore. This is too hard. I'm never going to be myself again. I have no hope. If this is how my life is always going to be, then I would rather be dead."

This may have been the first, but it certainly wasn't the last time I had this conversation with God. Nor was it the only time I drove away angry, wishing another car would hit me and put me out of my misery.

I never thought seriously about taking my own life, even though when I was angry, sometimes I would shout at Chris that I wanted to kill myself or that I didn't want to be alive anymore. He knew I wasn't serious and that I was trying to get a big reaction out of him. Life felt so hard, but I knew I could never do that to my family. If it weren't for them, I realized I wouldn't have hesitated.

Fights like this happened on a more regular basis as our relationship spiraled downward. The more we fought, the worse I felt about myself, and life in general. The fog of despair became even denser, and my energy completely disappeared. I stopped going to physical therapy with Chris—it was too much. I stayed in bed each morning until the last possible second before I had to get up and take Chris to Barwis Methods. Then I would drive home and take a nap, exhausted from the effort. Even after I picked up Chris, I'd head straight back to bed and just lie there, not sleeping but not wanting to get up. I started getting strange headaches too. They were always concentrated in one spot, in my temple.

I used to spend hours on the phone talking to Sophia and Whittley when they were having a difficult time. It didn't matter if I had something else to do or if I was tired. They always came first. Now talking to them about their problems was becoming a chore and left me emotionally drained. I knew that I was all they had, and I was never going to give up on helping them or being there for them. There had been way too many people who had left them, and I wasn't going to be one of those people, no matter how I was feeling, but staying connected to them became harder and harder. I wasn't getting the same fulfillment I once felt during these conversations, and I doubted if I was even helping them.

Every once in a while, I mustered up the energy to do something I thought might make me feel like my old self again. I arranged for the

Athletic Angels kids to go to a Detroit Tigers game, and I took an online life-coaching class. But none of it really helped. I was lost, without hope that I would ever be found.

My relationship with God fell away as I slipped deeper into the fog. All my life he'd been so important to me, but now I was pushing God away just as I did everyone else in my life. I was shutting down, and I had no idea how detrimental that would be to my relationships and my life. I didn't let God or anyone else help me. To accept help meant admitting I had a problem and that I wasn't strong enough to fix it myself. That was the last thing I was going to do. I'm extremely independent, and I always want to do everything myself. I always *hated* letting others help me, even God. I didn't think I needed any help. Why would I? I had a "perfect" life, and nothing bad ever happened to me. When I did try to pray, I would break down crying, then I would again shut my feelings off. I didn't want to deal with what I was feeling.

Deep down I wondered if I might be depressed, but I never allowed myself to come to that conclusion. *I can't be depressed*, I thought. *I haven't gone through anything hard in my life. I've got a great family. I'm engaged to somebody I really love. I've never gone through anything traumatic. Why would I be depressed?*

• CHRIS •

I hate to admit it, but I never thought depression was real. I assumed people who thought they were depressed simply had the wrong perspective on life or a bad attitude. After all, I had been through one of the most horrific things with my spinal cord injury, and I never crashed into depression.

So when Emily quickly went downhill, I thought I had the answers. First I thought I could fix her problems by easing her workload. "Let me hire someone to help us in our apartment," I said. "You can go get a job, and I'll use the insurance money to pay a nurse or hire someone to help with laundry or cooking. You don't have to do this."

Emily flat out refused.

Then I thought, *Hey, I'm a motivational speaker. I just need to be more motivational and encouraging to her. I'll commit to being a more positive force and always looking on the bright side.* As you can imagine, that didn't go over well.

After days of the strange headaches Emily was having, she wondered if they had anything to do with how tired she was. "I feel like maybe I should see a doctor," she said. "I mean, what if I have a brain tumor or something?"

Obviously, I didn't want her to have a brain tumor, but the idea that there might be a physical explanation for everything made sense to both of us.

"Let's get you a doctor's appointment," I said.

Doctors scanned her head and took vial after vial of blood for multiple tests. Everything came back normal.

As hard as our relationship got, and as frustrated as I was that nothing was helping, I never considered leaving Emily. Despite the fighting, I loved her. She was still the girl I first met, the girl I proposed to not that long ago. She was just struggling right now with something I did not understand. It felt like a roller-coaster ride for both of us. For a few days she'd be her best self, as though she didn't have any problems in the world. Then we'd go through a few days of her being easily irritated. That was always followed by days where she completely shut down and spiraled out of control. Then, just as quickly, she'd be back to her best self. When she was her best self, I always thought we were through with the fighting, but the cycle always continued. I still believed that Emily would beat this. I just didn't know how.

▪ EMILY ▪

Within a few months, I had fallen deep into a pit and had no idea how to climb out. Chris kept suggesting that I start running again or spend more time with kids. Part of me wondered if that might help, but I just didn't have the energy or the will to try. I went through the motions, taking care of Chris and our apartment, always one wrong word from him away from a total breakdown.

At the same time, I was also an excellent actor. No one but Chris had any idea that something was wrong. I never let on when I talked to my parents or when I saw Chris's trainers. But putting on a show in front of friends got to be too much, so I stopped going out with friends and let Chris go by himself.

But even Chris didn't understand the full extent of what was happening. He saw me get angry or lying around the apartment, but I didn't tell him how I actually felt. I was used to being strong and self-reliant. The last thing I wanted was to open up and be vulnerable.

"Why don't you talk to your mom?" Chris asked me. "You can't just act like everything is fine."

I whirled around and glared at him. "If you ever tell anyone about any of this, or if my family finds out, I'm leaving," I said, dead serious. "I will turn off my phone. I will take all my money out of my bank account. I will leave, and you will never see me again."

Chris didn't say a word, but the fear on his face said everything. He could see I wasn't joking. I would rather lose everything than get help.

I didn't understand why I was feeling like this. I completely understood why the kids I had worked with and mentored needed help and why they were struggling with depression and other mental health problems, because they had gone through the most terrible things you can imagine. But if I couldn't help myself when I had never gone through anything difficult, how was I going to survive in life when something bad happened to me? There was nothing I hated more than being vulnerable and getting help. . I was extremely independent, stubborn, and a perfectionist. It was a dangerous combination that led to a lot of unneeded suffering.

I kept telling myself I could handle this. I had no idea how wrong I was.

14

Searching for Hope
in a New Place

· EMILY ·

"So, Nick told me he's moving to Florida," Chris said.

I had just picked him up from another therapy session. I still didn't have it in me to go to the sessions anymore. My mind wasn't fully awake, since I had dragged myself from the couch, where I'd spent my morning rotating between sleeping and watching bad morning television, to pick Chris up from Barwis Methods. But when I heard him say the word "Florida," I was suddenly wide-awake.

"Wait, what? What is he doing in Florida? Why did he quit?"

"No, no, no, it's not like that," Chris explained. "They're opening another Barwis Methods in Port St. Lucie. Nick is moving down there to get it started and help run it."

Instantly, my mind raced. Chris started working out with Nick rather than Rhoades shortly before the graduation walk, and they really clicked. Nick explained things in a way that was helpful to Chris, and he saw progress right away once they joined forces. I didn't want Chris to have to switch trainers again, but living in Florida sure sounded nice.

"Alright," I said, glancing at Chris as I gripped the steering wheel. "Let's go. Let's move to Florida."

Chris's jaw nearly fell into his lap. "Are you serious? You want to move just like that?"

I laughed. "Why not? There's no reason for us to stay in Michigan, and Nick is your trainer. Don't you want to keep working with him?"

"Well, yeah, but there are plenty of good trainers in Michigan too."

"Maybe," I said, gesturing out the window to the snow already coating the ground, even though it was only November. "But don't you want to get away from this?"

Chris stared ahead thoughtfully and slowly nodded. "Our lease is just about up," he said.

"Right? This could be perfect timing! You could keep working with Nick, and we could live in the warmer weather and go to the beach all the time. It would be like living on vacation!" After months of sleepwalking through life, it felt good to have excitement stirring in me. I desperately needed a change, and moving to Florida sounded like the chance I was waiting for. *Maybe life isn't hopeless after all*, I thought. *Maybe I've just had too much of the Midwestern gloom. Maybe everything will look better in the Florida sunshine.*

▪ CHRIS ▪

I never thought Emily might want to move to Florida. The idea came to me as soon as Nick told me he was moving, but I didn't want to uproot Emily again. If a move was going to happen, she needed to be the one driving it. Seeing her excited about something for the first time in forever gave me hope for her and our relationship. The more we talked about it, the more it seemed like fate.

Ever since the graduation walk, we'd lived in a state of limbo. We talked about moving back to Iowa since our families were there, but Iowa didn't offer the incredible training I was receiving in Michigan. But we had never really thought about making Michigan our permanent home either. We had signed a short lease for that very reason.

By now I realized that training at Barwis Methods wasn't going to be my ticket to complete physical independence, at least not anytime soon. I moved to Michigan really hoping it would be my magic bullet. I'd never forgotten what Mike Barwis said to me during that first evaluation there more than a year before. "If you were in this program for five or six weeks, you'd be a changed man," he said. I really believed that, and in many respects, he was right. I grew much stronger and made incredible progress, even beyond my graduation walk. In my mind, though, being a changed man meant walking on my own. Period. I'd be okay with walking with a cane, but I wanted my independence back.

Six months of intense training since the graduation walk had made it clear that full independence wasn't going to happen no matter where I worked out. But I wasn't ready to throw in the towel. Nick and I made such a great team, and he drew so much out of me that I knew I needed to keep working with him. I also wanted to be ready for the day I walked with Emily back up the aisle at our wedding, even though we hadn't talked about the wedding in a while. As our relationship deteriorated, so did my drive to walk on our wedding day. If it took moving to Florida to get our lives back on track, so be it.

"I think it's an amazing idea," I said to Emily right there in the car. "Let's look into it, and if it works out, I'm all in."

What I didn't say was that the training was only my secondary reason for moving. Emily clearly needed a change. Nothing I'd tried had helped pull her out of her funk. She still showed no passion for the things that used to set her on fire. She still had zero energy. Most days she only lay around or slept whenever we weren't fighting. I constantly walked, mostly rolled, on eggshells, trying as hard as I could not to say the wrong thing to set her off. I felt sick as I thought of all those nights when she drove away, screaming that she didn't want to be alive. If I didn't do something to help her, I was terrified that she just might get her wish.

By now neither of us talked much about our wedding. I brought it up every once in a while, but the idea of planning a wedding was too overwhelming for Emily. From time to time, my parents asked if we'd set a date or if we'd looked into any venues. Six months had passed since the proposal. I always told them we weren't going to rush into anything. I wanted Emily to be excited about planning a wedding, and if she wasn't enthused, I didn't want to push it. With all the fighting, our relationship wasn't in the best place anyway.

That evening Emily chatted much more than usual. There was a light in her eyes that I hadn't seen in months. Instead of slinking back to bed, she typed furiously on her laptop. I could tell she was in research mode, Googling everything. I smiled as I felt my shoulders relax. Emily's spark seemed to have returned. Maybe, just maybe, this move would be what she needed to snap out of whatever was going on.

"Chris, they have some amazing group homes there!" Emily called from the family room. "They're set up like a family home, and they have live-in parents actually stay with them. The idea seemed so much better than group homes where staff are constantly coming in and out. That's such a smart idea! I would love to get involved with that."

We made a few calls over the next couple of days and decided that since our lease would be up in a month, we had to move quickly. Emily flew to Florida to scope out apartments and found a brand-new complex with a nice pool and workout facility. It even had a little movie theater and pool table in the clubhouse. "It feels like a vacation home, Chris!" she raved on the phone. "It's not perfectly wheelchair accessible, but they have a ground-floor apartment available, and the doors are pretty wide. I think it's the best we can do."

Both of our parents supported the move. I think they were sad we would now be a plane ride away, but they definitely didn't mind having an excuse to visit Florida in the winter, not to mention having a free place to stay.

Emily almost seemed back to normal as she mapped out the details of our move. She seemed to be regaining the energy she'd lost in recent months. She got me on the Barwis Port St. Lucie training schedule. She hired movers to haul our boxes and furniture down to the new place. Then we spent Christmas in Iowa and headed down to Florida with my family. My parents, my sister, and one of her friends came down and helped us to unload and set up our new place.

As we waved goodbye and their car disappeared into the horizon, I looked at Emily and grinned. "Well, we did it. I think this is going to be a great change for us."

• EMILY •

At first living in Florida did feel like a vacation. I was surprised every time I saw palm trees out my window. It didn't take long to get used to walking outside without a coat in the middle of January. We found it amusing when the locals wore jackets and pants when the temperature was in the sixties.

During that crazy month of planning and preparing for our move, I felt energized, as if the fog had finally lifted and I could be myself again. I carried that momentum into the first few weeks in our new home. I reached out to the group home that had intrigued me and met with the lady who founded it. I toured the facility to see if it was right for me, and I worked with the founder and the trainers at Barwis Methods to get the kids from the group home to work out at their facility. Chris was visibly relieved to see me getting out and pursuing my dreams again. I was too. Maybe whatever was wrong with me had disappeared.

Then my Grandma Max's health deteriorated.

My mom called and told me that my grandmother was in the hospital. My grandma and I had a special relationship and remained very close even after I moved away. She was the strongest person I knew. Her faith in God was incredible, even though she'd lived through the kinds of trials that cause a lot of people to give up on God. My grandmother meant the world to me. I always wrote her long letters every birthday or Christmas or Mother's Day, telling her how much I loved her and how special she was to me. Now she was sick and in the hospital, and I was more than a thousand miles away.

In February I flew with Chris to Iowa for a speaking engagement—he was getting more and more of them lately. Grandma Max, who lived in Wisconsin, was two hours away from my parents, who still lived in Iowa. Grandma ended up coming home from the hospital on our first day back. We all hoped she'd turned a corner. But the very next day, her condition plunged downhill. My aunt told us that my grandmother struggled to get in and out of bed and couldn't even stand up to get herself into her wheelchair.

I looked at Chris with fear in my eyes. "I need to be with her," I told him. Instead of going with him to his speech, I drove up to Wisconsin with my mom to take care of Grandma Max. We made her fruit smoothies and chicken noodle soup, trying to coax her into eating and drinking when she didn't feel like it. We begged my grandma to return to the hospital, but she was adamant that she wanted to stay home.

When she was ready for bed, I jumped into action. "Grandma, I'll transfer you from your wheelchair into bed," I told her confidently. "I do it with Chris all the time."

She looked at me skeptically and sized up my five-feet-four frame. Just the day before, she had fallen when one of my cousins and a few larger guys tried moving her out of her chair. "Honey, I don't think that's going to work."

"Come on, I can do this." I felt as if I was at one of Chris's training sessions. "I can get you up. Just trust me. All you've got to do is sit up a little bit, and I'll do the rest."

She was still nervous—I heard her gasp a few times during the transfer process. But we did it. I was even able to help her adjust her position in bed to help her sleep better than she had in days.

We didn't know it at the time, but that would be the last night she would ever spend in her home. When I transferred her to bed, she asked me to stay with her, which gave me one last, special night snuggling up next to my grandma. She cried out in her sleep multiple times about seeing heaven, worrying me that she was going to die right then and there.

"Grandma, can I help you with anything?" I asked her at one point.

She sighed. "All I need is you, Emily." I still replay that moment in my head sometimes.

She made it through the night, but the next day she woke up struggling to breathe. Her oxygen levels were so low that my aunt, who's a volunteer EMT, found an oxygen tank for her at the place where she volunteered. My mom and I realized that Grandma's time was running out.

My family and I talked my grandmother into going to the hospital. We called for an ambulance, and three EMTs and a police officer arrived, all trying to help her onto a stretcher. I couldn't believe it when I saw them nearly drop her as they struggled to hoist her up. My grandma was terrified.

"Stop!" I finally said, taking control. "Let me do this." I marched in, looked my grandmother in the eyes, and said, "It's okay, Grandma. Trust me. I can do this." I then stood her up and transferred her onto the stretcher by myself.

At the hospital, though, all the doctors could do was make her comfortable. She'd had a heart attack, and one by one her organs were shutting down. When the doctors gave us some privacy, I lay in her hospital bed next to her, my face on her chest, hugging her with all my might. I had stayed so strong up until that point. I took care of her. I transferred her. I kept her spirits up. I was upbeat for my mom, aunts, and uncles, who were devastated at the thought of losing their mom. After all that, I couldn't take it anymore. I crept into the bathroom, shut the door, and sat on the floor, sobbing uncontrollably. I knew everyone in the hospital room could hear me, but I was too upset to care. My grandma was mostly unconscious during the last days in the hospital. She woke up a few times. She was able to tell us she loved us, and it was nice because she still had her sense of humor. The priest came in to give her a blessing, and we asked her how it was. She said, "It was better than nothing." We all cracked up! Now she had been unconscious for a while, and I kept praying that she would wake up just one more time.

I still had a burning question I had to ask my grandmother before it was too late. I kept thinking about Whittley. She was still really struggling, and I felt so out of control since I was in Florida and she was in Iowa. I knew that if my grandma was Whittley's guardian angel, I would feel more peace. And I knew my grandma would be the best guardian angel, since she was so strong. I was so thankful when she woke up, and I asked her, "Grandma, will you please watch over Whittley?" She looked me straight in the eyes and said, "Of course I will, Emily." Those were the last words we shared, and she fell back asleep.

Grandma Max passed away in that hospital room. I was with her the whole time, never leaving even to shower. I was going to be there for my grandmother no matter what. I got the chance to speak at her funeral and share how special she was to me. When I stepped down from the podium and took my seat, I could feel myself closing down again. I cried a little, but not as much as I normally would, considering how close I was to my grandma. I didn't want to feel the pain and sadness. I wanted to be numb again. The wall I thought was gone had suddenly returned, just like that.

As the fog set in again, I chose to feel anger instead of grief. I even got angry at my Grandma Max for dying. *You could still be here if you were healthier!* I thought. *Now you won't be here for my wedding. How can I get married when you won't be here to see it?*

▪ CHRIS ▪

Emily's grandmother's death sent Emily spiraling down into a new low. Just a few months earlier, Emily had almost seemed back to normal, laughing and smiling and pursuing a career that would ignite her passion. Within a few weeks, though, cracks began to form. An angry response here, a sluggish day there. When her grandmother died, Emily crumbled. I knew how much Emily and her grandmother adored each other. They were so much alike—deep, thoughtful people who love with their whole heart. The two of them had a strong connection. I knew Emily would be devastated, especially since it was her first experience with losing a loved one.

Even so, it was hard not to be discouraged when the anger and personal attacks returned. I tried to be understanding, knowing I wasn't the real reason behind her anger, but it wasn't easy.

Then Emily told me she got a job at the Hibiscus Children's Center. This wasn't like the group home where she'd done her traumatic internship but was instead a shelter for kids from the time they're newborn to twelve years old. I was thrilled for her. For months I thought Emily simply needed to do something where she could use her degree and that ignited her passion. This job checked all the boxes. *This could really help turn things around*, I thought.

At first the new job seemed to do the trick. Emily came home from work with a spark in her eyes. She told me about two girls, Cali and Sara, five and six years old. When they came into care, they were separated from their two younger sisters. Emily had an immediate connection with them, and I could already see that she cared a lot about these girls. She shared with me that one night Cali was struggling to sleep. No one was able to get her calmed down, but she opened up to Emily about how much she missed her grandmother who had passed away. Emily opened up about her grandma, and they cried together.

Because Emily was working, I hired a caregiver who helped me in the mornings and drove me to therapy. Now Emily was not only doing what she loved but also was relieved of doing everything for me. I was very optimistic that we'd turned a corner.

I shouldn't have been.

Emily and I still went around and around over whether I gave her the love that she needed or whether she respected me. It didn't even help when her sister, Marisa, moved to the same apartment complex as we did, as did my friend A.P. I thought for sure that having family and friends around would help pull Emily out of whatever she was going through. We didn't fight nearly as much because she just buried everything down deeper and hid how she was feeling. Things only got worse when her new job had her working crazy hours. She started working double shifts and sometimes only slept a couple of hours a night.

Then anxiety set in. She became paranoid about everything I did, like if I texted her that my plane was about to take off. If I didn't take off within seconds, she'd text back, "Well why couldn't you talk to me right now? Clearly you haven't taken off yet."

"The plane is ready for takeoff, but we're not yet in the air," I'd say. In the three minutes before I turned off my phone, a major fight would ensue.

"Oh, you don't want to talk to me? You obviously don't care about me." she'd say.

I was baffled. Now she scrutinized everything I said or did. Everything always came back to whether I really loved her and cared about her. Her doubts about how I felt left me beating myself up and feeling guilty that I wasn't better at expressing my love for her. I knew I needed to do a better job. If I could show her that I loved her and how much I appreciated her, perhaps at least half of our fights could be avoided.

But her blowups only became more unpredictable. One day I went grocery shopping with one of my friends in an attempt to take something off Emily's plate. When I came back, she went through the grocery list and carefully compared it to the items I'd brought home.

"Wait a minute," she said, holding up what looked to me like bananas. "These are plantains. Why the heck would you buy plantains?"

I took a closer look at them. Now that she mentioned it, they did look a little different from the bananas I was used to eating. But since I had zero experience with grocery shopping, I had no idea that there were different types of fruit that looked like bananas. In my head, a banana was a banana, so I grabbed the first bunch I saw.

I laughed as I tried to explain. Emily was not amused. "I asked you to get bananas, Chris," she snapped. "That's pretty much the most basic thing on the planet. How can you possibly get that wrong!?"

"Wait, are you really upset?" I thought she would see the humor in the situation too. Apparently, I was wrong. "We can pick up something else. It's not a big deal."

"It is a big deal, because you don't listen to anything I say. You don't care about me. You don't care about what I want. Why even go grocery shopping if you're going to buy the wrong stuff just so you can get out of there as fast as humanly possible?" She looked at me disgustedly and shook her head. "You can't do anything right."

Is this really happening? I thought. *Why are we fighting about bananas?*

All along, I kept thinking that if we just tried one more thing, just crossed off one more box, then things would get better. But the boxes were running out. We moved to a new place. Emily got a job. She wasn't responsible for all my care anymore. And yet nothing was better. If anything, it had gotten worse. I wondered if all relationships went through times like this. I had little to no experience to draw from. I tried reading blogs and listening to podcasts, looking for a nugget of inspiration.

Slowly, though, I began to lose hope. And that's not a normal posture for me. I'm the guy who was determined to beat those three percent odds, the guy who worked out five-plus hours a day just to walk when everyone said I couldn't. I knew to focus on the positive, to concentrate on what I could do instead of what I couldn't. But now I'd done everything I knew to do. I didn't know how to stay positive when nothing helped. I felt completely unable to control the situation, and it was infuriating. I didn't understand how our relationship falling apart or Emily's depression was part of God's plan. Honestly, this time in my life was even lower than when I went through my spinal cord injury.

There was, however, another line of help we'd forgotten about. Emily and I were far from God at this point in our lives. We had never gotten involved in a church community since we had moved to Michigan together; we didn't pray together or seek God's help with much of anything. Our faith had been so important to both of us when we first started dating, but now it had faded into the background. Deep down I knew that was the opposite of what we should be doing. I was trying to keep from doing anything that would add to Emily's plate, and going to church seemed as if it would be one more task and responsibility that would overwhelm her. I was looking for a quick fix. I didn't think mere service attendance would be enough to address our issues and problems.

It turned out we needed God even more than I thought, because our lives were about to take yet another wild turn.

15

Instant Parents to a Seventeen-Year-Old

· EMILY ·

"Emily?" The sniffling voice on the other line was hoarse from sobbing. I sighed. A tearful call in the middle of the night could only mean one thing—Whittley was in trouble again.

"What's going on, Whitt?" I asked, not sure if I wanted to know.

"It's really bad this time," she whispered. "I'm in big trouble. My sister kicked me out. The cops are involved. They're putting me in a group home. They might even send me to . . . to . . . to juvie!" Her voice broke into sobs as she choked out the dreaded *J* word.

I closed my eyes. This was much worse than usual. "Oh, honey, I'm so sorry."

"I can't go to juvie, Emily. I'm so scared. You don't know what they do to people there. I'm never going to have a normal life if I end up there."

"Okay," I said, my mind racing.

"Emily?" Whittley said, then hesitated. "Will you and Chris be my foster parents?"

I was caught off guard, but I wasn't surprised because I knew Chris and I were her only good option left.

"You know me better than anyone," Whittley continued. "You believe in me. I know that if you take me in, I can actually turn my life around. Otherwise, I'll be stuck in group homes or juvie until I turn eighteen, and then who knows what I'll do?"

This wasn't the first time I'd considered fostering Whittley. I hated watching her bounce from house to house, group home to group home, never getting the help she needed. The idea of her aging out of the foster care system without a real family scared me. I hated to think what might happen to her if she was left to her own devices.

My knee-jerk reaction was to say yes. Everything inside me screamed, *We've got to do this!* But I also had to ask myself, could I handle it? I knew I had changed dramatically in the past few months. Investing in Whittley, even long-distance, was exhausting, as I slogged my way through this never-ending fog. But what choice did I have? Her life literally was on the line. But what would Chris say? He was just as caring as I was, but he was also the realist in our relationship. He would have questions, to say the least.

"I'm not saying no," I said slowly. "Chris and I have a lot of talking and thinking to do. But Whitt, even if we want to, I don't know if it will work. We live in Florida, and you are in Iowa. We can't just drive and pick you up. Both states require lots of classes and other hoops to jump through before we could be licensed to take you in. Even then I don't know if the state of Iowa would let us bring you here."

"I know, I know," Whittley said, as if she didn't hear anything beyond me saying I'm not saying no.

"But I'm not saying yes either," I said. I didn't want her to get her hopes up only for them to come crashing down. "You have a lot of work to do if you want to come live with us. You have to stop hurting yourself and quit all the stuff that keeps getting you into trouble."

"I will!" Whittley sounded desperate. "I'll do anything!"

"I'm serious. I will not put up with anything like that in our house. You need to show me you're serious and start working on this now."

Chris looked completely confused as I hung up. I turned to him and shook my head, wondering where to begin.

• CHRIS •

I wanted to help Whittley as much as Emily did, but I was hesitant. Obviously, on paper, Whittley needed a dramatic change. Even with Emily and me stuck in a rough place, we could still provide Whittley with a better home environment than any other option she had. But Emily was fragile right now. Many times she had told me that she could not handle anything happening to Whittley. While that would be bad enough from a distance, I wondered what might happen to Emily if Whittley attempted suicide while living with us. A traumatic loss like that could completely destroy Emily.

Then there was the idea of becoming a dad to a seventeen-year-old at the ripe old age of twenty-four. Just typing out that sentence reminds me how insane that sounded to me then. It still does now! How could I possibly parent a teenage girl when it wasn't that long ago that I was a teenager myself? What would my family and friends say and think? They would all think we were crazy, which, hey, I thought it too. Yet I didn't dismiss the idea out of hand. Emily and I decided to take our time with this decision and talk it over during our vacation to Aruba with my family.

The trip was great. Both of us were able to relax. The problems with which we'd lived for what felt like forever seemed to disappear. We were both ourselves again. In the middle of this dream vacation, while relaxing on the beach, Emily turned to me, looked me in the eye, and said, "We're her last hope, Chris. We've got to do this."

I knew she was right. If anyone could help Whittley, it was Emily. I imagined Emily throwing herself into getting Whittley here and doing everything she could to make sure Whittley graduated from high school and started down the right path. *We might not just save Whittley,* I thought. *This might just save Emily too.*

"Okay," I said. "I'm in. Let's do it."

Emily threw her arms around me and held me tight. When she finally pulled away, I saw tears running down her cheeks. "Thank you," she said simply.

"So how do you want to tell her?"

"Oh, we can't tell her. Not yet." Emily was already all business. "We can't say anything until we've checked off every single box. She would be beyond devastated if it didn't work out for some reason. We can't risk it."

I nodded, impressed yet again by her wisdom. I felt certain that if anyone could make this work, it was Emily.

"I wonder what my parents will say," I wondered aloud. I didn't have to wait long to find out. When we told them what we were thinking about doing, my family was skeptical, to say the least. It's not that they didn't want me to help a girl who desperately needed it. Since my injury, though, they were overprotective and overly concerned about everything I did. My parents asked if I'd thought this through—I'm in a wheelchair, we're not married, we live in an apartment, and we'd be taking in a seventeen-year-old with a laundry list of behavior issues. I assured them I had, but they still worried about me. Emily's family wasn't surprised when we told them. After all, she tried to talk them into fostering Whittley when Emily was still in high school.

When we returned home from spring break, a tear-stained letter from Whittley awaited us in our mailbox. She spoke of how deeply she wanted to turn her life around and how moving in with us would give her the fresh start she needed. Emily read and reread the letter multiple times before she sat down with her laptop, that all-business look on her face. I couldn't help but smile. It looked like this decision was already paying off for Emily.

We were up against a tight deadline. Whittley had contacted us at the end of March, and our goal was to move her into our apartment in time to start school that August. Navigating the foster care system and the approval process was more time consuming than either of us expected. We had to take classes in which other couples always looked at us, shook their heads, and said, "God bless your souls," which is Southern code for "we think you are nuts."

Once we finished all the classes, we still had to wait for the Florida and Iowa Departments of Human Services offices to work out the details between them. Waiting on our approval to come through was agonizing. Meanwhile, we still hadn't told Whittley what we were doing. All we told her was that we would try to figure something out and that she had to keep making good decisions in the meantime.

The months leading up to Whittley coming to live with us were jam-packed and insane, but they were also a breath of fresh air. Emily had a new sense of purpose, energy, and direction that I hadn't seen since she took charge of our move to Florida. For the first time in months, we even stopped fighting. When we finally got approved to become Whittley's foster parents, Emily and I went away for one last weekend together on the beach, simply to enjoy each other's company. We spent long hours talking through the house rules and boundaries we would set for Whittley. We felt like a team again. I remembered how much I had missed moments like these. I hoped they were here to stay.

• EMILY •

Whittley moved into our guest room one week before the start of her senior year. We got some funny looks when we enrolled her in the local high school. Not many seniors have parents in their early twenties. From the start, Whittley made all sorts of promises about how she had turned her life around. I wanted to believe her, but I was not delusional. I expected her to fall into the wrong crowd or start making poor choices again. I prepared myself for some tough love and set boundaries right off the bat. Our biggest rule, our one deal-breaker, was simple: if she wanted to live with us, she had to stay in school. If she ever dropped out, we'd send her straight back to Iowa.

Those first few weeks, everything went shockingly smooth. Whittley wanted to make me happy, which led her to make better life choices. Somehow, I brought out the best in her.

Before she moved in, I worried about how Chris and I would handle taking in a teenager when our relationship was under so much strain already. But with Whittley in the apartment, we barely had time to argue. I still worked at the children's shelter, Whittley was always home after school, and Marisa and Chris's friend A.P. were over all the time. On the surface it looked like our life—and my mental well-being—had improved drastically.

The truth was, I was a great actress. I stuffed every dark thought and negative feeling deep inside when Whittley was around. I plastered a smile on my face when we went out with friends. I was as determined as ever to make sure no one had any idea what was going on. But putting up this front was exhausting. I felt suffocated from wearing this mask and trying to pretend that everything was okay when it definitely was not.

Before long, cracks broke through my façade. I still hid my feelings from most of the world, but Chris and I started fighting again. We kept it behind closed doors. I didn't want Whittley to see what was going on. Anytime Whittley was gone or asleep, I fell into my bed to rest up for my next grand performance of how fine I really was.

Meanwhile, the honeymoon with Whittley ended quickly. The principal's office called and called and called with one behavior problem after another. Whittley always told a completely different story than her teacher, so figuring out the truth was exhausting. I had known Whittley long enough to be onto her game. I knew that every authority figure in her life had let her slide through with a slap on the wrist unless she did something truly inexcusable, like punching someone. Chris and I decided early on to stop that cycle once and for all. We didn't care how small the offense was, there were going to be consequences. Once I grounded her from her phone. Another time I took away her TV so she could only watch shows with Chris and me in our living room. The party was over, and Whittley was furious.

"Are you kidding me?" she fumed. "No one has ever punished me like this just for cussing at a teacher."

No matter how I was feeling internally, I was always compelled to stay strong for Whittley. I was all she had, and I had to step up to the plate of parenting her. "You are not going to disrespect your teacher," I calmly explained. "That will not be allowed here."

Sometimes Whittley took the drama up a notch and made a big show of hauling out a suitcase. "I'm packing my bags," she yelled. "I know you're going to kick me out now. My life is over."

"Whittley, you're not going anywhere," I said calmly. "You're not getting kicked out just because you got in trouble at school today."

"I'll call my caseworker," she said, mustering up a tear or two. "I'm going back to Iowa."

I could see she wanted to give up simply because of one mistake, but that's not how it worked in our family. "No," I said. "We're going to make it right, and then we'll move on. You made a bad choice, but you're not a bad person. You're going to write an apology letter to your teacher, and then we're going to move forward."

She made good on her threats to run away more than once. I knew it was a ploy for attention, and I wasn't having it. I told her I wouldn't chase her but would just call the cops and have them pick her up. That didn't stop her from storming out the door in a big show. I would watch her hang around the apartment complex parking lot, glancing toward our building every so often to see if I was coming after her. I was determined to make good on my promise that I wouldn't go after her, but obviously I'm not completely heartless. Instead, I would call Marisa, who lived in the same apartment complex as we did. She was always good at talking Whittley down and getting her to come home.

Every once in a while, I saw signs of progress. One evening Whittley had just finished helping me clean up the apartment when I reached out and patted her shoulder. "Whittley, I really appreciate you," I said. "Thank you so much."

The next day in the car, I could tell Whittley had something on her mind. Finally, she spoke up. "Emily, can I talk to you about something?"

"Well, of course you can. You can talk to me about anything."

Her face was serious as she looked at me. "I felt really uncomfortable when you told me that you appreciate me."

I waited for her to tell me the bad part, but I finally realized she was done speaking. "Wait, what? Can you explain what you mean?"

She looked indignant. "No one has ever told me that before, and it made me uncomfortable."

It hit me—Whittley had never felt appreciated. I couldn't count the number of fights I had picked with Chris over the fact that I didn't feel appreciated. Now here was Whittley confronting me about expressing that very feeling.

"Okay, Whitt, this is insane. No one has ever told you they appreciate you before?" She just stared at me. "Well, they should have! Listen to me. You have value. You are so special and loved. You deserve to feel appreciated." She listened, but I could tell she didn't truly believe it. She had never heard that in seventeen years. In fact, she had many people in her life tell her the complete opposite and who made her feel as though she didn't matter. This was the first time she had ever heard that someone appreciated her. Why would she believe me?

· CHRIS ·

Bonding with Whittley did not come easily for me. When Emily was around, Whittley was as relaxed and happy as can be. Anytime I was alone with her, though, she clammed right up. I wondered what I did to offend her until Emily explained that it wasn't only me. Whittley had a long history of terrible experiences with men. She wasn't comfortable around any man.

A few weeks after Whittley arrived, Emily had to work a Saturday, and Whittley and I were on our own for lunch. I told her we could order a pizza, but she shook her head. "I'm going to make you pancakes," she declared. "Not from a mix either. Homemade."

I smiled. "Pancakes sound great, Whitt. Thank you so much."

I don't claim to be a cook, but when I took one look at the plate she set on the table, I knew something was off. The pancake's color did not look right. But I kept my mouth shut and dug in.

I have no idea what she did to those pancakes. Maybe she mixed up the baking powder with baking soda or salt with sugar. Whatever it was, this was the most disgusting batch of pancakes I'd ever put in my mouth. Even so, I forced them down. Whittley watched me eagerly. I didn't want to make her feel bad, so I dutifully finished off the two cakes on my plate.

By the time I finished, Whittley was done cleaning up and sat down to eat her lunch. She took one bite and spit it into her napkin.

"That is disgusting!" she shrieked. "Ugh! Chris, how could you eat that? What is wrong with you?"

We were still laughing when Emily came home from work. From that moment, Whittley began to trust me. I'd eat those pancakes again today if it meant they'd bring us closer like they did that day.

· EMILY ·

Even with the bumps in the road, I was always confident that Chris and I were the best thing for Whittley, but we still felt that nothing we were saying or doing was making a huge impact on her life. I was determined to push back my struggles and dark feelings to be the best mother possible, and that included making sure she had no idea that I struggled behind closed doors.

But it wasn't working. My life was spiraling downward. First came the insomnia. I struggled to sleep more than two hours a night. Every night, I laid down and tried to go to sleep, but my mind raced as my anxiety ramped up to a new level. The worst part was that I wanted to sleep, desperately. I was exhausted all the time, but I couldn't do the one thing I knew would help. I took melatonin, but it didn't help. Nothing did. As the sleepless nights piled up, I was losing my mind.

My lack of sleep took a toll on my emotions. That Thanksgiving we went to Sarasota to visit my brother Michael. I volunteered to make the meal. I dug up the best recipes I could find and made everything from scratch to give Whittley an amazing Thanksgiving. We spent all day in the kitchen, making turkey, ham, stuffing cooked inside the turkey the traditional way, green bean casserole, mashed potatoes and gravy, pumpkin pie, and rolls. We had a candlelight dinner. When dinner was over, though, I broke down in tears in front of Michael. It was unlike me to break my cover, but I couldn't stop myself. Later I cried to my mom on the phone about how I couldn't sleep.

As if the insomnia wasn't enough, my heart started racing. My heart rate wouldn't dip below the nineties, even if I was resting in bed. I clocked a heart rate of 118 just standing in front of the sink doing dishes. If I went for a run, my heart rate skyrocketed into the two hundreds. Fear gripped my body, and I felt as though I couldn't breathe.

My family convinced me to see a doctor. Deep down I hoped something was physically wrong with me. At least then I'd have an answer. But once again, the doctor gave me a clean bill of health.

That left me with only one conclusion: my mental struggles were now taking a physical toll on my body. *I can't ignore this forever*, I thought. *But I don't know if I have it in me to fix it.*

I still thought I should be able to pick myself up by my bootstraps and help myself. After all, I've always been a take-charge person. I'm an independent woman. That's what independent people do, right? The fact that I couldn't was an obvious sign of weakness in my mind. I was so intent on helping others that I forgot I was allowed to ask for help for myself. When I look back at those days, I see a woman who desperately needed God. I needed him to give me courage and strength to get the help I needed. I needed him to fill the void in my soul that I didn't realize existed. I had turned away from him at the exact moment my soul cried out for him.

I was still so blind, but my eyes were about to be opened.

16

Finding Faith Again

· CHRIS ·

By the end of the year, I had run out of ideas of how to help Emily. I tried everything—encouraging her to do the things that made her come alive, telling her to exercise, giving her motivational speeches, freeing her of caregiving responsibilities, and even moving her to Florida. Nothing worked. She even saw a doctor who looked for any medical reason for her mood changes and exhaustion, but every test came back normal. From time to time, she'd perk up long enough to make me think she was better, but the changes never lasted. Within a few days, she always came crashing back down. I'm a fixer, but I couldn't fix this. Emily was clearly suffering from depression, and no amount of motivational speeches, exercise, or time pursuing her passion was going to snap her out of it.

I begged Emily to seek professional help. I told her I'd help her research the right mental health specialist to visit. I'd even go to the appointment with her if she wanted me there. I offered to do couples therapy. I think on some level Emily knew she needed help. She hated feeling like a different person, and I knew that the headaches and rapid heartbeat scared her. That made it harder for me to understand why she continually refused to seek help.

One night, weeks after we argued over her need to see someone who specialized in depression and anxiety, she casually mentioned right in the middle of lunch that she had made an appointment. I could barely contain my excitement. *She's going to get better*, I thought. *Our lives are going to get back to normal.*

But just one day later, in the middle of yet another fight, Emily dropped a bomb. "You know what?" she yelled, anger flashing in her eyes. "I'm canceling my appointment." I froze. *Is she serious?* Her face was hard, with an expression I didn't recognize. That look told me she didn't care how much canceling the appointment would hurt herself, as long as it hurt me too.

"Emily." I hoped she couldn't tell I had tears in my eyes. "Please. Don't do this."

"I'm doing it," she said defiantly. "I'm not going."

I couldn't believe what I was hearing. I had held out so much hope for this appointment. Since I worked at home, our apartment was a daily battle zone until Whittley came home from school, and I felt helpless to fix it. Every morning one of my first thoughts was, *Will we make it through today without a fight?* I braced myself for a confrontation every time I returned home from my workouts. The time I spent away from our apartment felt like a breath of fresh air.

Don't get me wrong. I was not an innocent victim. Emily's struggles often brought out the worst in me. When she blew up at me, I would blow up right back at her. She often called me out, saying, "When was the last time you went out of your way to do something thoughtful or romantic? Like taking me out on a date, writing a note, getting me flowers?" She was right. Although we spent a lot of time together, I rarely went out of my way to show her how special and meaningful she was to me. I felt as if I were failing her. But with all our fighting, it was hard to get motivated to do something like that, although I knew she needed it more than ever.

We also often fought about her feeling as though I did not acknowledge her or notice her efforts to make our house a home. I'd come home, and she'd ask, "Do you notice anything different?" I would look around trying to figure out what was new, but I never noticed, not even when the changes should have been obvious, like new lamps or pictures on the wall.

Emily also felt I did not appreciate her or actively listen to her without getting sidetracked by reading a sports article or scrolling through Twitter. I was at my worst after a workout. I'd get home exhausted and only want to do something mind-numbing, like scroll through social media. Emily would start a conversation, and I would listen at first, then slowly get sucked into looking at my phone. "Are you even listening to me? Then what did I just say?" And I could never remember. She'd say, "You care more about sports than listening to me." She was right. My ignoring her was rude. But to her, that meant I didn't love her, which was very frustrating for me. I loved her more than anything; I just didn't show it consistently enough.

I made so many mistakes, and I wish I could have handled the tense moments better. While it's certainly not an excuse, I was exhausted. I didn't always have it in me to handle another argument calmly and gracefully. After more than a year of a few highs mixed with extreme lows, something had to give.

▪ EMILY ▪

By the end of the year, I had hit the lowest point of my life. I couldn't sleep. My heart raced all the time. And I lived in a fog that I feared might never lift. Every instinct in me told me to run away from feeling vulnerable. That fear of vulnerability kept me from seeking help. I made multiple doctors' appointments, some that Chris didn't even know about—but I always ended up canceling. I knew that if I sat down with a mental health specialist, all the pain and emotion and weakness I had locked up for so long would come pouring out, and I couldn't let that happen. I thought if I got help for this when nothing bad had happened to me, that would mean I was weak and not strong enough to handle things on my own. Just the thought of that made me sick to my stomach. I also believed that if I let the pain and emotions out of the box, I could never put them back in. I would be forced to feel all the emptiness and sorrow that I had refused to let myself fully experience since my grandma's death. I could not let myself do that.

Getting help would also force me to give up my current coping mechanism—anger. Chris always got the worst of my outbursts. I'd get mad because he didn't love me or appreciate me enough or never went out of his way to show he cared about me or didn't clean up after himself or when he paid more attention to his phone than me. Basically, I was mad all the time, but in my mind, my anger was completely justified.

Once, in the middle of a fight, Chris looked at me and asked, "Do you realize how your anger is affecting me?"

I shrugged and raised my eyebrows. "I don't care. Do you understand how I feel when I'm not angry? If you really knew, you'd be happy I'm mad and not something else."

With time my anger grew into something more dangerous. I claimed I loved Chris, but he had now become the scapegoat for all my problems. This gaping, gnawing hole I felt inside had to be his fault. If he were just more romantic or more appreciative or more helpful around the house or just more something, anything, I'd feel right again. Not once did it occur to me that Chris was never meant to fill that void. Only God could do that. But I wasn't ready to admit that my relationship with God was as messed up as my relationship with my fiancé. Instead, I found it easier to keep blaming Chris.

Everything came to a head one night when Chris went over to watch a basketball game with his friend A.P. rather than hanging out with Whittley and me. The longer he was gone, the angrier I became that he'd rather watch a stupid game than be with me. I tried to go to bed, but I can't sleep when he isn't home. My anxiety kicked in, and worry nearly drowned me.

Finally, Chris came rolling back into our apartment around midnight. A.P. came in and helped Chris into bed so that they wouldn't disturb me, but I still heard them, which made me even more angry. I was having enough trouble trying to sleep, and I had to be up at 4:30 a.m. for work the next morning and now *this*!

As soon as A.P. left, I let Chris have it for how, once again, all he thought about was himself and how he was always choosing sports over me. I decided I'd had enough. I was sick of Chris ruining my life. I was done being the victim. I looked him right in the eyes and said, "Chris, I want you gone."

He closed his eyes for a moment, then looked at me. "You know you don't mean that."

"I do mean it." My voice was cold and hard. I didn't feel a thing. "I am so done with this relationship. You need to leave. I want you out of here."

I stomped to the kitchen and grabbed a handful of trash bags before heading straight for his closet. I yanked his clothes off the rack and jammed them into the bags as I spoke. "I'm taking you over to A.P.'s," I said, stuffing a blue collared shirt into the bag, the hanger still attached. "Tell him whatever you want. I don't care."

I wanted Chris to argue or put up a fight, but he was silent. That told me everything I needed to know. If he really cared, he'd fight for me. I pulled out another bag and started packing his pants. Chris just watched me without saying a word. I couldn't believe he wasn't going to stop me. *I must have been right all this time. He never loved me.*

Then, in the middle of packing another bag, I stopped. It hit me out of the blue—if Chris were gone, what would I have? I had no one else. But I had just made this big show out of packing up his clothes. I felt too stupid to say, *Oh, wait, never mind, I was just kidding, I really want you to stay.* So instead I sat down on the floor by all of Chris's clothes, frozen, as tears welled up in my eyes. I tried to stop them from escaping but failed miserably. Before long I was sobbing.

I didn't look at Chris. I was too embarrassed. Then I heard him say, "Emily, come here."

Sobs bubbled up in my throat as I curled up in his arms. I buried my face in his shoulder and cried unabashedly. How could I have ever thought I didn't want him? How could I have come so close to throwing away everything we had?

I felt him hold me closer as he whispered, "Em, I don't want to leave."

"I don't want you to leave either," I sniffled.

In that moment I realized I had become a person I never wanted to be. I needed to change, not just for me, but for everyone else in my life. I knew I couldn't change by myself. Something told me that only God could help.

But I didn't know where to start. I used to feel so close to God, back when I was helping others and writing almost every day in my prayer journal. I could look back and see all that he had done for me and how I had relied on him. Those prayers stopped right after our graduation walk. The only prayers I prayed now were usually just asking why, or were sometimes the dark prayers I prayed on my worst days. I could hardly admit to myself that I'd prayed them, much less told anyone else, but I had. More than once I pleaded with God to take my life because I didn't want to live anymore. How could I go back to God now and start over?

But I knew I had to take a step somehow.

A short time after nearly throwing Chris out of our apartment, I drove to a Catholic church and slipped silently into a pew. Chris was out of town at a speaking engagement. A Catholic church felt like home to me—it was the denomination I grew up attending, but more than that, it represented my grandma's faith. My grandma was devoted to the Catholic church her whole life, and I never knew anyone with a stronger faith.

I was amazed at how the old habits came back to me. I remembered the proper responses and when to kneel. When the priest began his sermon, it was obvious God wanted me there. His whole message was about prayer—the very thing missing from my life. The feelings I spent so much energy pushing down came bubbling up, and I couldn't stop the tears from flowing. *This is where I need to start,* I thought. *I need to just start praying. God can help me with the rest.*

Right after church I stayed in my car and listened to Christian music. The song "Tell Your Heart to Beat Again" by Danny Gokey came on. The words expressed exactly what I felt. Like the song, I felt shattered, as if my life were broken into a thousand pieces scattered across the floor. I sobbed. It was as though God was speaking directly to me, telling me to get back up, to take a step out of the darkness in which I'd lived for far too long, and to follow him on the journey he had laid out for me. "Tell your heart to beat again," the song said, and that's exactly what I needed to do.

Tears poured down my face. For the first time in almost two years, I wrote in my prayer journal, pouring out my heart to God. I wrote:

> I hate admitting that I'm not strong enough and that I need help. I know how detrimental it is to not only me but everyone around me. Somehow I still do it because I have this terrible fear of being vulnerable. It's honestly why I feel like I've been struggling with depression for over a year and a half now. I feel like I have lost myself, and most days I

feel completely hopeless about ever becoming "me" again. I wonder if it's been too long and I have forgotten who I am. If I can't be me, then what's the point of being alive? I have stopped living, but life has not stopped. I want to be me again! I know the only way to do this is to let you back into my life and to let you take away my pain and help me feel alive again. I think I have tried to be strong, hiding my insecurities and vulnerabilities for too long. It's time to know I can't do this alone and I am not alone. I have Jesus, and Jesus is all I need. I believe that all the hard days and the pain I have had and I am experiencing are for a reason. I don't know what that reason is, but I sure hope I find out soon.

I felt myself wanting to pray. I kept opening my prayer journal again and again. Something stirred inside me that I hadn't felt in ages. I also knew one church service wasn't enough. If I wanted to get closer to God, I needed to find a church to attend regularly.

I liked the idea of going to a Catholic church. I liked the traditions and felt closer to God there. Plus, there was a parish near our apartment that would be perfect. Chris, on the other hand, wasn't interested in a traditional service, and I knew Whittley would be bored out of her mind. I wanted to do this together. All of us desperately needed God in our lives, and I would go anywhere that made them happy.

Then one day I noticed a new church open up across the road from our apartment as I drove home. It didn't really look like a church, but the sign outside read "Christ Fellowship Church." *Maybe this would be a good place for us,* I thought.

▪ CHRIS ▪

"We should go check out this church I found," Emily said out of the blue.

Emily's words should have surprised me, but something told me this was exactly what was missing from our lives. When we first started dating, we both talked about our faith and how important God was to both of us, but our lives hadn't reflected that priority in a long time. God was more of a last resort; faith had become something we'd turn to only when we needed to break glass in case of an emergency. I never questioned

God's existence or the Bible's truth. But up until this point, God had never been a vital part of my everyday life. I turned to him when something bad happened, like my football injury, but I never made an intimate relationship with him a priority in my day-to-day life. Our relationship was more like the one I had with my fire extinguisher. It was there if I needed it, but it's not as if I took it out and used it every day.

I knew this needed to change. Emily and I had also talked about how important it was for Whittley to find a relationship with God. Until this point in her life, every experience with God had been negative. I knew she was angry at God for all the horrible things that had happened to her. She'd also gone to church a few times before she came to live with us, and had horror stories to show for it. Yet, in spite of the bad she'd encountered, I knew nothing would be better for Whittley than discovering who God really is and developing a relationship with him.

So when Emily mentioned checking out a church she'd found, I was open to it. "What church is it?" I asked her.

"Christ Fellowship. It's literally half a mile from our place."

I thought for a minute. "Is that the building that doesn't look like a church?"

"I think it used to be some sort of film studio. But now it's a church. We should go check it out."

I nodded. "Okay, let's do it. Let's go this Sunday."

I was excited for the three of us to attend together. Not surprisingly, Whittley was less than enthused. I expected a battle, and she did not disappoint. We ended up bribing her with Dunkin' Donuts and coffee if she came with us. Begrudgingly, she agreed.

The next Sunday was New Year's Day. That seemed like God's perfect timing. What better day for making a fresh start than the day everyone in America is busy making New Year's resolutions? We dragged ourselves out of bed and made it to church only a few minutes before the service started. We were stunned by how many people were there. We immediately felt welcomed by the greeters, who said, "Welcome home."

As we walked into the church, a gentleman with a Christ Fellowship polo and a name badge asked us how many spots we needed. Within seconds two chairs were pulled up to make an extra row to accommodate us. A countdown appeared on the projection screens, and I glanced around nervously. I hadn't sat through a church service in a long time. Sitting here felt so familiar and yet strange all at once.

Energy filled the auditorium as young families, elderly couples, and everyone in between packed into the seats. Music swelled, and a worship leader invited us to stand and praise God with them.

I looked at Emily, amazed. I could tell from the tears rolling down her face that she felt the same way I did. I'd been to my share of church services that felt forced and fake, and even more that were lifeless and boring. Christ Fellowship was none of those things. Everyone in the room worshipped as though God was right there in the room. I had never experienced anything like that. I couldn't help but wonder what I had been missing out on.

The service didn't let up when the pastor took the stage full of energy and joy. He then directed our attention to the screen to watch today's service, which was live from the main church campus in Palm Beach Gardens. Emily and I looked at each other with furrowed brows. *We are seriously going to watch church on a screen while at church?* I'll be honest. I was a skeptic. However, I had never heard a message that was so relatable and easily applicable. I expected to be bored but instead found myself wishing I had taken notes. The message was about new beginnings and fresh starts, that if you want to see things you have never seen before, then you need to start doing things you have never done before. Don't let your past keep you from getting to your purpose. It was the best message I had ever heard at church. As I looked at Emily, neither of us had to say a word. We both knew we would definitely be coming back the next week.

Afterward, we took Whittley out for the coffee and donuts we had promised her. "So, what did you think of the sermon, Whitt?" Emily asked between sips of her iced coffee. "What did you take away from it?"

Whittley didn't look up from her box of donut holes. "Nothing. It was boring."

I forced myself not to roll my eyes. Her answer was so predictable.

"I really liked the part where Pastor Todd said we need to align our thoughts with God's Word. That really hit me hard." I said.

Emily chimed in, "I also loved the Bible verse 2 Corinthians 5:17, about how if anyone is in Christ the old is gone and your life is new."

Whittley shrugged. "Whatever."

▪ EMILY ▪

Over the next couple of months, I cried through more church services than I can count. For longer than I could admit, I had felt so unloved and worthless, as if I would be better off dead. Now I heard God telling me I was loved and accepted just as I was. Even in my darkest moments, God was right there all along. The One who gave his Son for me had never abandoned me. I was the one who had turned away from him, but now I knew I didn't have to stay that way. All I had to do was give him my life and lean on him, and he'd do the rest.

My prayers that first began after that Catholic mass became integrated into my everyday life. The more I prayed, the more I realized how desperately I needed God. I wanted to spend time reading his Word and listening to his voice. I wanted to take my deepest needs and concerns to him. For the first time in years, God didn't seem far away.

The tears that started at the New Year's Day service didn't let up. After nearly a year of numbing myself to my grandma's death, I finally allowed myself to grieve. I allowed myself to cry hysterically and unleash the feelings that I was convinced would make me weak.

As I spent time with God, I couldn't stop thinking about Philippians 4:13 (NKJV): "I can do all things through Christ who strengthens me." That verse means so many things to so many people, but I knew exactly what God was telling me to do. The verse does not mean that all I had to do was pray more and trust God more and my anxiety and depression would magically disappear. Meditating on the verse assured me that God would give me the strength I needed to seek help. I felt him telling me, *You can do this. I'll help you. We're in this together. I won't leave you.*

My hands shook as I dialed the mental health clinic I'd researched. When the office manager told me the therapist was booked, I didn't panic and hang up but made an appointment with a nurse practitioner who specialized in mental health.

"Now, we have an automatic one-hundred-dollar charge in case of no-shows," the office manager told me. "So if for some reason you need to cancel, we need a twenty-four hour notice or you'll be charged one hundred dollars."

Ha. That is the least of my worries.

I promised myself I wouldn't cancel no matter what. But when the day came, I sat in my car in the parking lot of our apartment, my hands glued to the steering wheel, unable to move. *I can't do this*, I thought.

My stomach lurched as I thought about being vulnerable. Then I remembered the one-hundred-dollar charge for no-shows. *I don't care*, I thought. *This is the hardest thing I've ever done. I can't do this.*

I was so sick of the fog, the panicked thoughts, the racing heart, and sleepless nights. Still, the idea of telling a stranger what was happening inside my head terrified me. No one knew the extent of my depression, not even Chris. How could I make myself vulnerable and admit everything? *God, I can't do this alone*, I prayed. *I need you to be strong for me.* Philippians 4:13 flooded my heart once again. "I can do all things through Christ who strengthens me." Somehow, those words gave me the push I needed to turn my keys in the ignition and pull out of the parking lot.

I cried the whole way to the clinic. *This is going to be awful*, I thought. *I don't know how I'll get through this.*

I could barely see through my tears as I parked my car and climbed the stairs to the office. My heart pounded, and I took a deep breath as I opened the door and sat sniffling in the lobby. *Help me, God*, I prayed. *Give me the strength to get through this.*

"Emily?" a nurse called. She took me through a hallway to an exam room and asked me a few preliminary questions. I managed to hold it together until the nurse practitioner knocked on the door and sat down in front of me.

"So, what seems to be the problem?" she asked.

Where do I even start? I thought. I couldn't talk. Instead, I completely broke down.

"It's okay, it's okay," she said. "Let's just start with easy questions."

I calmed myself as we talked through my family history. When she asked me again about my problems that had brought me to her office, it all came pouring out. "I haven't been myself for almost two years," I told her. "I'm depressed, and super tired, and I just want to sleep. But I can't sleep. Sometimes I only sleep an hour a night. My heart rate is way too fast, and I feel anxious, like something is really wrong all the time, even though there's no reason for it. I feel like I'm suffocating and can't come up for air."

She listened so kindly, and patiently asked questions. Her diagnosis wasn't surprising—I had read enough articles to know I probably had depression and anxiety. But hearing someone else confirm how I felt gave me a sense of relief. "Sometimes our bodies don't make enough of the chemicals we need to feel happy and at peace," the nurse practitioner said. "A lot of people think you can only be depressed if something bad happens to you, but it's not true. Anyone can have a chemical imbalance that makes them depressed or anxious, or sometimes both. It's a medical condition that requires a medical response." I understood now that you don't have to have something happen to you to feel depressed. All the fears I had that something was wrong with me and that I was weak disappeared. I felt so thankful that I finally had the strength to accept help.

I went home with antidepressants and antianxiety medicine in my purse. The nurse practitioner told me they wouldn't work overnight, but I could expect to feel more like myself within three weeks.

Three weeks. I was miserable for two years, and all it would take was three weeks of pills to feel better? *How could that be possible?*

▪ CHRIS ▪

I was stunned when Emily told me she'd seen a doctor. I knew both of us had changed since we started going to Christ Fellowship, but I never expected her to take such a major step without telling me.

I was almost afraid to get my hopes up. I'd experienced too many moments when I thought Emily was back to her passionate, healthy self only to be crushed when the anger and depression quickly returned. I had thought moving to Florida or taking in Whittley might be catalysts for change. Each time, I was bitterly disappointed. But this time seemed different.

I watched Emily anxiously as the days and weeks went by, analyzing every conversation. *Are we fighting less than usual? Does she seem happy? She seems more like herself, but will it last?*

Three weeks passed—the magic timeline when Emily said her medication would fully kick in. And suddenly, Emily was smiling. She went to sleep easily and didn't toss and turn or get up in the middle of the night. She didn't rip me apart for not hearing what she said. Maybe I was imagining things, but Emily seemed better. And the change in her wasn't going away.

One night Emily drove me to pick up Panera for the two of us and Whittley. I noticed she was quiet as she helped me roll my chair into the van. She stared at the floor as she buckled her seatbelt, and I heard her sigh.

"Em? What's wrong?" Fear gripped my heart when I saw she was crying.

"Chris, I'm so sorry," she sobbed. "I said so many awful things to you. I feel like such a terrible person. I keep thinking about all the times I lashed out at you for no reason, and I feel so guilty. If I were you, I would have left me."

I grabbed her hand, choking back tears. "Emily, I forgive you. You were not yourself. That was not you."

She fell across the console and laid her head on my shoulder. "But I don't deserve it. I did so many awful things to you."

I wiped a tear from her cheek. "None of that matters now. You made a bad choice, but that was not you. God doesn't hold that against you. You have to forgive yourself too."

I held her hand as we prayed together. *This is for real*, I thought. *This is a new start.*

17

Peace At Last

· EMILY ·

It was an ordinary evening. Chris and I were playing cards with Whittley and Chris's friend A.P. Whittley laughed as Chris teased her playfully. The look in Chris's eye told me how much he loved Whittley. Even though she wasn't that much younger than we were, she wasn't just a foster daughter to the two of us now. We both loved Whittley as a daughter. In spite of the hard times she sometimes gave us—she still was, after all, a teenaged girl—she loved us as well. Watching Chris and Whittley go back and forth, her guard completely down, an overwhelming sense of gratitude and peace came over me. *I am so lucky*, I thought. *I really have a great life.*

My eyes welled with tears as I saw my life clearly for the first time in years. Chris noticed the look on my face and put his hand on my knee, with concern.

"Em, what's wrong?"

"Nothing. Nothing at all." And I meant it. "We just have such a great life."

My life had changed so dramatically in such a short time that I was still in shock. Yes, the medication pulled me out of the fog of depression, but that was only half of the equation. Since that first Sunday at Christ Fellowship, my relationship with God had grown exponentially. I wasn't simply the person I was before. I was even better.

Back in high school, most of my prayers were focused on other people. While that sounds like a good thing, it also meant I never leaned on God for my own needs. I thought of myself as an independent person who could handle any situation life threw at her. I knew other people needed God, and I prayed for them constantly, but my life was so easy that it didn't occur to me to pray for myself.

My depression forced me to realize that I couldn't handle life on my own. I had tried, and I failed miserably. I didn't realize God was trying to teach me something until a sermon one Sunday seemed as though it was directed straight at me. "Sometimes, God brings people through difficult times to refine them in his image," the pastor said. "If you're very independent and you think you can do everything on your own, he might bring you through a dark time to show you that you need him."

For a moment I thought someone had told the pastor my story. Every word he said resonated with me. God threw me into a situation that was impossible for me to escape alone. Without him and his strength, I never would have called the mental health clinic. I would still be in the fog of depression, angry and bitter. My prayers for death could have taken an even bleaker turn. When God rescued me, it was as if he was saying, "I've got this, Emily. I always have. And I always will. You don't have to carry your burdens yourself."

Once I grew closer to God, my relationship with Chris took off to a new level. All those fights over whether he really loved me or whether he did enough to show me he cared boiled down to one thing—I had looked to Chris to fill the void that only God can fill. No one in the world can make me feel truly valued or loved. And, frankly, that's not their job. As I grew closer to God, I stopped looking for Chris to fill me up. Instead, I meditated on what God says about me. His Word tells me I am chosen, I am loved, I am made in God's image, I am part of God's plan. The truest thing about me is what God says about me. I stopped pressuring myself to be perfect and allowed myself to rest in God's love.

Filling myself with God's Word enabled me to recognize my negative thoughts for the lies that they were and showed me how God's promises could stop them in their tracks. Sometimes I felt overwhelmed with shame and guilt when I thought of the old me, the girl living in the fog, ready to explode at anyone who crossed her. I thought of those wasted years I could have spent fulfilling his purpose for me instead of sitting around feeling sorry for myself. In those moments God brought his words to my mind from 2 Corinthians 5:17 (NIV): "If anyone is in Christ, the new creation has come: The old has gone, the new is here!"

I truly believed God had made me a new creation, but I was also clear on what this meant and what it didn't mean. I didn't overcome depression because I prayed the right prayer or believed strongly enough. Depression is an illness that requires medical attention. If I had had a brain tumor, I would have seen a doctor and treated the condition aggressively. No one would ever suggest that I simply change my attitude or try to have enough faith to make the cancer go away. Prayer goes hand in hand with medical treatment. Taking medication cleared the fog while my relationship with God renewed my mind and transformed me into a new person. I was finally ready to fulfill my purpose. Now I just needed to figure out what that was.

• CHRIS •

For most of my life, Jesus sat on the bench like a pinch hitter. He was ready to take the field in case disaster struck, but he wasn't on the roster. I only prayed when I really needed help, but most of the time I tried to handle whatever life threw at me on my own. God wasn't a priority, and he certainly wasn't part of my day-to-day life unless I was desperate.

Everything changed when Emily and I got our lives right with God. Attending church on Sunday turned into thinking about the sermon throughout the week and trying to implement it in my life. Christ took his rightful place at the center of our relationship. Emily and I started doing devotions and praying together. When struggles and challenges came up in our relationship, we took them to God instead of battling like we used to. Finally, we had peace.

We dove into the church community, trying to surround ourselves with Christians to help support us on our journey. I joined a men's Bible study and downloaded a Bible app to keep my time in the Word at the forefront of my mind. I felt God laying on my heart the need to step up and be the godly leader he calls me to be for my family.

God had done so much in our lives, but that doesn't mean we didn't face challenges. Our number one challenge at the time was to get Whittley to graduate from high school. She started her senior year behind in the credits she needed to graduate, especially in math. It didn't help that Whittley hated math. We tried to help her, but like most every other kid, her favorite kind of help was us doing her work for her. That was not going to happen. Even when we helped her and showed her how to do certain problems, our method was often different from her teacher's. Who knew math had changed so much in such a short time?

Even with the challenges in math, we didn't let Whitt give up. We continually stressed the importance of a high school diploma. Emily and I worked tirelessly to motivate her to do the work, knowing full well that someday she would thank us even if she hated us now. We tried to get Whittley to understand that a diploma meant a foundation she could always fall back on. Without it, she'd limit herself on the kinds of jobs she could pursue, to say nothing of eliminating the chance to go to college.

Less than one day away from Whittley's eighteenth birthday and six weeks before graduation, Emily overheard Whittley talking on the phone with her caseworker in Iowa.

"Tomorrow I'll be eighteen and I can finally drop out of school, right?" Whittley said.

Emily barged in and said, "Wait, you are dropping out of school!? You are going to waste all the countless days and years of going to school just to drop out six weeks before graduating? Plus, you manipulated Chris and me into thinking you were serious about wanting a better life for yourself when the whole time you were just planning on dropping out?"

Whittley didn't have an answer.

Over the next hour or so, Emily and Marisa pleaded with Whittley to realize how big of a mistake she was about to make. I sat on the couch listening through the wall, praying that Whittley would listen. I knew she hated having uncomfortable conversations around me, which is why I didn't join in. If there is another thing Whittley hates, it's being told what to do.

This day was no exception. She shouted back at Marisa, saying, "Emily hasn't done anything for me. She has never helped me. I hate it here. I would be better off in a group home. Anywhere would be better than here. I don't need any of you in my life. I'd be better off without you. As soon as I get my ID, I'm gone."

Knowing how Emily had poured her heart and soul into Whittley, Whitt's saying those things to her was too much for me to take.

Whitt came storming out of one room and walked right past me in the family room on her way to her bedroom. I looked up at her and simply said, "Whitt, I am so disappointed in you," as tears rolled down my face.

She stopped, and I could tell she was taken aback but then kept walking.

The next day, Emily picked Whittley up early from school so that she could get her state identification card. Emily did this even though Whittley claimed she was going to leave the next day. From there Emily dropped her off at work. While on break, Whittley called Emily sobbing. "I can't lose you. I'm so sorry for everything I have said and done. I want to stay and graduate. I promise I'll make it right. You are all I have and all I have ever had."

I think the thought of losing Emily was too much for Whittley. For me, the entire episode was nearly a beat-for-beat rerun of Emily throwing all my things in garbage bags when she told me we were through forever. Like Emily, the very real possibility of losing both of us made Whittley realized that we both truly loved her. When she stormed through the living room the day before, she had fully expected me to yell at her. But by calmly telling her how disappointed I was with her, she saw my compassion and love. This episode proved to be a major turning point for all of us and our relationship. Whitt had a much better attitude the following weeks with her school work. There were times she said, "I can't do this," but she eventually got back after it. She only had to push through for six weeks, and that's exactly what Whittley did to graduate on time!

• EMILY •

Now that Chris and I were right with one another and with God, I had a feeling that God wanted us to do more than sit back and be happy and comfortable. I knew he had more in store for us to do, and I had a pretty good idea what that was. One night after Whittley went to sleep, I said to Chris, "What would you think of taking in another foster kid?"

I didn't know what he might say. This wasn't the first time I'd mentioned fostering more children. The two of us had talked about it several times over the years we'd been together. My heart and passion had always been to help kids in need.

"You mean now?" Chris asked, sputtering. "But Whittley still lives with us. We don't have room in our apartment. Where would we put them?"

"It could be only a short-term placement," I said. "We could take in a baby under the age of one who could sleep in our room."

"Emily, do you have any idea how much stuff we would have to buy?" Chris replied and shook his head. "Babies need cribs and diapers and formula. Our apartment is tiny as it is. We have no place to put everything. Overloading it with baby stuff just doesn't seem like a good idea."

"Well, yeah, I know, but I just would love to do something like that; it sounds so fun," I said. I knew that if God was calling us to do this, I would have more conviction and would push it if it felt right. The Holy Spirit would take care of all the convincing Chris might need.

"It's not that I don't want to foster," Chris explained. "I just don't think it's the right time yet."

"I get it," I said. He was right. I left it at that.

▪ CHRIS ▪

It wasn't just the timing that made me hesitant about becoming full-fledged foster parents. Even though I knew nothing about teenage girls, Emily at least had a long history with Whitt. On top of that, I knew the arrangement was only temporary. Whittley planned to move back to Iowa right after graduating from high school. But now Emily wanted us to take in more kids. I hesitated and came up with excuses as to why now wasn't the right time, but the truth is I was super scared of fostering any kids, whether it was one or ten. We would have no idea what they had been through or how they would react to being in our house. That level of uncertainty would change everything, not to mention the fact that our day-to-day lives would be drastically different with kids in the house.

Then there was the whole issue of me being in a wheelchair. As much as I wanted to help, I was extremely limited in what I could do. If one of the kids acted out, I had no way to get them to listen to me beyond attempting to reason with them, which isn't exactly an effective method for any child, much less one who has lived through trauma. I worried about the amount of work fostering was going to put on Emily's shoulders.

But in spite of my hesitations, I had a strong sense that Emily was right. God wanted us to do this. I did my best to ignore him. I held on to all my reasons why we needed to wait, but I knew my reasons were just excuses. If I was serious about following God's will for our lives, I had to get past my excuses and trust him, then do whatever he wanted us to do.

· EMILY ·

I didn't press the issue with Chris. Instead, I prayed. Every time I went to God in prayer, I had this overwhelming sense that we needed to start the process of fostering younger kids not in a year or so, but soon. Very soon. I hesitated to say anything more to Chris, but finally I couldn't keep it in. "Chris, I really feel like God wants us to do this," I said. "I know in my heart that I'm supposed to be a foster mom. And I truly believe you're supposed to be a foster dad too."

"I know," Chris sighed. "I just keep thinking of all the reasons why it doesn't make sense right now. Why can't we do it in a few years when we are married and have more space?"

"There are kids who need help now," I said desperately. "It doesn't matter that we're young. We could change their lives."

Chris looked around our cramped living room. "I just keep coming back to the fact that our apartment is tiny."

"Well . . ." I paused. "What if we moved into a house?"

"I still don't know, Em. I don't know if it's a good idea right now. I don't think waiting is a bad thing. We don't want to rush into this."

I agreed with Chris, but the next time I got alone with God, I could barely write in my prayer journal fast enough. My brain was moving one hundred miles an hour, and I needed God to tell me what to do. *Do you want us to become foster parents now? Should we move? If we move, where should we go?*

I didn't know the answers yet, but I decided it wouldn't hurt to do a little research and make an informed decision. I checked out houses online to see what was available in our area at a price we could afford. I still couldn't shake the idea that we should help kids sooner, not later, and I wanted to get the ball rolling. I was full of life again, and I couldn't contain it. I knew there was more we could be doing to help kids in foster care. Chris wasn't so sure it was the right time, but sometimes Chris just needs a little push.

Since we were already licensed in the foster care system, all we needed to do was apply to foster younger children. I connected with our licensing agent and told her, "Chris and I would really like to foster toddlers and young children. We don't have the space right now, but I'm sure once we move into a house that could change." I had only casually browsed a few real estate websites, but the caseworker took what I said to mean that we were days away from closing on a house.

"Oh, you're moving?" She perked up. "Why don't you just wait until you're moved and settled? Then you can open up your home to some other ages. We'll definitely be able to get kids placed with you."

That was all I needed to hear. If Chris wouldn't feel comfortable fostering more kids until we were in a house, and the caseworker thought it was a good idea, then I would find us a house.

For weeks I scrolled through real estate websites every chance I got. Finding exactly what we wanted in a house wouldn't be easy. Wherever we moved had to be fairly wheelchair accessible. For some reason I could not explain, I kept lingering on listings for homes with way more bedrooms than we needed. One night I was about to shut down my computer after staring at house listings for so long that my eyes were practically crossing, when I came across a house that was really close to Barwis Methods. *That would be perfect for Chris*, I thought. But this house had four bedrooms, not two or three. Chris and I had talked about taking in no more than one child once we got a house, but I had this nagging feeling God had something bigger in store, as if he wanted to stretch us in ways we couldn't imagine.

18

Tackling Two New Challenges

· CHRIS ·

"Em, have you ever heard of Now I've Seen Everything?"

The name almost sounded like a tabloid when I saw it pop up in my email. I came close to deleting the message before I noticed that it mentioned my graduation walk.

"It looks like they're some kind of media company," Emily said after a quick Google search. "They post inspirational videos on Facebook and other social media sites. Why do you ask?"

I handed her my phone. "They emailed me out of the blue. They found the video of my graduation walk. They want to know if they could post it."

Emily shrugged. "Hey, the more people who see it, the better, right?"

"Yeah, definitely. Who knows, maybe it'll go viral?" We both laughed.

No one had asked me about my graduation walk in quite a long time. It'd been nearly two years since graduation. After our initial media frenzy subsided, life returned to normal. Besides an occasional article in the *Des Moines Register*, I didn't get calls for interviews anymore. I didn't think much of it as I typed a response giving the group my permission.

But when I checked Facebook the next day, my eyes practically bulged out of my head when I saw that this new post of my video had more than one million views. *What?* I thought. *How is this even possible?*

We thought that was huge, but there was more to come.

Someone with the Facebook profile name Mighty Duck posted the video of my graduation walk with the quote, "True friends know your weaknesses but stick by your side." Within a few days his post had over twenty million views. When it was all said and done, the video reached 250 million views!

This was the second time my graduation walk video had gone viral. The first time it happened, Emily and I were so caught up in the excitement of it all that we failed to see the opportunity God had given us. We knew the video inspired people, but now we wanted to make sure we clearly communicated the message that anything is possible when you keep pushing forward, stay faithful to God, and don't give up. God's timing for this latest round of exposure couldn't have been more perfect. Right after Emily came out of her depression, God gave us this platform to make a difference. We knew our story had the power to inspire others going through tragedy or facing difficulty. Now we were given a second chance to do something with it.

▪ EMILY ▪

After Mighty Duck shared Chris's graduation walk video, we stayed glued to our social media accounts for days. We responded to as many comments as we could and stayed on top of any video shares so we could get involved on those threads as well. Our work paid off. Emails flooded in from other social media news groups and podcasts. Within days, Chris's personal Facebook account went from zero followers to seventy-five thousand. We knew God had opened this door for us to use our story to give hope to others. He had a much bigger plan for us than we had planned for ourselves.

What struck us were not the likes or shares but the stories people wrote to us. People we had never met poured out their hearts about battles with cancer, abuse, divorce, depression, anxiety, tragedy, you name it. One woman messaged us with the story of her four-year-old daughter who was kidnapped, and all the horrible things that happened to her while her daughter was gone but thankfully was found. One gentleman had attempted suicide and was depressed, but seeing this video gave him hope for his future for the first time. After my own struggles with suicidal thoughts, this gentleman's response really encouraged me.

As I read the messages, I felt a growing sense of responsibility. I knew how it felt to be stuck in a dark place with no hope. I remembered all too well what it was like to feel all alone without God in my life. By taking Chris's graduation walk video viral a second time, God grew our platform and gave us an opportunity to help others realize there is always hope and anything is possible when you lean on God. Now it was our job to step up and communicate this message even more clearly. *The wedding walk would do it*, I thought.

When was the last time I thought about the wedding? Chris had given up asking me about it long ago. We had been engaged for nearly two years now. Our families had not-so-subtly asked us many times what we were waiting for, or if we were ever actually going to get married. At the time, we told them we didn't want to rush it. Our relationship was so rocky then that planning a wedding almost made me feel like a fraud. And as a prisoner of my depression, everything from choosing a color scheme to creating seating charts felt overwhelming. It was too much. Now, thinking about the wedding for the first time in a long time, I felt a jolt of excitement. *I wonder what kind of venues they have around here*, I thought. I searched for a place that had the right look but didn't have stairs and was also affordable.

"Do you think you'd rather get married inside or outside?" I asked Chris a couple of nights later.

His head snapped up from looking at his phone, and he stared at me as if my hair were on fire. "What?"

"Would you rather have an indoor or outdoor wedding ceremony? I like the way outdoor ceremonies look, but it's so hot here that I just don't know if it would work."

Chris grinned at me and grabbed my hand. "Wait, you're researching wedding venues?"

I shrugged and nodded. "I mean, we need to plan the wedding if we're going to do the wedding walk. The two pretty much go together, right? And we have to do the wedding walk now that the graduation walk has gone viral again."

He laughed. "Yeah, I think so."

"This is not for me," I said. "I could not care less if you walk me down the aisle. This is about all those people watching your graduation video. They are looking to us for hope. We have to give it to them."

Then I caught myself, realizing how that must have sounded. "And things are good, right?" I searched his eyes for reassurance. "I know I'm happy. I think we're stronger than ever. I just want to be married."

I could see a tear in Chris's eyes as he nodded. "That's exactly what I want."

"Well, good. But you didn't answer my question! Indoor or outdoor?" We both cracked up at my not-so-graceful segue.

"Definitely outdoor. We could always have the wedding in the early spring when it's not so hot."

I laid my arm on Chris's shoulders and closed my eyes. I still couldn't believe how close I had come to throwing away our relationship. For months I had convinced myself that Chris was ruining my life, that he was the reason I felt lost and dead inside. Now I didn't want to imagine my life without him. Chris was my rock, my cheerleader, my biggest fan. He was steady when I was all over the place. He was the brake to my gas pedal. He was my perfect balance, and we needed each other. I could see that now.

I turned to him and grinned. "Let's get married."

Chris kissed my forehead. "I can't wait."

▪ CHRIS ▪

Even though I continued working out with Nick at Barwis, I hadn't put in nearly as many hours as I did right after I proposed to Emily. Why train for something that may not happen? I told myself. But now that she had brought it back up and was excited about getting married, I quickly kicked my training back into gear. My motivation for the wedding walk was nothing like my graduation walk. Then I needed to prove something to myself. Now I wanted to show how faith in God can overcome any obstacle. And I discovered that I was more motivated to do something for others than I had done for myself.

I like a challenge. I didn't want the walk to be the same as my graduation walk. Whatever I did had to force me to train harder than I ever had before. And that gave me an idea. For my graduation walk, Emily stood in front of me, supporting me and walking backward as I took each step forward. "What if we walked side by side?" I said to Emily one day. "That's what couples normally do at the end of a wedding ceremony."

Emily was excited, "Let's do it! We will make it work. We always do."

"I know we can't do it now. But I could work up to it."

"If you want to do it, I know it's going to happen," she said, smiling at me. "Let's try it and see how it goes!"

"Now?" I asked, startled.

"Why not?" she shrugged. "I can walk you to bed, just like I used to."

Slowly I stood up and leaned against her as we slipped our arms around each other. I pushed my weight onto my left leg as I tried to hoist my right foot up to take a step. Nothing happened. I gritted my teeth, tightening every muscle in my body. My foot wouldn't budge. I underestimated how much I had counted on that supporting person in front of me.

"Em, I can't move." I tried to pretend it didn't bother me, but I had to fight back tears. "Just help me get in bed. I don't want to do this right now."

But we kept trying. We reinstated our nightly walk ritual, and eventually I could take one step, then two. I cranked up my hours at the gym, working out three hours each Monday, Wednesday, and Friday and another hour on Tuesdays and Thursdays with my friend A.P. Later, when A.P. moved to Minnesota, I bumped up my gym hours even higher, to two hours on Tuesdays and Thursdays.

My exercises didn't necessarily change beyond focusing more on a side support. What was different was my intensity. I had a renewed focus and attention to detail that I hadn't brought to Barwis Methods in far too long. I was all in and pushed myself every step of the way.

Over time I learned how to pick up my legs to take a step without leaning on someone in front of me to help me leverage my weight and shift my body. Walking one single step was a battle. Once I mastered that feat, I had to figure out how to sustain it for seven yards—the length

I set out to accomplish for our wedding. Reaching this goal took major commitment. It took until two weeks before the wedding before I was confident I could complete the walk.

Training this time around was different for another reason. Before, Emily was extremely involved and was at the gym with me every single day. That didn't happen this time. It wasn't because she was depressed or too tired to come to my training sessions. Instead, she was busy with the next big chapter of our lives—our application to become foster parents to young children had finally been approved.

▪ EMILY ▪

Whittley graduated on time at the end of May. On June 9 we moved into the four bedroom house I'd found near the Barwis gym. We were ready to move out of our apartment. We had gone through the most substantial changes of our lives in that apartment. We had grown up so much over the past year and a half, so much so that we outgrew our apartment and needed to move into something bigger. Our bright yellow house was the perfect place to continue our journey.

When we moved into our new house, I wondered how long we'd have to wait before we got our first foster placement. We didn't have to wait long to find out. Almost immediately we did respite care for a two-and-a-half-year-old little girl for a week while her foster family went on vacation. I thought it would be a good way to dip our toes into the water and get used to having a kid in the house.

Then on July 5, while the little girl was still at our house, my phone rang.

"We've got a sibling group placement coming in," our licensing agent said. "Two kids—a three-year-old boy and a two-month-old girl."

"Yes!" I cried. "That sounds great!" Then I caught myself. It wasn't just my decision to make. "Hold on. Let me talk to Chris, and I'll call you back."

"Emily, that's too much," Chris said when I filled him in. "We were only planning on taking in one child under the age of two."

"I know," I said, my voice trailing off. "But it's only one more than we planned, and the baby will just sleep all the time."

"Didn't you say three-year-old boys had the worst behavior in your group home?"

I sighed. "Yes. Okay. Well, what if we just took them until they can find someone else? I don't want to just tell her we can't do it right off the bat."

"I can do that. As long as it's only temporary."

Our caseworker found another family who was on vacation but could take the kids when they returned in ten days. I hung up the phone and looked at the clock. It was 9:30 p.m., and two small children would be here in a matter of hours. We needed car seats, a bassinet, a bed rail, diapers, formula, clothes—basically everything. Meanwhile, the little girl already in our care was asleep in her room, and it was her last night with us. I couldn't leave her alone with Chris while I ran to the store because he couldn't pick her up if she needed him. And he couldn't exactly run to the store by himself. So I did what I had to do. I loaded the sleeping girl into my car, bare feet and all, and drove to Walmart. It wasn't ideal, but when we signed up to be foster parents, I fully expected that late night car seat runs might be part of the gig.

At 1:00 a.m. we heard a knock on our door. I had prepared myself to find devastated children on our porch, and I had steeled myself for a rough night. But when the little boy, Trevor, walked into our living room, he was silent and looked scared. He was the tallest three-year-old I had ever seen. He then immediately spotted the toys I had bought for him and darted toward them. He was smiling and happy, as if he hadn't just been yanked from his home. I made him a snack and played with the toy trucks with him. I wanted him to get a little more comfortable with his surroundings before immediately putting him to bed. I laid Ella, the two-month-old, in her crib, which we had put next to our bed. I had to pinch myself as they went down to bed like it was nothing. Was this real life?

Both kids kept up their good behavior the next day. Our only problem was their clothes—they came with nothing, and none of the clothes I had bought Trevor fit, since he was the size of a five-year-old and I had bought him 3T clothes.

Trevor held it together until the moment we brought him into his room for bedtime the second night. His little lips quivered, and his eyes welled before he burst into tears. My heart broke for him. This poor guy was trying to be so strong after he was ripped from his mom and taken to live with strangers. Now he lay on the floor, sobbing the saddest cry I had ever heard, completely devastated.

I was holding back tears as I brought the boy to Chris in the living room. His two-month-old sister was crying and hungry. I had to get her a bottle.

Chris held out his arms. "Give him to me." The boy curled up on Chris's lap as if he was meant to be there and buried his face in Chris's shoulder. Within minutes, he fell asleep.

Chris stayed with him the entire night. As I watched the two of them together, I knew we could not let these kids go somewhere else. These poor children had gone through so much already. Putting them through another transition and confusing them seemed cruel. I couldn't do that to them, not when I felt this instant connection to them.

▪ CHRIS ▪

A couple of days later, I went out of town for a speaking conference. Emily called me between sessions. *Oh no*, I thought. *Something happened with one of the kids.*

"Emily? Are the kids okay?"

"Everything's fine," she said. "I was just thinking about how that other family is coming back soon. But I've been thinking . . . we should just keep them. They've been through enough already without being uprooted again. We've just got to keep them."

"Whoa, whoa, whoa. We agreed that taking in two kids was only temporary. Where is this coming from?"

"I don't know." Her voice sounded wistful. "They're just such great kids, and it's going so well. We thought it would be crazy to have two kids, but they're about as easy as it gets."

"Yeah, but that's going to change," I said, trying to be the reasonable one. "This is the honeymoon phase with them. Sure, it's easy now, but it's going to get harder." When we got the call about the three-year-old and two-month-old, I was dead set against taking them. Why would we jump right in with two when our plan was one kid all along? The fact that it was only temporary helped ease my mind. But now Emily wanted to remove the "temporary" from the placement.

We talked for a while without coming to an agreement. After we hung up, I started thinking through my reasons for not agreeing to a possible long-term placement with these two. I had to admit that the experience with them had been much better than I had expected. Ella was a ridiculously good sleeper and wasn't fussy at all. I bonded quickly with the three-year-old—he was a friendly, playful kid who loved taking rides on my wheelchair. I couldn't be active and playful with him the way I had imagined, but as we grew closer, we found other ways to keep him busy. I was surprised to find myself developing strong feelings for them too.

The more I thought about it, the more I realized what I needed to do. I called Emily back. "Okay. They can stay with us," I said.

"Seriously?" she cried. "Really? I can call our caseworker?"

"You can call our caseworker. I love these kids too. You're totally right. We can't disrupt their lives again. They need stability, and they have that with us."

I didn't know how long these children would be with us or what God had in store for us and them. Less than a week into our foster care journey, God was already stretching us. We had our own plan going into this. God had another. Frankly, his plan scared the heck out of me. I worried it was too much, that we couldn't handle it, that we weren't ready. And yet God asked us to step out in faith and trust that he would take care of us. We just needed to keep saying yes.

"Two kids is a lot," I remember saying. "I don't know how we're going to handle it." I look back on those words now and laugh. It turned out I could handle a lot more than I thought. It would just take saying yes to God a few more times.

· EMILY ·

I couldn't believe how quickly these kids began to feel like our own. And from the way the kids acted, it certainly seemed like the feeling was mutual. We kissed them to bed, told them we loved them, sang to them. Trevor was extremely attached to me, and Ella didn't remember a mother before me. Trevor *loved* to dance. We would play the "Happy Song" or the *Jungle Book*'s "The Bare Necessities," and he would start dancing like Baloo. Chris would ask to be transferred to the couch so he could be in a stable spot to hold Ella, and she would lie in his arms while he watched football. I knew the placement was only temporary, but it looked like they wouldn't leave our care anytime soon, especially since their grandmother had applied for custody, only to have her home study denied.

One day I was on the phone with our caseworker, trying to find out how we could get permission to take the kids on a trip. "Oh, by the way, did you hear about the grandmother?" she mentioned casually.

"Um, no," I said, wondering where this was going. Who else would have mentioned anything about these kids' grandma except their caseworker?

"Well, it turns out her home study is now approved, so they're going to move in with her as soon as the judge signs off on it."

I sat frozen, completely stunned. I thought we had way more time with these kids, and now they could be gone within days. Not only did I want them to stay, I felt instinctively protective of them. Who was this woman, and how was she getting the kids when her home study had been denied?

As soon as I hung up, I broke down in tears, completely devastated. Chris was just as upset as I was when I told him. I knew this was what we had signed up for when we agreed to become foster parents, but the reality hit hard.

Once we had worked through our emotions, we laid out a plan of what we should do next. The kids were going to go to the grandmother. We had no say in that. But we hoped to still have some part in these children's lives. I set up a meeting with their grandmother so we could start a relationship with her. I had to meet her and help her see how much we loved these kids!

When the time came to actually meet, I had so many concerns. I was very protective of these kids, and I wanted them to have the best, so I immediately prepared for the worst. To my surprise, the grandmother turned out to be the nicest lady in the world, who obviously cared for and loved these children. Her home study was denied by mistake. There was no reason she shouldn't have custody. She was also extremely appreciative of the care we'd provided for her grandkids and told us she wanted us to be part of their lives.

"Here's my address," she said, handing me a slip of paper. "You can come visit whenever you want."

When the day came for these two precious children to move out, our house felt so empty that I ached with loneliness. I couldn't sleep. I would wake up in the middle of the night crying. I was sick to my stomach. It felt as though I were grieving the loss of my own flesh and blood. *God, I know this is the plan you have for us,* I prayed. *But it's so much harder than I imagined. I really need you right now, because I can't do this on my own. I trust that you've got this in your hands.*

Chris held me on his lap as I sobbed. "Emily, these two little ones are going to a place where they are loved," he whispered, stroking my hair. "There are kids out there right now who will come to our home who don't have that love and are in much worse situations. They need our love more than those two do."

I knew he was right. God was opening our home at just the right time so we could take in more kids who needed us. Not knowing who that would be made me feel jumpy. We were foster parents with no kids, and I desperately wanted kids in my house. *What's next, God?* I prayed. I should have known that his answer was already on the way.

19

Learning to Walk by Faith

· EMILY ·

As it turned out, I really didn't have to worry about being a foster family without foster children. The need for foster parents is so great that long waits between placements never happen. Ever. The day we said goodbye to Trevor and Ella, we were asked to take on a short-term placement for a two-year-old boy and his newborn baby brother going through drug withdrawals. At the same time, we also committed to taking in a three-year-old boy with behavior problems.

The two-year-old came to us first—his brother was still in the NICU. I visited the baby in the hospital for snuggles and love as often as I could. The two-year-old had his own struggles. His caseworker warned us that he was extremely small for his age and most likely malnourished. I had a sandwich, cookies, and chocolate PediaSure shakes waiting for him the day he arrived. As soon as he came into our home, we could see the tiny boy's ribs through his shirt. He barely said a word but looked around wide-eyed, quiet and withdrawn. He clapped and smiled when he saw the food but still could barely even pick at the cookie.

The three-year-old came the next day. The first few days he was pretty good, but we had a feeling we were in the "honeymoon phase."

This is what they refer to when you first get a foster child. They are on their best behavior because they aren't yet comfortable enough to reveal their true feelings and behaviors. After the honeymoon period, maybe three days, this boy blew around our house like a tornado. His caseworker wasn't kidding about behavior problems. Multiple times a day he went into full-blown screaming, panic mode. He hit, scratched, and pulled hair every day. Once, he picked up a Pyrex glass bowl and launched it at the two-year-old's feet. I was grateful when the two-year-old and his brother were taken to a different home, solely because I feared for what could happen when the three-year-old was in one of his destructive moods. He had to have our full and undivided attention, which meant we could not take on any more placements.

Within a month the three-year-old's behavior started to calm down. We saw small changes, along with far less physical aggression. Day by day he started to trust us. He stopped fighting as much. Let me also add that the little guy's behavior did not shock us, nor did it scare us off. We knew that kids who need the most love ask for it in the most unloving ways. Every child who finds himself or herself in foster care has gone through trauma. They need love and stability in their lives even though they often don't know how to respond to either. When the three-year-old lashed out at us, we knew it wasn't about us. He'd been through a lot. No foster parent in their right mind ever expects a child to come into their home and behave like a perfect angel. I knew from experience how God loves me when I am at my worst and how his love can change a life. That's why he called us to be foster parents, so that he can love hurting children through us.

Once the three-year-old's behavior improved, Chris and I felt God leading us to do more. We'd already been contacted about taking on more placements. Before saying yes or no, we always prayed over each call. We said no to a few that didn't feel right while we were working through our little boy's behavior. We wanted our next placement to feel as though it was part of God's plan.

We went through a few weeks where we received no placement calls. Rather than fret, we waited for God to bring the right children to us. Then a call came about a sibling group—a one-year-old boy, a three-year-old girl, and a four-year-old girl. Chris and I looked at one another and instantly knew we would take them. I was very surprised when Chris was willing to say yes to this placement. He was starting to love foster care as much as I did.

The thought of caring for three more kids in addition to the three-year-old already living with us was very intimidating. Even though Chris and I felt ready and willing to help other kids, every placement brings a new set of challenges and unknowns. What will the kids be like? How will this affect our three-year-old? How will our lives change? Do we have what it takes? We kept reminding each other of a message we had recently heard at church: "God doesn't call the qualified; he qualifies the called." Both of us had peace that if God wanted us to do something, he would equip us with what we needed and would take care of the details.

The only problem was, we didn't have a vehicle big enough to carry all our new children. Both Chris's van and my car only had three seats in the back. But that wasn't a problem we couldn't overcome. "We are going to get a bigger vehicle," I told the caseworker. "We'll take the two oldest kids, then get the younger brother as soon as we get the car."

We drove to a car dealership as soon as we could and bought a giant used SUV that fit eight people. We then went on a shopping spree and practically bought a new wardrobe for each of our new foster kids. Since Christmas was right around the corner, I also hurried to shop and wrap as many presents as I could so the kids would have a nice holiday.

The kids hadn't lived with us for a week when we found out an aunt had stepped forward to take them. We had everything ready to care for four kids, and now they were leaving. Even the Christmas presents I'd bought were left behind.

Somehow, I wasn't discouraged. "This was not a waste," I said to Chris. "I know God had us do this for a reason. I just have a feeling that we're going to get another placement that will make all this work worth the effort."

• CHRIS •

By the end of the year, my apprehension toward foster parenting had completely evaporated. I had given up on my idea of only taking in one child under two long ago. Caring for the three-year-old with behavior problems gave me the trial by fire I needed to get comfortable with being uncomfortable. Our lives became like foster parenting boot camp. Emily read child development books and offered me tips and ideas to help us cope with the boy's destructive behavior. Saying yes to the three-child placement was a huge step for me. Had we received that call even a week or two earlier, I don't think I could have said yes. God still had work to do in preparing my heart.

When the three kids went to live with their aunt, Emily and I left our three-year-old in respite care and joined Emily's family on vacation in Turks and Caicos. We had just arrived at the beach and were in the middle of transferring me out of the car when I noticed Emily checking her phone.

"Chris, you need to take a look at this," she said, her voice serious.

I grabbed her phone and noticed she had a text message from our licensing agency. "Sorry to bother you on vacation," she said. "We had four girls come into care, ages one, four, six, and eight. Can you help at all?"

I gulped. "Four is a lot."

As much as I had grown comfortable with living outside my comfort zone, the idea of having five kids in our house scared me. Plus, caring for school-age children was not what I had in mind. Besides taking care of Whittley, I had zero experience with kids older than three and before that had zero experience with kids under three.

"I don't know, Chris," Emily sighed. "It sounds like these kids really need help." Our caseworker gave us more details about their case. The children's mother had passed away, and now their grandpa who had taken them in was dying. As Emily read these details to me, tears welled up in her eyes. I could tell she was doing her best not to cry, but it wasn't working.

"I know they need help," I said, trying not to seem heartless, but I had some real concerns. "I just don't know anything about how to raise school-age kids. I don't know how parenting them from a wheelchair would even work. We'd have to figure all that out while we're also trying to get the hang of juggling five kids."

"Okay," Emily replied. Emily received a message saying they think they found placement for the oldest child. The look in her eyes told me her mind was racing. "Well, what if we take the three younger kids? We were going to have four kids anyway before the other kids went to live with their aunt."

"I can live with that," I said.

Emily whipped out her phone to text our caseworker. "Wait a second," she said a few moments later. "I recognize these names."

"What?"

"The caseworker just told me the three youngest kids' names, and the name of the six-year-old sounds so familiar." Emily frowned, deep in thought. "There was a girl with that name when I worked at the group home." Emily had since quit the group home to devote herself to being a full-time foster mother. "I doubt it could be them, but I'm just going to ask her for the eight-year-old's name."

"There's no way it could possibly be them," I said. "That would be nuts."

Moments later, Emily burst into tears. "Oh my gosh, Chris, it's them."

I stared at her in disbelief. "But . . . how could this happen?"

"It's Cali and Sara," she sobbed. "You know when I quit that I was sadder about leaving them than anyone else."

I held her silently as she cried on my chest right there on the beach. It was hard not to believe that somehow God had arranged all this, but I couldn't shake the feeling that caring for five kids was more than we could handle.

"We can't let them separate these girls," Emily said, looking up at me. "We've got to do something. We've got to take these girls."

As much as it killed me, I had to put my foot down, or as I like to say, put my tire down. "Absolutely not, Emily," I said. This was how our relationship worked. Emily followed her heart; I followed my logic. "We cannot take in four kids. Especially not four kids who have been through so much. We would be crazy to do that."

I thought Emily would nod in agreement and acknowledge that I was right. But instead, she stood back and stared at me in disbelief. "How can you not want to help them when you know they need us?"

I had every reason to say no. "It's not just the extra four kids. I love fostering, but taking care of all of them with my physical limitations ... Emily, you would have to take care of all of us, cook seven meals, get seven people up in the morning, grocery shop for seven, drive everyone everywhere they need to go and, oh, on top of that, take care of our dog just for starters. I also feel guilty because when you need a break or get overwhelmed, I can't take over for you, to say nothing of the stress it will put on our relationship and how little time we could spend together.

"Our families live in Iowa, and we are in Florida," I continued. "Think about how it might impact me and my speaking career. That's what I love and what gives me purpose. We are months away from our wedding. We still have a lot of planning to do. I just don't see how this can work." After I finished, I thought to myself, *How could anyone disagree with my logic?*

Emily looked at me, completely disgusted. "I can't even talk to you right now," she sobbed before she turned and ran down the beach.

▪ EMILY ▪

As soon as I heard those girls' names, I felt in my bones that we were supposed to take them. It all made sense. God had clearly placed me at the group home at exactly the right time so I could meet them and bond with them. And it wasn't a coincidence that months earlier, I had this feeling that God wanted us to take on more kids. Literally the night before, Chris and I had been outside, looking at stars, when I told him I had this strong feeling God was about to use us in a huge way. I thought we might get a call about twins, a drug addicted baby, or a sibling group of four kids. At that moment, Chris obviously thought I was crazy. But I thought back to the night before and just knew this was God's plan. Why else would we have bought the eight-passenger SUV or all those Christmas presents with no one to receive them? All our preparation was to get us ready for these girls. But Chris didn't see it.

I cried hysterically as I ran down the beach, eventually collapsing to my knees. I was devastated to hear what these girls had gone through since I last saw them. My heart was shattered, thinking about all the pain and loss they had endured in their short lives. *God, I know in my heart you want us to take these kids,* I prayed. *Please give Chris strength to know that we can do this and give him peace that this is all part of your plan.*

I saw my older brother Michael running down to the beach toward me. "Emily, what's wrong? Let's talk."

I told him about the text I'd received. "Chris doesn't want to take in the four kids. He thinks it's too much."

"You've got to do this the right way, Em," Michael said. "Don't fight him. You need to go down there and explain to him more in depth about how much you care about these girls and how connected you are."

I knew Michael was right. My mind-set switched from devastation to action. I was going to do everything in my power to help these kids heal and know God. And that began with talking to Chris and trying to change his mind.

· CHRIS ·

I felt I'd made a convincing case until Emily took off running down the beach, crying. Then I thought about one of the key verses at our church, Isaiah 54:2 (NIV): "Enlarge the place of your tent, stretch your tent curtains wide, do not hold back; lengthen your cords, strengthen your stakes." The verse sounded so inspirational before. Now it sounded convicting. It was as if God was asking me to stretch out my tent and trust him to take care of the rest. I realized I wasn't saying no to Emily. I was saying no to God.

I thought back through my winning logic. I said I was worried about Emily, but I had already witnessed the incredible transformations in kids' lives she'd already made. I had no doubt God made her for this. *Then why did I say no?* Plus, Emily had been so right about Whittley, and every other child we had brought into our care. I needed to step out in faith once more.

Emily returned a few minutes later, much calmer now. She laid out her case for me. Rather than shoot her down, I took a deep breath and said, "If you think we can do this, then I think we can too. Let's do it."

· EMILY ·

We returned home from Turks and Caicos just three days before the girls were set to move in. Chris's parents were in town celebrating Christmas with us, and meanwhile, we had to round up the supplies we'd need for our exploding family while also caring for the three-year-old already in our home.

One particularly pressing need was bunk beds. We didn't have enough places for everyone to sleep, and there wasn't enough time to order beds online, where they were much cheaper than the local furniture stores. I posted in a Facebook group for local foster families, asking if anyone had a bunk bed I could use, not really expecting a response. Within an hour a woman texted me saying she had brand new bunk beds sitting in her garage that we could have for free. I felt chills down my spine. This was confirmation from God once again that we were following his will.

The girls arrived on December 26—Cali, Sara, Sam, Haley. The only clothes they had were what they were wearing. All four each only brought one Christmas present. They left everything else behind. I found out later that their aunt purposely didn't send anything for fear that whoever they were placed with would steal their belongings. Luckily, we already had piles of presents waiting for them. We expected them to be emotional messes after leaving their family, their grandpa passing away, and all they had endured. We braced ourselves for the worst, but surprisingly, they were excited to be here. When the two oldest, Cali and Sara, got here, they screamed, "Miss Emily! Miss Emily!" and ran to give me a hug. Cali, the oldest, was used to being the mom. When the caseworker left, the youngest, Haley, screamed and cried, so Cali quickly picked her up. Haley was feisty—she hit, scratched, and would spit at you if she got mad. Sara had a loud and big personality. Sam was sweet, quiet, and much more reserved than her sisters.

The next few days were an intense rush of finding clothes that fit everyone and getting the girls settled in their rooms. The girls' grandpa had died on Christmas Eve. A few days later, I drove the girls nearly four hours so they could be there for his funeral. I had to bring the girls to the funeral to let them grieve and be with family. I thought back to losing my Grandma Max, and my heart ached even more for these girls.

All of this was just the beginning. There was no getting around it—having five kids was crazy, but I loved it. There were so many moments when I threw up my hands and prayed, *God, I need you right now because I absolutely cannot do this alone.* But even in the midst of the insanity,

I felt this overwhelming sense of peace. I knew God brought us these girls for a reason, and I was determined to give them all the love and help they needed.

▪ CHRIS ▪

Before we brought foster children into our home, I thought parenting younger kids from a wheelchair would be next to impossible. I couldn't pick them up to comfort them or even yank them out of harm's way. But in time I realized there are also major advantages. They're too young to give my wheelchair a second thought, beyond getting excited about riding in it with me.

When the girls moved in, it was a different story. I don't know if they had ever met someone in a wheelchair. They looked at me with an attitude of "You're weird. You're in a wheelchair." They made blunt, offhand comments as if they were nothing. "Why are you marrying him?" they'd ask Emily, even though I was right there. "He can't even walk."

The first few years after my injury, while I was searching for self-worth, I certainly would have been offended, but I have learned walking isn't the most important thing in life and wasn't important to a woman like Emily. I brushed it off because I knew they didn't know any better. I also knew we could use this conversation to show how your adversity or circumstances don't define you or dictate your worth, which these girls needed to know, given what they had been through.

Once, in the middle of a conversation about Halloween, I mentioned how much I loved trick-or-treating. The oldest girl put her hand on her hip and scowled at me. "How can *you* have fun?" she asked scornfully. "You can't walk."

I told her, "The best part of trick or treating has nothing to do with walking. It's about dressing up, spending time with family and friends, and getting candy. How you get there is irrelevant. I focus on what I can do instead of what I can't. You don't have to walk to have fun." I think it clicked for her.

Once we got past their shock of having a new foster dad who couldn't walk, my being in a wheelchair gave me something in common with the kids. I understood what it was like for life to be unfair and to experience a terrible situation I didn't deserve. I was living proof that adversity doesn't have to define you and that, with God, you can overcome anything life throws at you. The kids' reactions to my wheelchair also gave me a healthy dose of perspective. I looked at their situations and felt they had it worse than me. They looked at me and thought I was way worse off than they were, hands down.

Because of my limitations, I was forced to get creative. I became an expert at describing how to dress yourself, or how to adjust a toy or open a jar. I learned that if I built strong relationships with them, they would listen and obey, even though I couldn't physically force them to do anything.

I came to see myself as the family cheerleader who tried to stay upbeat as much as possible, which is actually what I felt I had to be, since my injury, with Emily, family, and friends. Sometimes, though, I found myself wishing I could play with the kids in the pool, or wrestle in the living room, or toss a football in the backyard. It was easy for me to fall into a victim mind-set, even after years of life in a wheelchair. Once again, I forced myself to remember that lesson I'd learned in the helicopter, struggling to breathe. *Don't focus on what you can't do. Focus on what you can do.*

▪ EMILY ▪

Becoming a foster parent was the best thing I have ever done. I finally found my purpose and reason for being alive. After so many years of pretending I had it all together and relying on myself for everything, I now didn't have a choice but to put everything in God's hands. Taking in kids who needed help removed any charade of knowing what the future held or controlling my own destiny. We had five children with challenging behaviors and no clue when or if they would be reunited with their families. I had to let God take control, because there was no way I could navigate these waters on my own.

Not so long ago, that kind of surrender would have been impossible. If I had attempted to foster while I was in the throes of my depression or before I gave my life to God, I would still be grasping for any shred of control I could get. I could not have continued to be a foster parent if I carried the weight on my shoulders like I used to. I knew God had me wait for exactly this moment. As crazy as it might sound, I was actually grateful for my experience with depression because it prepared me to let God take the reins.

Parenting school-age children also revealed that God allowed me to go through my depression for a specific purpose. I remembered what it was like to bury my feelings and refuse to talk about my struggles. I had pushed away everyone who cared about me. When our oldest foster daughter did the same thing, I saw right through it.

One night I was hanging out with Marisa in our living room and listening to music when it turned into a dance party, as music often does when you have kids. Out of nowhere, the two oldest girls broke into dance moves they must have seen on TV or from an older girl, because they were inappropriate for girls their age. All I said was, "You can't dance like that. That's not appropriate," but I might as well have told them to get out of my house, because the oldest completely freaked out. She became so upset, I could not reason with her. I could tell from the look on her face that she had shut down and entered full-on fight mode.

I took her in the other room as she screamed at me, "I hate you! This is the worst place I've ever been." There was a time those words would have stabbed me in the heart, but I didn't flinch. I knew exactly what she was trying to do. "I bet if I hit you, you wouldn't love me anymore," she said, her eyes flashing.

How many times had I put Chris through crazy ultimatums? I knew better than to take her seriously. She was trying with all her might to push me away, but I wasn't having it. I kept my voice completely calm. "It doesn't matter what you do. I will always love you. I'm always going to be here."

My foster daughter didn't know what to do. She was used to her words cutting right through and getting the response she wanted. She'd never seen anyone refuse to react, so she took it up a notch.

"I bet if I cut off your head and buried you, you wouldn't love me," she sputtered, the pitch of her voice rising. Her eyes locked with mine as if to say, *What are you going to say now, huh?*

"I would still love you," I said calmly. I knew she wasn't a violent person and didn't mean a word she said. Everything she said was meant to push me away. "You can't say or do anything to make me leave this room," I said, gripping her shoulders in my hands and looking into her eyes. "I will not leave you in this place. I know what it's like to push people who love me away. I know what you're trying to do. But I am telling you here and now, I'm not going anywhere."

She didn't say a word, but I saw tears welling in her eyes, and she squeezed them shut, willing the tears not to fall.

"You've been fighting this for too long," I said gently. "But you don't have to fight this by yourself anymore."

"No," she insisted. "This has always worked. I've always been able to push people away." She was trying to protect herself from being let down again. Why would she trust me and let me in? She had built a wall around her heart because she had been hurt too many times.

"Honey." By now I was sobbing, but she still held back her tears. "You are not alone anymore, and no matter how hard you try, I will never let you push me away!"

Then, somehow, the two of us had our first heart-to-heart conversation. We opened the Bible, and I read her verses that had spoken to me when I came out of my depression that I hoped would be powerful for her. The Holy Spirit was in the room that night. God spoke to both of us so clearly as she finally dropped her defenses and opened up to me.

That night alone didn't solve her problems. More often than not, she told us she was fine when she clearly wasn't. But because of my experience, I knew not to take those answers at face value. I learned to keep asking the questions and to help her dig deep.

As horrific as my depression was while going through it, I would go through it again in a heartbeat if it meant I could help more kids like my foster daughter, Cali. My experience allowed me to understand her in an intimate way that has transformed my life. Chris always says of his injury that given the way life has turned out, he would not change a thing. After my conversation with Cali, I realized for the first time that I could love these kids where they were—with walls arounds their hearts—because I had been there too.

20

Planning a Wedding

When the Wedding Is the Least
Important Thing You Have to Do

· CHRIS ·

When I proposed to Emily, I imagined her diving into choosing a color scheme, tasting cake samples, and scouting out venues. I couldn't wait to see what she came up with—she had such great style and had decorated our apartment like a pro. I knew she'd dreamed of the perfect wedding growing up, and planning was in her blood. She practically told me how she wanted me to propose to her, for crying out loud. So shortly after we got engaged, I was caught off guard when suddenly selecting invitations and mapping out seating charts became as appealing to her as a root canal. Even the mention of our wedding visibly overwhelmed her. She told me she just couldn't think about it right then.

I understood why, but I would be lying if I said I wasn't hurt. Part of me wondered if I should plan the wedding myself. It didn't help that my family constantly pestered me to set a date. I couldn't tell them that Emily wasn't herself and that our relationship was in shreds. My mom was ready to take over the planning simply to see us make it down the aisle.

Then the clouds parted, and Emily emerged from her depression. Even after she seemed like herself again, I didn't bring up the wedding. I didn't want to push it. I knew how much it took for her to break free and seek help. The last thing I wanted was to overwhelm her with wedding planning and send her spiraling back into the fog. I was enjoying our relationship again, and a wedding wasn't on my radar.

That's why I could barely contain my excitement as I watched Emily slowly begin to Google venues and ask me about possible dates. I had never lost faith that one day we would get married, and now it was becoming a reality. *Emily's finally going to have the engagement experience she always wanted*, I thought. *I can't wait to see her throw herself into planning mode.*

But then life threw us another curveball. Not only were we foster parents, but we were parents to five children who had experienced the most unimaginable abuse, neglect, trauma, and loss. Our life was a series of shuttling kids to school; juggling appointments; helping them through difficult moments, of which there were many; and fielding incredulous looks when we dared to take them all out in public together. Everywhere we went someone invariably commented, "You sure have your hands full!" or "Are those your kids?"

Emily fully embraced her new role as their foster mother. And, not surprisingly, the kids were crazy about her. When she wasn't kissing a scraped knee or helping someone with math homework, she was busy sweeping up crumbs, wiping off counters, or shopping for groceries. There wasn't exactly a lot of extra time for her to plan a wedding. All we had was a date—April 21, 2018—and a golf course we'd reserved as our venue.

I wasn't much help around the house, and while I shared as many parenting duties as I could, Emily had to shoulder most of it. I could, however, pick up the phone and make wedding calls. I could handle online venue searches and signing caterer contracts. All of this meant that when I wasn't training for our wedding walk or speaking in front of crowds, I was busy taking on a role I had never expected—wedding planner.

I had figured that even if Emily wasn't the one planning the wedding, she would still be stressed about making sure I didn't accidentally pick carnations instead of roses or order white tablecloths instead of ivory. I still had the infamous banana-versus-plantain incident in the back of my mind. But Emily was surprisingly relaxed and chill. She didn't seem worried that I was in charge of everything. I, on the other hand, was terrified.

"Em, this is a little scary, having me decide everything," I said to her multiple times.

"You'll be fine," she assured me. "At the end of the day, all that matters is that we're married. Everything else is just a bonus."

• EMILY •

I knew Chris struggled to understand how I could possibly be so nonchalant about the details of our wedding. Believe me, that's not normally my personality. When I had imagined planning my wedding in the past, I thought I would freak out and not be able to sleep, worrying that the flowers wouldn't look right or the decorations wouldn't be perfect.

Becoming a foster mom put everything in perspective. As much as I had always struggled with perfectionism, I realized that those tiny details didn't matter when I had five kids who needed my attention. Chris worried that I didn't care about the wedding, but that wasn't the case at all. I was unbelievably excited about marrying him, and I was looking forward to our big day. But I also knew that the flowers and decorations didn't matter as long as we became husband and wife.

Chris isn't the planner in our relationship, so I knew he was nervous about possibly letting something fall through the cracks. I wasn't worried. I knew God had this, and over and over he kept showing up for us. The documentary company Fotolanthropy had contacted us after they saw Chris's graduation walk to tell us they would take care of our wedding photography and videography. We reached out to them to see if they were still interested in capturing our story since so much time had passed. Not only was it perfect timing for them, but their producer and founder, Katie, told us she wanted to do even more. "I feel like God has placed it on my heart to do a full-length documentary titled 7 *Yards* on your story and to find someone to help you with wedding planning and decorations," she said.

Katie found a world-class wedding designer and planner, GRO Designs, who planned and designed everything, including the floral arrangements and bouquets. I got chills every time I thought about it. To me, it was another sign that God was right there watching out for us, and that we were doing exactly what he wanted us to do. Like most engaged couples, we were hit with sticker shock when we first began researching venues and vendors. I wasn't sure we'd be able to afford flowers beyond a couple of minimal arrangements. GRO Designs showed us their plan to heap tables with the most beautiful all-white roses and hydrangeas I'd ever seen, at no cost to us. The planner freed Chris up to focus more on his growing speaking business while also putting in the hours he needed at the gym.

With the wedding plans in motion, I could focus on helping our foster children work through the trauma and loss they carried. On top of the long list of other reasons they were in foster care, the four girls had lost their mother as well as their grandpa, who had cared for them for a year before he passed away.

Many nights I woke up to the sound of our five-year-old, Sam, crying for her mommy. My heart broke as I picked her up and let her sob in my arms. I wished I could take away the pain she felt, but all I could do was hold her and love her.

A therapist told us it takes around six months for a child in foster care to fully open up and act like themselves. We took in the group of four sisters less than five months before our wedding. With each month that went by, another layer of their shells fell away. As they became more comfortable, they told me more of their tragic story, filled with abuse, neglect, and more loss than most adults face in their lifetimes. As a foster parent, I could not do what I do if I didn't put the weight on God.

With time, we saw changes in the girls that I can only chalk up to being the work of God. We were tested one night when Cali was told that she wasn't going to be able to live with a family member as she had hoped. Since bad news always goes down better with ice cream, we went to Culver's. While there, the two of us talked about how to handle this news and how to move forward.

I told her, "You have two choices. You can feel sorry for yourself and think why me? You can be angry and let it bring you down. Or you can choose to be happy, trust that your life is in God's hands, and be thankful for what you have."

Cali sat there a moment, then said, "I'm going to choose to be happy."

A few minutes later, a firefighter walked in and ordered ice cream. Cali walked up and boldly said, "You don't need to use your money. Use mine because you risk your life for all of us."

"You don't need to do that," the firefighter said, a little taken aback.

Cali looked back with a smile on her face and said, "Yes, I do. You risk your life for other people."

The firefighter was almost speechless. He had the biggest smile when he said, "Thank you, sweetheart. I hope you have a blessed night."

I could barely hold back my tears. Here was this precious girl who so easily could have sulked and felt sorry for herself, but instead, she thought about others.

As the wedding grew closer, I had to step away from caring for the kids every once in a while to take care of wedding details that had to have my input. I would ask Marisa to watch the girls, or I would have the girls play outside so I could finish up a last-minute detail. Every time, the kids broke down crying. "Miss Emily, I want you," they'd cry—Miss Emily was their name for me since that's what the oldest two called me at the group home. "I need you to hang out with me. I miss you." Their cries killed me. The last thing I wanted was for our kids to question their value and worth, and that's exactly what the wedding was doing to them, despite my best efforts.

"Chris, we've got to have these kids in our wedding," I said as I sat on his lap one night after the kids were in bed.

Chris nodded slowly, deep in thought. "I was thinking the same thing," he said. "But there will be logistics we have to figure out. We'll have to get approval from their caseworker for the kids to be in photos and videos. Because they are in the foster care system, their identities must remain private. What if the film crew accidentally captures one of them in the wedding walk shot?"

I leaned into his chest and sighed. "I know, but we can make sure we come up with a plan for the film crew and have the kids in places where they won't get into the shot for the wedding walk. They're always going to be a part of our lives, one way or another. Regardless of any logistics, we have to make this work. They have to know they are family forever."

The kids were thrilled when we told them that the little ones would be flower girls and ring bearers, while the older ones would be junior bridesmaids. And, of course, I called Whittley to tell her she had to fly down to be in my wedding party too.

▪ CHRIS ▪

Even with me in charge, the wedding was falling into place. People stepped up and offered their services in ways that left me in awe. Don't get the idea that the whole planning process was smooth or that Emily and I never had any disagreements. More than once, Emily thought of a song she wanted in the ceremony or another random idea almost immediately after I had solidified a plan. As much as I tried not to, I felt uncomfortable taking on the role I had imagined Emily filling. Many times I wished she would take more initiative. Sometimes I threw up my hands and said, "Do you actually care about the wedding or not? Because I really wish you were more excited." Then there was the moment we realized we hadn't ordered my wedding ring yet and went to the mall jewelry store with all five kids in tow.

Yes, taking over wedding planning was uncomfortable for me and watching cartoons and playing with dolls was never on my to-do list, but as I grew as a foster parent, I discovered life has more meaning when you give up your comfort for something greater. These minor inconveniences didn't compare to the transformation I saw happening each day with our foster children. I loved being a foster parent, and if this was what it took to fulfill my purpose, then I would do it.

Throughout the planning process, our wedding walk was at the front of my mind. This walk was very different from my graduation walk, not just because it was longer or because Emily and I planned to walk side by side. At my college graduation, my walk was really about me. I wanted to prove that I could do what everyone said I couldn't. This time, my focus was on God. Emily and I wanted our walk, and our wedding, to point everyone who saw it toward God.

Of course, we wanted our church, Christ Fellowship, to be involved. We asked one of the pastors to perform our ceremony. He'd been so supportive of us and was happy to be involved. Emily and I also picked a theme verse for our wedding—1 Peter 4:8 (NIV): "Above all, love each other deeply."

I was already working with GRO Designs to design a walkway for our aisle to make sure I didn't roll my ankle walking on the turf. They came up with an aisle runner that would stay completely flat and solid so I didn't have to worry about hitting an uneven patch of ground during the walk. They spaced each of the words of our theme verse over the seven yards of our aisle runner. Every time I thought about it, I had to close my eyes and shake my head. God's hand was so evident in every part of our wedding. I had no doubt that he had put Emily in my life at exactly the right time. All the trials, all the struggles had brought us to this moment.

▪ EMILY ▪

The one wedding detail I couldn't let Chris handle was my dress. I still wanted that experience of finding the perfect gown and sharing that moment with my family. I had watched the show *Say Yes to the Dress* for years and imagined what it would be like in front of that mirror in the Kleinfeld's showroom. *How great would it be to share our story on that show?* I thought. *I could talk about foster care and maybe even encourage other brides to become foster parents.*

On a whim, I applied online for the show and told them our story. A producer reached out almost immediately and set up a time to do a Skype interview. They told me it was all preliminary and I wouldn't find out until later if I would be on the show, but I could tell from the producer's smile that it was a done deal.

A few weeks later, Chris and I flew to New York City with all our parents and sisters to tape a segment. With this type of reality show, you might expect the producers to stir up drama or ask me to pretend that I couldn't decide on a dress. But that was not the case at all. The producers, as well as the consultants, seemed genuinely interested in us. They interviewed both Chris and me, and I got to talk about foster care. Chris left the showroom, and my consultant helped me select a few gowns to try on. She had barely laced up the back of the first dress when I said, "This is it." The lace, sweetheart neckline, and sweeping train looked like they were made for me. When the consultant completed the look with a sparkling crystal belt, I was sold. I tried on a few more dresses, but none of them compared to the first.

We found out later that *Say Yes to the Dress* wanted to film our wedding—and our walk—to feature on their show. Chris and I were thrilled. Getting on the show wasn't about the money. They don't pay for your dress or travel expenses, and we only received a small stipend when they decided to feature our wedding. To us, this show was another way God could use us to share his message and bring inspiration and hope to more people, while also encouraging other couples to open their homes to foster children.

Every once in a while, in the midst of the chaos that comes with parenting five children while also planning a wedding, I would look at Chris and be transported back to that moment in his dorm room all those years ago. Before we moved across the country, before my depression, before we were foster parents, I sat in his lap and felt in my soul that if I had Chris, everything would be okay. Now, weeks away from our wedding, his ring on my finger, that feeling was even stronger. I never imagined Chris and I would overcome so many obstacles before we even said "I do." We still had our whole lives ahead of us, and a whole slate of new obstacles I couldn't begin to fathom. Life might be uncertain, but my love for Chris was not. I felt incredibly lucky that God placed us together, and that he had used us in such amazing ways already. I couldn't wait for the moment we promised to love each other for the rest of our lives.

21

The Wedding Walk

"Okay, Chris, keep your eyes closed."

Our little girls squealed and clapped with excitement as I trailed into the living room in my ivory lace wedding dress. Chris sat in the living room waiting for me, still wearing the blindfold I had tied around him a few minutes earlier.

"Miss Emily, you look so pretty!" Sara, our now seven-year-old, sighed. I grinned at her as I stood behind Chris.

"Are you ready?" I asked.

"Ready."

In ten months Chris went from being unable to take a single step to walking side by side with me well beyond seven yards. He poured everything he had into his hours of training, teaching his body to put one foot in front of the other without the support of someone walking in front of him. Now, one week out from our wedding, it was time for a dress rehearsal. We remembered from Chris's graduation walk that every detail, from the length of my dress to the shoes we wore, could mean the difference between successfully walking and tripping and falling. I purposely picked a dress that wasn't too poofy and didn't have a crazy hemline. The only catch was, I still didn't want him to see me before our wedding day. That's where the blindfold came in.

I helped Chris place his hands in mine and stood him up. "This will probably be a little easier when you can actually see," I laughed.

I slipped my arm around his waist and placed my other hand in front for support while Chris held onto my shoulders with one arm. I carefully shuffled my dress out of his way, and we took a step forward. Then another. Then another. I held Chris's midsection steady as he moved across our living room.

"Feeling good?"

He nodded. "We've got this," he said confidently.

"I think we're good," I agreed. "I'm comfortable in my dress. And if you step on it, I'd rather that happen after we've already taken photos."

Chris laughed. "Agreed."

Our oldest foster daughter, Cali, stared at us. "You're not going to practice more?"

I shrugged. "I know we can do it. And anyway, that's not what our wedding day is about."

I wasn't exaggerating. I almost felt eerily calm about our wedding day. I wasn't worried that we couldn't make the walk or whether the kids would act up or if some detail had fallen through the cracks. Up until now everything had clicked into place, and not because of Chris or me. God's hand had already been all over our wedding. I knew he had a plan and was going to see it through to the end.

For the weekend of the wedding, we planned for everyone, including the seven of us, to stay at a hotel next to our venue. Those plans seemed so simple when I made them. But getting all five kids and everything everyone needed for the weekend proved to be just a little more difficult, which is a huge understatement. I ran around like a crazy person, rounding up the flower girl dresses and ring bearer tuxedos and making sure everyone had their hair ribbons and shoes. But the chaos was totally worth it. Chris and I were so excited to have everyone in one place where we could spend time with our family and friends.

In the madness of packing up the kids, I turned to Chris every so often and grinned. "I can't wait to marry you."

· CHRIS ·

The week before our wedding, I had to fly out of state for a few speaking engagements. Each flight, I spent the entire time in the air working on a special wedding surprise for Emily: I wrote out our love story in the form of a poem. By the time I was finished, my wrist was worn out to the point where I had to wear a brace. I told Emily I wrote too many emails, but I don't know how convincing I was.

As the day of our wedding drew closer, I continued training for the wedding walk. This time around, the walk was a goal, but it wasn't the point. The point was celebrating a new beginning. Seven years ago, when I found myself lying on a stretcher, unable to move anything except my head, I worried I was doomed to spend the rest of my life alone. I wondered who could possibly love me when I couldn't take care of myself. Now God had blessed me with a girl way out of my league, who not only loved me but also pushed me to live for others and gave me a richer, more satisfying life than I could have imagined. I only got one shot at marrying this girl. One shot at a wedding. I could barely even nibble on fruit or carrots, my stomach was so full of nervous butterflies. I couldn't wait for that moment when I saw Emily in her dress. I knew my excited nerves would turn to pure joy.

· EMILY ·

My eyes fluttered open the morning of April 21, and I immediately checked the weather. My app predicted overcast skies and a high in the low eighties. *Perfect*, I thought.

When I imagined my wedding day, I always thought I would feel nervous. Isn't that what brides are supposed to feel? But I didn't. Instead, I felt overwhelmed with a sense of peace. I knew I was supposed to marry Chris. And I wasn't nervous about everyone watching me as I vowed to be his wife.

Marisa, Whittley, and my mom joined me in my hotel room for breakfast, along with the other ladies in my bridal party. We laughed and chatted as a stylist curled and coiffed my hair and a makeup artist finished my makeup.

My mom zipped up my dress, then stood back with tears in her eyes. "Oh, Emily," she cried. "You look so beautiful."

"Stop! Don't make my eye makeup run!" I said, fanning my eyes as if I could dry my tears. "Chris hasn't seen me yet."

Originally, I told Chris I didn't want him to see me until I walked down the aisle. I love traditions, and that's what I had imagined for my wedding. But as the day crept closer, we realized that would mean we barely saw each other on our own wedding day. We wouldn't have time to talk, much less enjoy the day. We changed gears and instead decided on what photographers call a "first look."

Three hours before the wedding, our photographer led me to a quiet, secluded area away from the rest of the wedding party, surrounded by trees and flowers. I broke into a smile as I saw Chris waiting there in his navy suit, facing away from me.

"Chris," I said, tapping him on the shoulder.

The look on his face as he turned around was priceless. He took in every inch of me as he smiled, his face practically glowing.

"You look amazing!" he said as I knelt down to hug him. I climbed into his lap and closed my eyes, placing my forehead on his. *This right here is what it's all about*, I thought.

"I have a surprise for you," Chris said.

"What?" I said, genuinely surprised.

"I wrote you a poem; it's inside my jacket," he said.

Now I was downright shocked. "You wrote what? When did you even have time to do that?" I reached inside his jacket and grabbed the poem.

"Remember when I had to wear that brace? This is why."

I laughed as his poem began with our awkward text messages and our first date at a hot dog stand. My laughter turned to tears as he described how he felt about me in those early days, and how deeply he loves me now.

"Although you scare me with your ideas, I'm excited for our future and what lies ahead, even if it means taking on more than five kids," he read.

Then he added, "That was a joke. Don't take that seriously."

I burst out laughing. "I do take that seriously."

"Let's never forget, our strength comes from God. Faith is what is most important. I love you so much," his poem ended.

I held his face in my hands and kissed him. "I love you too, Chris," I whispered. "I'm so thankful for you and for how far we've come."

"It's crazy to think of where we were just a year ago," he said. "I have never had more confidence in us than I do today. I can't wait to see what the future has for us. This feels so right."

All I could do was nod as I wiped tears from my eyes. "I am so lucky I get to be your wife."

· CHRIS ·

My heart pounded as I heard the string quartet play their first few chords of the wedding music. My parents stood next to me, waiting for the wedding coordinator to give us the nod that it was time to go. *This is it*, I thought.

I could see the rows of white chairs set up on the golf green, each one filled with someone we loved. I searched until I could see our first foster daughter Ella sitting in the crowd—she was only eleven months old, so unfortunately, she wasn't able to be in the wedding. We'd invited Trevor and Ella along with their grandparents and mother, who was in the process of being reunited with them.

Our four-year-old foster son and previous foster son Trevor both shifted nervously next to me, playing with the box and the sign they were going to carry down the aisle. "Are you guys ready?" I asked them. They nodded seriously. It was obvious they didn't take their job as ring bearers lightly—even though the ring box was empty. No use telling them, though.

When we got the signal, my mom walked by my side as my dad pushed me down the aisle. My eyes soaked in each detail as we made our way toward the front. The aisle runner, the music, the flowers draped over the row ends and the arch—everything was beyond incredible. It was well outside the scope of what we could have afforded without everyone's generous donations. I couldn't believe this was actually our wedding.

My parents hugged me as we reached the front, and I turned to wait for Emily. As I watched our sisters and Whittley walk down the aisle, I thought back to what Emily had said for years: "You better cry when I walk down the aisle." Every time, I told her, "Ah, don't get your hopes up. I'm not a crier. If you cry, I might too, but don't bank on it."

Then, in the distance, I saw her standing arm in arm with her parents. Like so many years ago, when I first saw her walking toward the Super Dog hot dog stand, my heart pounded as I took in her beauty. I had seen her not an hour before this, but now, in this moment, I was completely overwhelmed with joy and happiness. Tears filled my eyes as I thought, *Oh my goodness. This is the girl I get to spend the rest of my life with.*

I locked eyes with her as she walked down the aisle, holding her bouquet and smiling ear to ear. *This woman is going to be my wife*, I thought. *Not my girlfriend. Not my fiancée. My wife.* I knew beyond a doubt that Emily was my match. There was no one else for me. I thought of the sacred vow we were about to make, the bond we would share as husband and wife. And then, to my surprise, the tears flowed.

Emily bent down to hug me when she reached the end of the aisle, and we held hands as the pastor prayed for us. We stole looks at one another and smiled as he delivered the wedding message. We promised to love each other for better or worse, in sickness and in health, 'til death do us part, and exchanged rings. But my favorite part of the ceremony came at the pastor's suggestion.

He had the idea that we take communion together and share a moment to ourselves. As someone from our church sang "When I Say I Do" by Matthew West, we turned our backs to the audience, ate of the bread, and drank from the cup to symbolize Christ's sacrifice for us. Then Emily sat in my lap and instantly started crying. She told me how thankful she was that I was going to be her husband. We held one another until the song was over.

"Look," I said, pointing to the sky. The clouds that had covered the sky in one gloomy gray mass broke apart for the first time all day. "It looks like heaven is looking down on our ceremony."

· EMILY ·

Before the wedding I told Chris I wanted our ceremony to feel like we were the only ones there. "I want it to be me and you," I said, "and it's just us coming together as one."

As the song played and Chris and I sat together, facing away from the audience, I had that feeling I'd always wanted. There in his arms, I knew once again that as long as I had him, everything would be okay. This man had pushed through one of the worst things imaginable but somehow still had a positive outlook on life. Instead of being defeated by his miniscule odds of moving anything below his neck again, Chris was motivated to defy them. Chris challenged me not to worry about the minor inconveniences of life but to look on the bright side. When I was at my lowest point, when I gave him every reason to leave, he stayed by my side. And he looked past his apprehension about foster parenting to welcome kids into our home and make a lasting difference in their lives.

Tears filled my eyes as I sat on his lap. God had brought us together; there was no doubt about that. Whatever we faced in the future, I knew we would get through it together, and I was overcome with peace and gratitude.

Finally, the pastor said the words I had longed to hear. "I now pronounce you husband and wife."

I threw my arms around Chris's neck and shouted, "We're married!" In my excitement, I forgot that Chris was wearing a microphone, and everyone in the crowd heard my outburst too. I threw back my head and laughed before kissing Chris—our first kiss as husband and wife.

"Ladies and gentlemen, I present to you Mr. and Mrs. Norton," the pastor said as the crowd cheered.

Just like we practiced, I took Chris's hands in mine and helped him push out of his chair and to a standing position. But when I looked down, I stifled a gasp. His pant leg was stuck halfway up his calf, and you could see his urinary leg bag and all its contents. *Oh my gosh!* I thought. *The photographer is here. The videographer is here.* People *magazine is here for crying out loud. Chris does not want his leg bag in* People *magazine.*

I knelt down as quickly as I could to pull down his pant leg. Either

I pulled too hard or his belt wasn't tight enough, because his shirt came untucked and his belly button popped out.

"Emily, get in front of me," Chris whispered.

"What? I'm not walking in front of you."

"No, my shirt. Fix my shirt."

I couldn't help but laugh. This was another reminder that life wasn't perfect, and that was okay. Instead of getting upset, I made a joke of it. "We don't want him to lose his pants!" I said as I moved in front of him, tightening his belt and fixing his shirt. Everyone in the audience was cracking up.

Finally, we stood side by side and prepared to walk. Then it hit me that we hadn't factored my veil into our practice. I was wearing a cathedral-length veil, and the wind was whipping it around. It was too risky to take the chance. At the last second, I ripped it out of my hair and handed it to Marisa. I used to hate imperfections like that, but that day, I was thankful they happened. The day wasn't about the walk or proving how hard we'd worked. It was about honoring God and celebrating what he had done.

▪ CHRIS ▪

A single ray of sunshine burst through the clouds as I gripped Emily's shoulder and took my first step. Any nerves or tension I felt completely disappeared. *We're going to crush this*, I thought.

Seven and a half years ago, those seven yards that stretched in front of me would have seemed insurmountable. On that day so long ago, the worst day of my life, I questioned God for taking away everything I loved and any hope I had for an independent, fulfilling future.

Today, on the best day of my life, I realized that what I thought was an ending was only the beginning. God's plan didn't look like mine, and I was so grateful for that. If I hadn't been injured, I never would have met Emily. God used my injury to change not only my life but also the lives of many others.

I smiled as Emily and I walked arm in arm, slowly clearing one yard, then another. Every inch felt like a triumph, not because of the applause but because I knew God was with us. These steps weren't for the people surrounding us or the cameras recording our every move. They were an act of surrender to God. Our lives wouldn't be comfortable. That was a guarantee. But when God said the word, we would say yes, whether that meant training a paralyzed man to walk or caring for five kids in one house. Walking wasn't scary as long as we stayed on his path.

I could have kept going, but when we reached the end of the aisle, Emily and I turned to one another and kissed as the crowd cheered. "We did it," she said to me, looking up into my eyes. "I love you."

Standing there, holding my new wife, I knew our life together was nothing short of a miracle. With God, all things truly are possible. The two of us are living proof of that.

Wouldn't Change a Thing

▪ EMILY AND CHRIS ▪

We'd be lying if we said there weren't times during our long journey to our wedding day that we didn't cry out to God and yell, *What are you doing? How could you let this happen to me?*

When we pictured our futures growing up, neither of us imagined catastrophic spinal cord injuries or crippling depression. We had our own plans for our lives, and we didn't consult God in the process. Clearly, we knew better than he did, and how dare he yank the rug out from under us and turn our lives upside down?

But as we walked down the aisle together at our wedding, our friends and family cheering with tears in their eyes, God's hand was evident. Every twist and turn in our lives had led us to this moment.

As crazy as it might sound, Chris is grateful that he found himself in the wrong place at the wrong time during that fateful Luther College football game. If life had continued as Chris had planned it, he might have settled for a normal life in the business world, spending his weekend at that lake house he dreamed of. God had something bigger in mind when he allowed Chris to lose all movement below his neck. What everyone else saw as a weakness, God saw as a strength. He stripped

Chris of everything he thought he knew and forced him to lean on God in radical new ways.

The determination Chris used to channel into practicing free throws in the driveway took on a new purpose—learning to walk again. He gritted his teeth and pushed himself to do one more rep, one more minute, one more hour. At the time, he thought his hours in physical therapy or at Barwis Methods would just prove the doctors wrong, and maybe even help him regain full mobility. Once again, God had a bigger plan. We never imagined that one simple goal of walking at a college graduation, and later, at our wedding, would end up reaching millions of people. God has used our story to inspire people who had lost hope that the Lord was still in the business of the impossible. We're still so incredibly humbled to be used by him in this way.

Emily never thought she could fall into depression. In her mind, depression was only for people who experienced something tragic, not an independent girl with a great life. We didn't understand why she seemingly became a different person overnight, bitterly angry and chronically exhausted. We didn't understand the constant fighting and bickering that suddenly plagued our relationship after two years of peace. And we certainly never thought we'd reach the low of Emily shoving Chris's belongings into trash bags and shouting that she never wanted to see him again.

But God refused to leave us in that dark place. Instead, he drew near to us as we attended Christ Fellowship Church, giving Emily the strength she needed to seek out help for her depression. Both of us learned what we had never understood—depression is a health issue that needs medical treatment, just as you would treat a broken bone. It's not something you can simply overcome by thinking positive thoughts. Emily's depression gave us a newfound understanding and empathy for the millions of people struggling with mental health every day. Not only can we relate to their struggle, but we're also committed to breaking the stigma of mental health and encouraging people to get help before it's too late. Anyone, regardless of their income or social status, can struggle with depression, anxiety, and a long list of illnesses. We thank God that Emily found help before it was too late. It's our prayer that God would use us to help others do the same.

As the fog cleared and the dust settled, we discovered that our relationship was stronger than ever. Giving up would have been so easy during those difficult days. It's easier to walk away than to fight for one another. By God's grace, we stuck together even when it hurt. We clung to faith in knowing these days would not last forever. Standing together on our wedding day, we knew that more dark days would come. We know our relationship will be tested again, that there will be days when one or both of us would rather walk away. But we also know that when God is the center of our relationship, we'll find the strength to stick together once again.

Most incredibly, God has used our love for each other to create a family. Neither of us could have imagined that we'd parent five children at one time in our early twenties and that we would foster fifteen kids. It's a testament to how God has grown our faith—because we relied on him, we bought a bigger place to live and a bigger vehicle to make room for more children.

We don't know what our family will always look like, but we could not be more excited about five more permanent additions. Whittley, who has been part of Emily's life for more than a decade, officially became our daughter a couple of months after we finished writing this book. We've always been her family. Then, only two months later, we adopted the four sisters, Cali, Sara, Sam, and Haley. Now, through the beautiful gift of adoption, our relationship is officially recognized by law.

By now it's safe to say we have no idea what the future holds. If the past is any indicator, it won't look anything like what we imagine even now. God's plans are always bigger and better than our own. We can't wait to see how God uses us next.